The Blue Box

Kristevan/Lacanian Readings of Contemporary Cinema

FRANCES RESTUCCIA

continuum

Continuum International Publishing Group

The Tower Building	80 Maiden Lane
11 York Road	Suite 704
London	New York
SE1 7NX	NY 10038

www.continuumbooks.com

A version of Chapter 4 was originally published in *lacanian ink*, The Symptom, issue 5, winter 2004. Sections of Chapter 5 were originally published in *Film-Philosophy* (14.1, 2010). And a version of Chapter 8 came out in *Symplokē* (18. 1-2, 2010), published by the University of Nebraska Press. Thanks to the editors for permission to reprint this material.

Library of Congress Cataloging-in-Publication Data
A catalog record for this book is available from the Library of Congress.

ISBN: HB: 978-1-4411-7744-5
PB:978-1-4411-0757-2

Typeset by Fakenham Prepress Solutions, Fakenham, Norfolk, NR21 8NN
Printed and bound in the United States of America

Dedicated to E. A. L.

Contents

Acknowledgments

One of the pleasures of having finished a book is to reflect on all the people who enhanced the project, whether they knew it or not. In some cases the debt for inspiration cannot even begin to be articulated. But to try now to express something in the way of gratitude, I will start with those who have had a direct impact on *The Blue Box*. Jean Wyatt and Todd McGowan have been invaluable in offering critiques of my work that transformed it, without a doubt, for the better, saving me from blunders. They have generously offered their critical eyes as well as a wealth of knowledge and insight. Jean has been meticulous and thorough, tactful and engaged—a life-long friend and nourishing intellectual companion. Todd was and is always ready to think. Whenever I had an issue, he gave an immediate extensive, often impassioned response. He put real energy into reading my book, took it all in, and offered extremely helpful, candid responses. I thank Judith Gurewich especially for mentioning the topic of anxiety in *Caché*—that comment, one of her innumerable unsurpassed intuitions, set off multiple versions of my chapter on this Haneke film, the last of which was most fully comprehended by Jodi Dean. Jodi's response to a conference paper I gave on *Caché*, because she "got it," was incredibly gratifying. Kalpana Seshadri needs to be deeply thanked, for holding up the most rigorous standards and for presenting her ideas to me in both professional and the most ordinary settings. It never seemed to matter if we were at a conference or riding in a car. Several of the films analyzed here were seen for the first time with Kalpana; her unparalleled discernment forcefully shaped many of my early responses, which went on to blossom from their inception at a site between the two of us. I thank Sam Girgus, one of the readers of my manuscript, for his enthusiasm and apologize to him for not calling it *Intimate Film*. (I almost did; his title seemed perfectly suited to me.) I continue to be grateful to Ewa Ziarek and Kelly Oliver for their steady support of my work on Kristeva. And Maria Margaroni (who teaches and lives in Cyprus) has become over the years a kind of intellectual guardian angel. Emma Limon has infused the project with theoretical knowledge drawn from her own film theory courses; as an artist she has enhanced my sensitivity to the non-diegetic dimension of film, to the images, colors, shapes, music—all the semiotic elements crucial to Kristevan readings. Judith Wilt has been an integral part of my film-life for decades, participating in Friday and Saturday night seminars that would have turned painful for most people after 15 minutes. John Limon usefully availed me of a sense of what I was up against yet also gave tremendous assistance in sorting out and clarifying concepts. I especially appreciate the interest in my work that Jeffrey R. Di Leo, editor of *Symplokē,* and David Sorfa, editor of *Film-Philosophy*, have shown, and thank Colette Soler for offering me the unique opportunity to present a paper on anxiety in *Caché* to a large group of very sophisticated psychoanalysts in Paris. Alan Richardson, Samir Dayal, and Charlie Shepherdson also imprinted this project. And dozens of students at this point deserve my appreciation, at Boston College as well as Venice International University, for plunging into my psychoanalytic world with fresh attention. I would be nothing without my bright students—perhaps my greatest resource. Speaking of resources, I have depended for years on the subtle mind of my close friend Kevin Ohi; our exchanges, many of which had to do with film, spun out the most intricate webs of thought I have experienced. Thanks too to Daniel Heller-Roazen for leading me, within the labyrinth of Venice, to grasp the infinite meaning of Lacan's "not-all." Reading the book will also reveal my indebtedness to Slavoj Žižek, a genius with whom it is necessary to argue.

Finally, it has been delightful to work with Katie Gallof, my dream editor, at Continuum; and thank you Haaris Naqvi for our conversation on that fortuitous bench outside the Bonaventure Hotel that led to my relationship with Continuum.

1

Introduction: intimate film in revolt

If we are to construct a civilization that is not solely one of production and commercial trade, we must redefine what we understand by 'freedom.' The freedom that we have to reconstruct together should be an autocommencement, to be sure, but with the other, and this not in order to produce the best causes for the best effects, but to share the power of beginning oneself anew with the other. The freedom of desire that is the desire for objects, knowledge, and production, joined with the freedom to withdraw into intimacy and mystical participation, are the two indissociable variants of European freedom. Because they have been separated, each of the two parts of the schism is vulnerable to impasses: the unbridled pursuit of objects of desire, even false ones; the stupidity of the media; the robotization of production; atomization; social insecurity; and the 'new maladies of the soul' on the one side; and the immobilization in painful narcissism; the hellish complacency outside of time; social amoralism; and pauperization on the other. Is a revision possible?

JULIA KRISTEVA, *CRISIS OF THE EURO/PEAN SUBJECT*

Informed by the theory of Julia Kristeva, *The Blue Box* analyzes a variety of contemporary films replete with psychoanalytic subject matter and styles—by Almodóvar, Haneke, Kieslowski, Lynch, Shainberg, Streitfeld, and von Trier. Lacanian theory also substantially supports this study, and the early as well as late work of Gilles Deleuze plays a part, but theoretically *The Blue Box* engages mainly Kristeva's *Black Sun: Depression and Melancholia* (1989) and *Intimate Revolt: The Powers and Limits of Psychoanalysis* (2002) as well as her newly translated *Hatred and Forgiveness* (2010).

The absence at the core of all the films taken up, with its potential to effect psychic reconfiguration—the transformation of psychic trouble to desiring subjectivity—is the book's fundamental unifying concept. Each film analysis in *The Blue Box* brings to light a darkness, the (Heideggerian) Nothing, an abyssal site of the Lacanian gaze, Kristevan "negativity," the "motor," as she calls it, "of psychical life" (Kristeva, 2010, 183). Hence the book's metaphoric title—*The Blue Box*—which signifies in David Lynch's *Mulholland Drive* both the bottomless site of the Lacanian Real and a crucial escape hatch, enabling release from debilitating fixations. The opening chapters locate what Kristeva calls "new maladies of the soul"—contemporary variations on melancholia, hysteria, obsessional neurosis, perversion, and psychosis—in recent films as well as in Hitchcock's *Psycho* (on both diegetic and non-diegetic levels) to show how a cinematic metamorphosis of such maladies can occur through an exposure of that abyss. And insofar as the early chapters focus on the capacity of film to access the space of the Nothing as an antidote to psychic disturbances, the film analyses in the first part of the book prepare for a more direct and detailed demonstration of films that snugly fit Kristeva's category of the "thought specular." That is: gradually, in the course of this study, a shift in emphasis takes place from psychoanalytic components within film to the spectator's psychoanalytic experience with film. In roughly the second half of *The Blue Box*, Kristeva's concept of the thought specular, from her fascinating chapter "Fantasy and Cinema" in *Intimate Revolt*, is elaborated and illustrated.

Kristeva's film theory is sparse; but what she has produced is revolutionary. Julia Kristeva deserves our full attention as a film theorist, as her work elucidates the capacity of thought-specular film to offer the spectator intense psychoanalytic experience that she calls "intimate revolt." This psychic rollercoaster ride has the ability to plunge into the abject to convert it to Nothing, thereby traversing fundamental fantasy, and to transport timeless trauma into time, ultimately to effect psychic reconfiguration.[1] *The Blue Box* looks at films that present elaborate fantasies and, through them, prompt the viewer to cut across a crippling fundamental fantasy—by enabling a mapping of his/her private fantasy onto the one being played out on the screen. Such absorption is a function of the semiotic dimension of the film, which offers the spectator an experience of intimacy, negativity, the gaze, and death. Thought-specular films have the capacity to absorb the spectator's traumatic psychic material, allowing desubjectification through filmic experience and a subsequent discovery of the drive, for the sake of its eventual transformation into desire.

What renders Kristeva's intimate revolt even more valuable is that this remarkable, cinematically induced transformation is set, in Kristeva's conception, within the context of the society of the spectacle (as defined by Guy Debord in his book of that title). In *Intimate Revolt,* the thought specular is perceived and privileged as a way of turning back the tide of our current dependency on tawdry, glossy images, the consumption of things, as well as speed and cold, technological efficiency. Ironically, the plethora of images that bombard us today within our society of the spectacle not only fails to liberate us but also deprives us of productive fantasy spaces. (Popular images may even be said to generate new maladies of the soul, which in turn require a curative fantasy space.) Nevertheless, Kristeva stresses that the visible is the port of registry of the drive and that cinema that celebrates our identity uncertainties has the potential to transform aggression to filmic seduction, to help us locate the drive and fold it into desire. Despite modern man's abuse of it, the specular is "the most advanced medium for the inscription of the drive" (Kristeva, 2002, 72). Kristeva's film theory, like *The Blue Box*, attempts to restore psychic life to the human subject, to remove its painful obstacles and unveil its riches, through an emphasis on the alluring cinematic semiotic, the gaze, and representation of the death drive—without which we are apt to impose our unconscious aggression on vulnerable human subjects. Opening up psychic life by restoring or inciting desire, therefore, has huge political significance.

Avowing maternal loss

The Blue Box commences with an examination of Krzysztof Kieslowski's *Blue*, a melancholic film that promotes staying connected to blueness and thus keeping the corpse of maternal memory warm. But eventually, as Chapter 2, "Black and *Blue*: Kieslowski's melancholia," argues, even the film *Blue* (exquisitely soaked in melancholia) transforms the reminder of loss, emblematized unforgettably by a fetishistic lamp of dazzling blue glass beads, into a remainder that carves out a lack, a space of Nothing crucial in psychoanalysis to discovery of the drive and the ensuing potential for desire. Kristeva's and Kieslowski's emphasis, however, is that such an emptiness—a lack/desire—bears an integral tie to the originally lost maternal object or maternal Thing. One's initial loss of the mOther, in fact, can only be *experienced* psychically through one's attempt to re-locate and thereby sustain the lost object in language. Our experience of loss/lack is necessarily paradoxical, then, insofar as our loss/lack constitutes a link with the lost object—and to refuse to acknowledge that lifeline is to miss out on an essential catalyst for desiring subjectivity. We re-encounter the maternal object through words and other forms of creativity in becoming desiring subjects. Desire depends on an active avowal of the lost mother.

The experience of the loss of the maternal object through the simultaneous carving out of a lack produces, what I will loosely call, a craving for something we assume and hope will be ultimately satisfying, our missing piece, Lacan's *objet a*, the cause of our desire. The very chiseling out of lack (enabling our experience of the loss of the lost object and in this way maintaining a delicate bridge to that loss or lost object) produces a desire for enjoyment or *jouissance*. Desire is therefore dependent on one's sense of loss and inheres in one's psychic effort to retrieve, in some Symbolic form, the lost object. Putting this idea in terms of signification or linguistic desire, we might claim that naming produces a wound, for which it simultaneously compensates us. The corpse of the lost object, the maternal object, the Thing (*das Ding*) therefore must be kept at a warm temperature, not of course at home, where Norman Bates in *Psycho* hoards his mother's literal corpse unburied and overheated, but at a sweet distance, in art and other forms of sublimation. Black, in other words, is ideally fringed with blue.

As Eastern Europeans, Kristeva and Kieslowski agree as well that this thread connecting us to the suffering maternal body ought to be maintained in the political arena, developed "in the domain of thought," to retard if not wipe out the society of the spectacle with its fixation on cheap images, consumerism, and "thought-as-calculation" that ultimately threaten the existence of psychic life altogether, as the human subject each day becomes more robotized (Kristeva, 2010, 19). In *Hatred and Forgiveness,* Kristeva poses vital questions that we ignore at the risk of the atrophying of our souls and the suffering of our bodies:

> modern man's psychical life seems to have been taken hostage between somatic symptoms (illness and the hospital) and the placing into images of his desires (reverie in front of the TV). No more psychical life then. Does this prefigure a new humanity that has gone beyond metaphysical inquietude and concern for the meaning of being, with psychological complacency? Isn't it wonderful that a person can be satisfied with a pill and a screen?
>
> (Kristeva, 2010, 157)

Framed by Julie, in *Blue*, who rediscovers her lost objects through classical music composed to celebrate the European Union, and Raimunda, in Almodóvar's *Volver*, who reunites with her lost maternal object through public song, discussion of the semiotic in *The Blue Box* insists on it in both the personal and socio-political spheres. Globalization would do well to acknowledge the Real maternal corpse in order to achieve an experience of Nothing for the sake of restoring desire to subjects who now docilely accept generic fantasies imposed on them by capitalism out to grab its profits. The films of *The Blue Box* all demonstrate that desire emerges through the representation of singular, rather than mass-produced, fantasies that equip the subject to traverse misery-producing attachments, locate the drive, and transport the timeless encrustations of trauma into time. All the films of this collection celebrate "moments of grace" (Kristeva's concept) in which *jouissance* is experienced at the intersection of atemporality and temporality, serving as a platform for desiring subjectivity. In this way desiring subjectivity is achieved through a kind of Eastern Orthodox mystical freedom—one that exceeds conventional boundaries by privileging the endless delights of silence, tenderness, beauty, passion, lament, and death. Kristeva persuades us to embrace Eastern Orthodox "intimacy and mystical participation" (Kristeva, 2000, 159–60).

A strain of mysticism certainly inheres in Kristeva's writing. Yet such mysticism never precludes or even overshadows, but instead complements, a political concern with the reduction of Others—e.g., Arabs, Jews, blacks, women, gays, etc.—relegated to the space of Nothing, excluded/included as *homines sacri*. In arguing for the dissolution of the fetish plugging that void, *The Blue Box* simultaneously advocates the removal of such Others from that space. Alterity within the subject must be recognized in its own right, to prevent its channeling of aggression toward the Other. Exposing that space as what it is—empty—rather than filled by the Imaginary Other, is central to this project. Unlike the obtuse Georges in Michael Haneke's *Caché*, we need to *confront* what Majid showcases—the vacant site of the drive—rather than inflict our unrepresented drive on the Majids of the world. Once trauma is articulated as constitutive of Being itself, racism and social conflict will no longer have to bear the burden of the trauma underlying history. Hanging on to the source of melancholia ensures that the basis of trauma stays located in the subject's *relation to the maternal Thing* rather than in a targeted ethnic or racial Other. *The Blue Box* promotes a cinematic encounter with one's constitutive lack, for the sake of an ensuing traversal of psychically crippling fundamental fantasies, and representation of the death drive, resulting in a healthy infusion of *jouissance* into the Symbolic—both on the personal and socio-political levels, the latter being absolutely contingent on the former.

New maladies of the soul

The early chapters of *The Blue Box* thus stake out particular psychic structures by locating them in films where they are put into relation with loss, lack, and Love—myriad forms of the Nothing. Chapter 3, "'The void of another enjoyment': *Breaking the Waves*," zeroes in on hysteria, which flirts with the desubjectification of Love. Chapter 4, "The use of perversion: *Secretary* or *The Piano Teacher*?" examines the therapeutic usefulness of perversion in escorting the subject to a zero-degree state. Propelled by fear of *aphanisis* (the eclipsing of the subject), obsessional neurosis is fleshed out in Chapter 5, "Unveiling fetishism in the society of the spectacle: *White, Female Perversions, Mulholland Drive*." And in Chapter 6, "*Psycho*: the ultimate seduction," psychosis is treated in a new Deleuzean reading of Hitchcock's most famous film, in which abjection leads homeopathically to a liberating dissolution. While Kristeva offers a profound theory of melancholia, we turn to Lacan for theory of the psychic structures—hysteria, obsessional neurosis, perversion—as well as for his notion of Love, given that psychoanalytic psychic configurations tend to define themselves in relation to that concept. The melancholic, for example, dodges Eros, whereas the hysteric charges up the amorous realm by insisting on her role as the object cause of desire or *objet a*. The obsessional neurotic wrestles with an impossible desire: fear of losing his boundaries, and collapsing into the cavernous maternal hole through Love, governs every move of his narcissistic romantic life. The pervert, on the other hand, longs to be the object of the Other's *jouissance* and so can abide a masochistic Love in this role of crucifixion.

"'The void of another enjoyment'" (Chapter 3), on Lars von Trier's *Breaking the Waves*, explores the capacity of film to exceed the limits of signification in its presentation of the desubjectification of Love. Propelled by the drive, Love would seem to be at home in contemporary film. In "Fantasy and Cinema," Kristeva offers an explanation for why: the visible or the specular, she theorizes, lends itself to "a primary and fragile synthesis of drives, to more supple, less controlled, riskier representability of instinctual dramas, the games of Eros and Thanatos" (Kristeva, 2002, 69). Is film, then, the place where Lacanian Love—that cannot stop *not* being written (to use a Lacanian formulation)—can be conveyed? And is the hysteria that leads to the hysteric's overstepping of the boundary between herself and her phallic master, whose desire she pretends to want to satisfy, equally at home in film, as the hysteric falls into the abyss of Love? A Woman beyond phallic language and law would seem to thrive in cinema—both the hysteric who coalesces with *objet a* and the Woman in Love situated in Lacan's infinite realm of not-all. In the form of

Kristeva's endless delights, mysticism weaves its way through *Breaking the Waves*, where the hysteric, the Woman in Love and the mystic flourish, as Stephen Heath puts it, in "the void of another enjoyment" (Heath, 1998, 105). And (most importantly for the psychoanalytic purposes of this book) that film has the capacity to convey *that* void, especially as it stands in for the unsignifiable experience of Love, indicates its potential to serve as an analytical site.

Chapter 4, "The use of perversion: *Secretary* or *The Piano Teacher?*" might appear to catapult us back to square one in that Erika Kohut in Michael Haneke's *The Piano Teacher* and the heroine of Steven Shainberg's *Secretary* (both like Julie in *Blue*) struggle to extricate themselves from parental attachments that bog them down in the Imaginary, barricading them from desire and motivating acts of self-mutilation. But the primary aim of this fourth chapter is to consider the merits of two psychoanalytic approaches to psychic trouble—enjoying one's symptom (by upgrading it to the level of the *sinthome*) or committing an authentic act (that reduces one to a zero point) to traverse a fundamental fantasy. In my argument, made through the juxtaposition of *Secretary* with *The Piano Teacher*, the authentic act proves to be the more effective therapy. Again the emphasis is on engaging the abject by encountering it as an agent of one's freedom.

The passionate attachment, one's most precious object, however, must initially be relinquished. In *The Piano Teacher*, this act of separation is shown to be excruciating, even to require that Erika reduce herself to a brutalized, corpse-like state, a "rape" victim, to clear the space for subjectivity. The mOther must be peeled away. Such a psychic denuding happens in this film through a woman's perverse play along the lines of Deleuzean masochism that, it turns out, because it is enacted by a woman, allows her to escape the Deleuzean masochist's incestuous bath with the maternal object, to move beyond his strategy designed to keep him luxuriating in maternal *jouissance*.[2] "The use of perversion" tests out the notion that Deleuzean masochism can escort women into the void or the Nothing by extricating them from the very maternal body the male masochist deploys Deleuzean masochism to enjoy.

Turning next to obsessional neurosis, *The Blue Box* revisits Christian Metz's classic *The Imaginary Signifier* and Kaja Silverman's provocative *The Acoustic Mirror* unabashed about analyzing obsessional "desire" that objectifies female figures in film (though a moral judgment is by no means implied). Fetishism, as Silverman explains, is marshaled to ensure the coherence of the male (obsessional) subject; being structured according to a lack, an absence at its heart, film is apt to provoke such a viewer to protect himself through the defensive mechanism of fetishistic disavowal. To generalize, mainstream (Hollywood) "movies" operate this way: the male spectator associates the female figure on the screen with lack (his paranoid projection) so as not to face "the absent real and the foreclosed site of production," losses inconsistent with the "phallic function" that defines the male subject; and sometimes, Silverman adds, "the male subject is even unable to tolerate the image of loss he has projected onto woman, and is obliged to cover it over with a fetish" (Silverman, 1988, 18). Working against this obsessional grain, Chapter 5, "Unveiling fetishism in the society of the spectacle," reads three films, Kieslowski's *White*, Streitfeld's *Female Perversions*, and Lynch's *Mulholland Drive*, as counters to the fetishism rampant in our capitalist economy.

These films push back against the globalizing tide of our spectacular, psychically diminished Western world. While most movies shrink the viewer to a pathetic consumer, the very deliberately targeted victim of the fantasies fully fashioned on the screen, Kristeva's genre of the thought specular—by distortedly depicting the spectator's desire—ethically works through and against the destructive fetishism that undergirds patriarchy, capitalism, and Hollywood. *White, Female Perversions,* and *Mulholland Drive* take up the task of a demystification of fetishism, putting in its place what has so much more potential for erotic life: negativity, the Nothing, absence—whose role in the essential unfolding of human beings has been undermined by the society of the spectacle. Western spectacular society, like science to Heidegger, "wishes to know nothing of the nothing," even though, or perhaps because, "from the nothing all beings as beings come to be" (Heidegger, 1929/1977, 96). The only "event," as Kristeva explains, that "seems to resist the remote control"—with which one "can go from the collapse of the World Trade Center to the arrest of Saddam Hussein to gay marriage and so on, each sequence effacing the previous one in a vertigo of the nullification of memory and subjects along with it"—is death. *Are* birth and death, she wonders, "the only values that retain the attention of our bodies made delirious by the acceleration of the spectacle?" (Kristeva, 2010, 279).

I situate the films of this fifth chapter in a brief historical trajectory beginning with the anti-fetishism protest of the 1970s, launched by feminists, Marxists, and modernist aesthetics. But, again, in *The Blue Box*, the socio-political dimension is grounded in the personal: Kieslowski's *White* condemns fetishism at the level of its obsessionally neurotic individual protagonist and *subsequently*, through Karol, takes on Poland's newly adopted commodity fetishism. Marx, Debord, and Žižek help us to link the fetishism of the obsessional terrified of an encounter with lack and Love—for fear that his egoistic, unbarred subjectivity will be eclipsed, his humanity exposed—with the fetishism of spectacular relationships, which disavow their true humanity. In both cases lack is avoided, and excess is rolled back into the system and controlled. But, in contrast, the film *White* itself implodes stylistically into the abyss in displaying screens overflowing with whiteness, perfectly happy to lose its diegetic bearings, to revel in the leftover. A site of the Lacanian gaze, *White*'s whiteness beckons the viewer to immerse him/herself in the film for the sake of experiencing the *jouissance* essential to the intimacy of psychic life, the void of another enjoyment.

What happens, regarding fetishism, in *Female Perversions* is more complicated, given that women's relation to fetishism is vexed. Women tend to be cast *as the fetish*, which in a sense precludes their "ability" to fetishize. *Female Perversions* therefore turns itself into an anti-fetish fetish so that women are no longer debarred from the act of fetishizing and at the same time are able to defend themselves against its objectification of them, as well as its suffocating closure of the vital gap between the subject and its origin—separation from which generates the lack essential to desire. Again, the abject needs to be put at a distance for the sake of the emergence of lack/desire, at the same time as lack/desire carries the signature of the lost abjected Thing, if desire is to be kept from becoming impossible. Loss thus converts to the lack or Nothing that ideally gets folded into Being in a way that leaves Being without the absolute loss of that loss. Lack, or the "acknowledgment" of a missing piece (left over upon separation from the mOther), therefore, testifies to the lost mOther-child bond, giving rise to Freud's libido, Lacan's lamella: "what the sexed being loses in sexuality"; "it is of this that all the forms of the *objet a* that can be enumerated are the representatives, the equivalents" (Lacan, 1981/1973, 197–8). Thus it enables our capacity to enjoy.

In the role of the fetish object, however, women are deprived of desiring subjectivity as well as of the enjoyment it seeks. Hence "cutters," as they have been appearing more frequently in contemporary film, attempt to carve out a lack on the body itself, to produce a wound, perhaps even in masochistic response to the sadistic obsessional's refusal to acknowledge his lack. *The Blue Box* is open to the idea of perversion as a therapeutic tool, the use to which it is put in *The Piano Teacher* and *Secretary* as well as in *Female Perversions*. Because perversion has access to the drive, as Kristeva proposes in *Intimate Revolt*, the "therapy of the sensorial cave ... often needs a perverse object as a pseudo-object in order to traverse its autistic enclosure" (Kristeva, 2002, 59). Such a deployment of perversion qualifies a film that engages in it as the thought specular, since this genre exhibits (rather than participates in) sadomasochistic drives in order to think, and work, them through. Thought-specular film, being the port of registry of the drive, has a special rapport with perversion that it refuses to abuse; instead, perversion is unleashed in ways that allow thought-specular film to hook the active drive operating in perverse acts and sew it together with desire. In *Hatred and Forgiveness*, Kristeva indicates the social benefits of such a strategy. After commending Freud for first locating and then playing on polymorphous perversion until it is teased out, Kristeva comments that such teasing out will result in fewer "perverse crimes" (Kristeva, 2010, 206). Thought-specular film contributes to that effort. "The artist," Kristeva claims, "is a pervert who has recaptured the polymorphous pervert within, the child, and uses perverse experiences not as an end in themselves, but to arrive at a new passion ... through the signs of reflexive consciousness (poetry, painting, novels, cinema)" (Kristeva, 2010, 92).

The "perversion" put to use in *Female Perversions* also has to do with adhering to patriarchal norms of femininity. Here it is a feminist *and* psychoanalytic concept. The heroine of *Female Perversions*, Eve, plays her perverse role of femininity, I argue, in a way that enables her ultimately to traverse her fundamental fantasy of being her father's fetish, his substitute phallus. Eve cuts herself loose from this fantasy through the film's "disavowal" of patriarchy's strategic obsessional conception of femininity along with its simultaneous "avowal" of femininity's appeal as a politically useful mask. Hence *Female Perversions* becomes a kind of conceptual fetish itself that works against the psychic demands of the father as well as against the daughter's fantasy of pleasing the father by becoming a Daddy's girl, thus meeting those demands. For *Female Perversions* as fetish object ironically exposes the cut at the heart of all fetishism and becomes in turn an anti-fetish fetish, thus slicing through the Daddy's-girl fundamental fantasy.

Noble fantasy

It is through art—literature, painting, and film—"including the most demonic and most tragic" creations—that we can resuscitate our intimacy, both our refuge from and resistance to the virtual world (Kristeva, 2002, 12). Cinema especially is a gateway to intimacy, given that it is a fantasy space and thus an Imaginary space, the Imaginary being Kristeva's designated path to intimacy. In the fifth chapter of *Intimate Revolt*, "Fantasy and Cinema," Kristeva establishes that the subject is constituted through the Imaginary (where the drive may be discovered) and that fantasy serves as a passageway to this psycho-analytic register. She accepts Freud's notion of fantasy as "the intimate creation of representations" (Kristeva, 2002, 63), rather than a fulfillment of desire. Such phantasmatic narratives need to be formulated and then inter-preted in order to dissolve symptoms. In this way access can be gained to unconscious fantasy, to keep it from being repressed. Dreams of course are a central place where fantasies come to light, bespeaking the reality of our desire or signaling why our desire is blocked. Likewise, film can serve as a dream-space for a spectator whose psychic life resonates with the semiotic components displayed on the screen.

In general, then, fantasy breaks down into the "sick" fundamental variety (such as Eve's in *Female Perversions*) and into what Kristeva calls "noble" fantasy that serves desire by offering an "escape hatch" from poisoned fantasies. Such an "escape hatch" assumes the form of a blue box in David Lynch's *Mulholland Drive*. Perfect for this study featuring Kristeva's thought specular, *Mulholland Drive* is, on the narrative level, *about* the use of fantasy to slice through a debilitating love fantasy, *and* the film also serves as a means of detachment, in offering itself to its spectator as a kind of blue box. Fantasy can evolve in one of two ways: it can become a fetish that plugs lack, or it can facilitate liberation from such an enclosure by leading to an abyss. Lynch's blue box is such an abyssal object that opens the way out of a vitality-diminishing fantasy. To extricate oneself from a destructive love relation, one needs to be reminded of the Nothing at the base of Love—to find, open up, and climb into the blue box. Such an "escape hatch" clarifies that the object of our desire (the beloved) is not, after all, synonymous with the *objet a*, or object cause of our desire—a structural absence, the missing piece that flies off when we detach from the maternal body. Entering the blue box allows one to leave the contingent cause of the lover's suffering (the beloved false object) behind. *Mulholland Drive* articulates all this psychoanalytic theory and simultaneously functions as just such an escape hatch.

Mulholland Drive also imbricates the illusion of love with the illusion of film, thus exposing Hollywood in particular, the centerpiece of the society of the spectacle, as a fetish concealing an absence, the Nothing—key to desiring subjectivity. Hollywood is condemned in this film for hiding the blue key to the blue box; *Mulholland Drive*, in indexing the Nothing, provides the key. Lynch's film's self-reflexivity insists that film is a Metzian imaginary signifier so that we can better comprehend how it can serve as Kristeva's Imaginary register, where (to Kristeva) the Real is inscribed so that engagement with the Imaginary can release the grip of an affliction-producing love. Kristeva celebrates the thought specular through films by Eisenstein, Godard, Bresson, Hitchcock, and Pasolini. I try to make the case that Kieslowski in *White*, Streitfeld in *Female Perversions*, and Lynch in *Mulholland Drive* carry on that legacy, that they too succeed where the fetishist fails, restoring psychic depth in part to overcome the contemporary demise of human Being.

Deleuze's abjection become splendor: *Psycho*'s gaze

A kind of dream-space, thought-specular cinema is a favored dwelling place of the gaze, the subject's constitutive lack. It is by luring the spectator into its fantasy space so that he/she can encounter the gaze, where our "impossible identities" all can collide "to the point of psychosis" (Kristeva, 2002, 73), that film gains the power to effect psychic reconfiguration. Hitchcock's *Psycho* emerges in the middle of *The Blue Box,* since it epitomizes the sort of film that can entrance the spectator as a way of offering an experience of the gaze emanating from the site of the maternal object, the gaze being the pivot on which the thought specular turns. By this time in *The Blue Box,* the emphasis has shifted to the spectator's rollercoaster ride of Kristeva's intimate revolt— which is, briefly for now, *anamnesis* or recollection through the unconscious with the goal of rebirth—experienced on the non-diegetic level of film. My focus in revisiting *Psycho,* in other words, is not on the character of Norman Bates as a psychotic melancholic, although it is necessary, in order to open up possible spectatorial psychoanalytic experiences with the film, to lay out Norman's psyche, and for this purpose Kristeva's *Black Sun* is illuminating. Instead, my stress is on how *Psycho* can be engaged as an antidote to melancholia as it reels in the viewer formally, in the end to distance him/ her cinematically from its sadomasochistic drives. Given its profuse semiotic components, *Psycho* well exemplifies how lektonic traces, semiotic express-ibles, operate in thought-specular cinema to capture the traumatic content of a spectator's psyche and spread it out across the film, interpreting it to demystify it. The spectator is then given ample opportunities to lose him/ herself in the abyss while watching this film, which from the beginning positions the viewer as a voyeur, so that the melancholic viewer is easily caught in its net. Black holes, sites of the gaze, pervasive in *Psycho,* summon the spectator in the grip of a depressing maternal psychic incorporation to experience the dark night of Norman's soul as a way of escaping his/her maternal prison.

Chapter 6, "*Psycho*: the ultimate seduction," in addition brings Deleuze further into the project, this time by way of his celebration of sensation and abjection. It is not, however, Deleuze's *Cinema I* and *Cinema II* books (the more obvious choice) that I invoke to coordinate Kristeva's theory of the thought specular with Deleuzean theory but his study *Francis Bacon: The Logic of Sensation. Psycho* serves as a perfect film for illustrating a perhaps unexpected but critical overlap between Kristeva's semiotic and Deleuze's logic of sensation. Hitchcock's film partakes in Francis Bacon's fascination with, in Deleuze's words, "invisible forces that model flesh or shake it" (Deleuze, 2003, xxix). *Psycho* shares Bacon's urge to flesh out such forces as well as Bacon's pity for people encased in their flesh—for whom abjection might provide relief. Just as painting—and certainly Bacon's painting—to Deleuze, avoids the figurative through abstraction and isolation, disrupting narrative and turning the figure into an image that eventually dissolves into the outer, infinite field, Hitchcock's film traces Norman's evolution from a figure closed in upon to his flight through dissolution. With his emphasis on becoming, Deleuze helps us to apprehend *Psycho* in a way that liberates it from the demands of representation by attending to its dynamic sensations. Thus we can better grasp what Kristeva means when she describes film as semiotic, as carrying lektonic traces with the potential to absorb the viewer's traumatic material, and in turn as the site of the dark night of the soul. St. John's dark night is Deleuze's pure and intense sensational life of abjection, become splendor.

Deleuzeans will want to stop there. Yet my aim is not only to reveal an overlap between Deleuze and Kristeva but also to deploy Deleuze to make a case for Kristeva's thought specular. Deleuze allows us to perceive the homeo-pathic psychoanalytic aspect of *Psycho*: how the film presents an intense portrait of abjection to move beyond abjection. Deleuze's theory of the Body without Organs helps us to grasp the ubiquitous spreading across *Psycho* of a *jouissance*-propelled *das Ding* on the non-diegetic level. And because Deleuzean theory ironically gets beyond suffering *through abjection*, it calls attention to the way in which abjection inheres in the move surpassing it to Kristeva's infinite re-creation essential to intimate revolt. *Psycho* grants the spectator this gift, as it inserts Norman's swamp into conscious temporality.

Intimate revolt: in-depth

But what, more elaborately, is intimate revolt, and why it is so pressing? Kristeva promotes a penetrating *return* to one's most intimate unconscious recesses. She puts the intimate revolt she is determined to foster quite dramatically: "A synonym of dignity, revolt is our mysticism" (Kristeva, 2002, 4). Kristeva's "mysticism" entails an interminable interrogation of one's being, a questioning and displacement of the past—as a function of the search for oneself. It is an "aptitude for return, which is simultaneously recol-lection, interrogation, and thought" (Kristeva, 2002, 5). One unlocks meaning and in turn achieves happiness through an intimate revolt that plumbs the depths of the unconscious since it is (only) through a profound *anamnesis* or recollection that psychical restructuring can occur. In *Intimate Revolt*, Kristeva explains that such a beneficial psychoanalytic journey or revolt involves, in fact, an interminable *repetition* of "retrospective return" that leads to "the limits of the representable/thinkable/tenable" (Kristeva, 2002, 7). Pushing up consistently against such radical limits, intimate revolt results in the *jousissance* essential to psychic life and thus has the capacity to fuel an unending process of re-creation, with positive reverberations throughout the social network.

It is because intimate revolt entails accessing the abyss that constitutes the subject, what exceeds the boundaries of representation, thought, and the tenable, that Kristevan psychoanalysis extends the philosophical tradition that celebrates Being as "wrought by nothingness" or in other words "the copresence of nothingness in being" (Kristeva, 2002, 8). In fact, Kristeva attaches the entire "psychoanalytic movement inaugurated by Freud" to the philosophical practice of interrogating Nothingness and negativity central to her psychoanalytic theory of intimate revolt (Kristeva, 2002, 9). She places Freud within a tradition that features Heidegger, concentrating on "What is Metaphysics?" (1929/1977) and *Being and Time* (1927/1962) as well as Sartre's *Being and Nothingness* (1943). Kristeva locates variations on her psychoanalytic theme of coming up against a psychical reality that threatens consciousness, exposing it to "the pulse of being," also in Heidegger's work on Hölderlin, in which (to Kristeva) the philosopher captures what borders on psychosis in being (Kristeva, 2002, 9).

A seminal psychoanalytic text in this trajectory is Freud's *Die Verneinung* (*Negation*), in which Freud explores the unbinding of the drive in the form of the symbol. The quintessential question here is how violence proper to the drive becomes the negativity necessary to symbolizing. Under what conditions does this transporting of the drive to symbolization occur? As Kristeva poses the question in *Powers of Horror*, "what type of repression yields symbolization, hence a signifiable object, and what other type, on the contrary, blocks the way toward symbolization and topples drive into the lack-of-object of asymbolia or the auto-object of somatization?" (Kristeva, 1982, 33). The implication seems to be that a "smooth," that is, an effective or productive, metamorphosis from the drive to symbolization would involve a lasting encounter with the psychotic space beyond the border on which subjectivity is founded. By putting consciousness in danger, intimate revolt threatens to dissolve subject/object borders and renders one open to an "assault of the drive" (Kristeva, 2002, 9) as a way of generating symbolization and, in the process, galvanizing desire.

Kristeva's revolt of intimacy, then, involves a provisional psychosis of being. Such a black hole can be encountered not only in analysis but also in writing and film that has the capacity to unfold meaning on the level of sensations and drives, finding its basis in the realm of the semiotic. Kristeva attributes especially to modernist literature and of course the thought specular the power to incite such a psychoanalytic experience for the reader and viewer. "Film in revolt," that is, has the potential to traverse evil—defined in Kristeva as an *unrepresented* drive—by staging a confrontation with the abyssal core of the self, by engaging unbound realms such as "the unnamable feminine, destructivity, psychosis," in the end to *articulate* the drive (Kristeva, 2002, 10). By leading the way to these arenas of disintegration, a semiotic film is able to reconcile the subject with the *Zeitlos* or timeless—the timelessness of the drive. Such an immersion and consequent hooking up with the drive, followed by its activation and *representation*, give birth to a newly constituted, thriving subject whose desire is set in motion.

This psychical "work"—well known as working through—softens the hard kernel of trauma by inserting non-life (the encrustations of trauma) into life. Working through, put another way, inscribes death in "lived actuality," contracting death and life, or the timeless and time, through Kristeva's "moment of grace that signals...the analysand's rebirth" (Kristeva, 2002, 36). Psychic as well as somatic pain is transported into time. The timeless traumatic psychic material is withdrawn from the excitation, where it has been lodged for a prolonged period, and invited to "work at the heart of an expressible, conscious temporality" (Kristeva, 2002, 38). Resituated at the intersection of the atemporal and the temporal, the memory-trace of the psychic trouble endures. It is by no means extinguished. But it is spread out within the "linear time of remembering" (Kristeva, 2002, 38). *Jouissance* ensues. After the arduous "journey to the end of the night," transmission produces joy.

To Kristeva, happiness depends on intimacy—intimacy both with oneself and with others. Intimacy with others and in turn the happiness it bestows, in fact, hinge on an initial inquiry into oneself—on the level of the unconscious. Therefore, with so much at stake, like Guy Debord in *The Society of the Spectacle,* Kristeva rails against our consumerist, image-obsessed, robotizing society of the spectacle—as it is anathema to intimacy, damaging to her highly cherished "culture of revolt," and ultimately threatening to psychic life. In *Intimate Revolt,* Kristeva insists (and who can disagree?) that "The conditions of modern lives—with the primacy of technology, image, speed, and so forth, inducing stress and depression—have a tendency to reduce psychical space and to abolish the faculty of representation" (Kristeva, 2002, 11) essential for working through psychic fixations. We are heading rapidly, in other words, toward psychic suicide. Years later, in *Hatred and Forgiveness,* this theme retains all its vitality and urgency: "[P]sychical life is atrophying"; suffering is taking over modern man's body: "he is somatizing" (Kristeva, 2010, 157). Satisfaction surely involves more than popping a pill and being plastered to a screen. As Kristeva spells out in *Intimate Revolt*, her goal is both a revived subjectivity and a reformed society, the latter depending on the former.

Intimate *Volver*

Chapter 7, "Intimate *Volver*," presents Pedro Almodóvar's *Volver* as the epitome of Kristeva's thought specular, as it articulates and enables working through, as well as condemns the society of the spectacle for mangling intimacy. Kristeva's semiotic is Almodóvar's signature. Just as *Mulholland Drive* is both *about* the psychoanalytic power of fantasy *and* a demonstration of such power, *Volver* is *about* intimate revolt *and* also provides an experience of intimate revolt for the spectator. The main character, Raimunda, serves as a model for the spectator, who, along with Raimunda, is invited to encounter the abjected maternal object, convert that maternal Thing into Nothing through the allure of the gaze, and traverse a fundamental fantasy by looping timelessness together with time, in other words by working through trauma. In *Volver* ("to return"), extreme personal trauma is painstakingly transported from the deep psychic cavity in which it is stored to the temporal world through the mediation of semiotic expressibles, the lektonic traces that draw in the spectator and lead to the gaze.

Surely Almodóvar designed *Volver* to fulfill Kristeva's theoretical dreams! Not only does this film lay out artistically Kristeva's concept of intimate revolt and offer itself to the spectator as a route for such a formidable return. But, with the wonderful aid of traditional Spanish customs (for example, belief in ghosts), *Volver* makes a charming, specifically Spanish case for the necessity of including death, the *Zeitlos*, and eventually the Nothing within the social fabric. The haunting of the maternal ghost, especially as it turns into a real maternal presence in the daughter's world in the end, extends the emphasis in Kieslowski's *Blue* that blackness must be fringed with blue and that a state of lack is achieved only through an experience of loss that takes place through the semiotic, art, and naming. Like many of the films treated in *The Blue Box*, *Volver* insists on the relation of lack/desire to the loss of the originary object in a way that braids the two together, in a lasting encounter. While *Blue, The Piano Teacher,* and *Psycho* reflect Kristevan theory up to the point of separation from the maternal Thing, *Volver* presents an achieved world of potential desire and community in the company of the mother, who is now signified and given a place herself in the Symbolic Order. The Symbolic itself is shown as coming into a new sensuous, women-centered, caring, death-inflected formation in relation to the maternal body.

Like Kristeva, *Volver* presents intimate revolt also as a critical and effective way of undermining the society of the spectacle. *Volver* attacks the forces of social robotization by parodying a TV talk show that, through bribery, attempts to turn intimate psychic material into entertainment. By focusing on Raimunda's journey to the dark night of her soul and annexing the pathetic social symptoms of failing to work through trauma (such as this brash TV show "Wherever You Are"), *Volver* indicates that deep and lasting social change depends on singular intimate revolts. The isolation and mechanization that the society of the spectacle induces, in order to keep itself alive as the best hope for (simulated) desire and a (pseudo-) feeling of connection, need to be eradicated first by restoring psychic layers to the individual subject.

Kristeva outlines a psychoanalytic mode of overcoming the widespread threat of the spectacle, centered in the West but steadily and stealthily creeping across, and in turn emptying, the globe—of subjectivity, psychic life, and meaning. As Giorgio Agamben testifies in *Means without End*, "Guy Debord's books constitute the clearest and most severe analysis of the miseries and slavery of a society that by now has extended its dominion over the whole planet—that is to say, the society of the spectacle in which we live" (Agamben, 2000, 73). The resultant freedom of the subject who enacts Kristeva's theory of intimate revolt fosters an "energetic urge into a dynamic of meaning with the other" (Kristeva, 2002, 233). The subject of intimate revolt, having encountered the otherness of him/herself in the guise of the otherness of the analyst or work of art, gains the capacity to establish "optimal connections with others" (Kristeva, 2002, 233) in communities that can in turn be questioned and transformed.

Shaming racism

"The virtue of blushing: turning anxiety into shame in Haneke's *Caché*" (Chapter 8) concludes *The Blue Box* by dramatizing this case for the necessity of encountering the unconscious alterity of oneself for the sake of embracing others—intriguingly through *Caché*'s privileging of shame over guilt. First of all, though, *Caché* is fraught with anxiety. The film serves as a microcosm of French racist society (of the spectacle) devoid of "living desire," lacking lack (Lacan's definition of anxiety)—the state in which Guy Debord in *The Society of the Spectacle* believes the "commodity's mechanical accumulation [that] unleashes a *limitless artificiality*" has trapped us (Debord, 1994, 45). The video camera within the film produces an eruption of anxiety, being itself (I argue) a product of the society of the spectacle. Given the political content of the film—the FLN massacre and all its horrific effects, including Majid's loss of his parents and Georges's rejection of Majid as his adoptive brother as well as Georges's shutting him out later in life—at first glance, the viewer is tempted to read *Caché* as a moral tale, as a didactic allegory that condemns France for its colonization of Algeria as well as the 1961 massacre, and therefore as a film that expects anxiety to be mitigated by guilt.

However, by turning to Agamben's conception of shame, we can begin to probe the depths of *Caché* beyond this superficial reading. While guilt transforms the enigma of anxiety into something knowable and controllable, shame preserves the inexplicable and hence leads to "a new ethical material" being "touched upon in the living being" (Agamben, 1999, 104). In the place of Agamben's remnant (in *Remnants of Auschwitz*), the site of shame, the videotape serves as a witness of the intersection of subjectification and desubjectification to open up the possibility of intimacy, between the French protagonist, Georges, and the French-Arab protagonist, Majid, whom Georges simply wants to shrug off. In carving out a space, a lack, insofar as it recognizes the desubjectification inherent in subjectification, thus removing Majid as Other from that space, *Caché* in addition resists our fetishistic society of the spectacle, predicated on lack of lack, or lack of living desire, and in turn on the erasure of human beings driven beyond the limit of dignity. When the film fixes its eye on Majid's suicide, it confronts the gaze to unveil and bring forth the incomprehensible—hardship, forms of desubjectification, suicide, death, all disavowed by the fetishistic society of the spectacle—again to witness living being massacred (both literally and figuratively) by the society of the spectacle.

It is a lack of intimacy that leads to the cruel elision of Majid. And in refusing to participate in the intimacy offered to him by Majid's invitation to his death, Georges buffoonishly misses the opportunity of an authentic act. He casually rejects the event Majid stages for him, absolutely numb to the grandeur of Majid as a human being. Georges loses out on the chance to engage the abject (Majid as well as his mother) for the sake of encountering it as an agent of his freedom of mystical participation. He runs away from an intimate revolt, a "retrospective return" that could have led to "the limits of the representable/thinkable/tenable." The dramatic scene of emptiness to which Majid invites Georges offers Georges a provisional psychosis of being with the potential to set in motion a psychic exploration that could have enhanced Georges's life and his social surroundings as well. By intimating that George's dismissal of his mother results in the aggressivity of his drive targeting Majid, *Caché* even reinforces the idea that maintaining a link to the mOther keeps trauma tied to the subject's experience of separation from the maternal Thing so that its violence is not foisted onto the ethnic or racial Other. In looking at issues of race through the story of one Frenchman, *Caché* also italicizes the Kristevan point that only by opening up individual psychic lives will political revolt occur. So long as the human subject remains closed to the unconscious, its drive, and the drive's accompanying aggressivity, the social order will be plagued by hatred of the Other. Intimate revolt, *Caché* suggests, can stamp out racism.

Diagnosing a new episteme

Sounding faintly psychoanalytic, in *The Society of the Spectacle*, Debord laments that the modern subject no longer knows his own desires, that he leads an inauthentic life with no real connection to time, language, or history, and that he lacks a sense of "moving toward self-realization" as well as toward death (Debord, 1995, 115). Debord urges the Western world to enter into a certain form of consciousness "to experience its reality" (Debord, 1995, 117). "Real life" has been negated and will remain negated until "false consciousness," along with "a false consciousness of encounter," is done away with (Debord, 1995, 152). Debord even suggests that the spectacle stages "a false way out of a generalized autism" (Debord, 1995, 153). So long as the intimate is neglected, so long as intimate revolts fail to transpire, our state of generalized autism will remain solidly intact. Kristeva takes up where Debord leaves off: the "unrepresentable sensations of the soul" (Kristeva, 2002, 52) must be thought and named. It is not only the analyst but also meditative writers and filmmakers who have the ability to mobilize socially frozen drives and thereby crack open our culturally pervasive sensorial cave, "this *spectacle* still called for now...a 'society.' The nonstop exhibition of intimacy, televising of values..." reinforces "a desire that all children who've been raised on video games since birth know full well is a desire for death" (Kristeva, 2006, 64–5).

While "psychic depth" is in many respects a strictly private matter, Kristeva's thought specular as a kind of mass movement has the power to inject the unseen, the unconscious, death into consciousness and as a result undo the dehumanization of society—even to militate against biopower by inscribing thanatology into the society of the spectacle.[3] For, as Foucault elaborates in *Society Must Be Defended*, with the predominance of the power of social regularization, death is gradually *disqualified*. A threat to the biopolitical, death has become, Foucault reminds us, "something to be hidden away" (Foucault, 2003, 247). Foucault's spooky assertion that "Power no longer recognizes death" (Foucault, 2003, 248) provides a further rationale for Kristeva's perspective that contemporary society needs to reintegrate thanatology into the logic of the living, to bring the conscious/unconscious subject back to life—in order to stave off the new episteme she appears to be diagnosing, in which the psychically complex subject has vanished and biopolitical robots rule.

Notes

1 Kristevan theory in relation to film has been taken up only fairly recently. To my knowledge, just one book-length study has been published on this topic, Katherine J. Goodnow's *Kristeva in Focus: From Theory to Film Analysis*. However, *Kristeva in Focus* does not engage Kristeva's theory of intimate revolt, her genre of the thought-specular film, or her chapter, in *Intimate Revolt*, titled "Fantasy and Cinema"—all of which is central to my project. Goodnow considers how two core concepts in Kristeva—"order and disturbances of order ... and texts of society and history"—are played out in contemporary New Zealand films. She concentrates especially on Kristeva's notions of the abject (in relation to horror), strangers, and love (Goodnow, 2010, xiv).

2 In referring here to a kind of *jouissance* tied to the mother, I subscribe to Bruce Fink's sense of two orders of *jouissance*. As he clearly spells them out in *The Lacanian Subject: Between Language and Jouissance*, "Jouissance is thus what comes to substitute for the lost 'mother-child unity,' ... a kind of jouissance before the letter, before the institution of the symbolic order (J1)—corresponding to an unmediated relation between mother and child, a *real* connection between them—which gives way before the signifier, being canceled out by the operation of the paternal function. Some modicum or portion of that real connection is refound in fantasy (a jouissance after the letter, J2), in the subject's relation to the leftover or byproduct of symbolization ... : object *a* .... This second-order jouissance takes the place of the former 'wholeness' or 'completeness,' and fantasy—which stages this second-order jouissance—takes the subject beyond his or her ... mere existence ... and supplies a sense of being" (Fink, 1995, 60).

3 Foucault defines biopower in *Society Must Be Defended* as a second wave of power, beyond "a first seizure of power over the body in an individualizing mode." Rather than being individualizing, biopower is "massifying, that is directed ... at man-as-species." Now we have a "'biopolitics of the human race," a "new technology of power" that targets processes such as "the birth rate, the mortality rate, longevity and so on—together with a whole series of related economic and political problems which, in the second half of the eighteenth century, [became] biopolitics' first objects of knowledge" and control (Foucault, 2003, 243).

Works cited

Agamben, Giorgio (1999) *Remnants of Auschwitz: The Witness and the Archive.* Trans. Daniel Heller-Roazen. New York: Zone Books.

—(2000) *Means without End: Notes on Politics.* Trans. Vincenzo Binetti and Cesare Casarino. Minneapolis: University of Minnesota Press.

Debord, Guy (1995) *The Society of the Spectacle.* Trans. Donald Nicholson-Smith. New York: Zone Books.

Deleuze, Gilles (2003) *Francis Bacon: The Logic of Sensation.* Trans. Daniel W. Smith. Minneapolis: University of Minnesota Press.

Fink, Bruce (1995) *The Lacanian Subject: Between Language and Jouissance.* Princeton: Princeton UP.

Foucault, Michel (2003) *Society Must Be Defended: Lectures at the College de France, 1975–1976.* Trans. David Macey. New York: Picador.

Goodnow, Katherine J. (2010) *Kristeva in Focus: From Theory to Film Analysis.* New York: Berghahn Books.

Heath, Stephen (1998) "God, Faith and Film: *Breaking the Waves.*" *Literature & Theology*, 12 (1): 93–107.

Heidegger, Martin (1929/1977) "What is Metaphysics?" In *Basic Writings.* Trans. David Farrell Krell. New York: HarperCollins Publishers.

Kristeva, Julia (1982) *Powers of Horror: An Essay on Abjection.* Trans. Leon S. Roudiez. New York: Columbia UP.

—(1989) *Black Sun: Depression and Melancholia.* Trans. Leon S. Roudiez. New York: Columbia UP.

—(2000) *Crisis of the Euro/pean Subject.* Trans. Susan Fairfield. New York: Other Press.

—(2002) *Intimate Revolt: The Power and Limits of Psychoanalysis.* Trans. Jeanine Herman. New York: Columbia UP.

—(2006) *Murder in Byzantium.* Trans. C. Jon Delogu. New York: Columbia UP.

—(2010) *Hatred and Forgiveness.* Trans. Jeanine Herman. New York: Columbia UP.

Lacan, Jacques (1981/1973) *The Four Fundamental Concepts of Psycho-analysis: The Seminar of Jacques Lacan: Book XI.* Ed. Jacques-Alain Miller. Trans. Alan Sheridan. New York: W. W. Norton & Co.

Silverman, Kaja (1988) *The Acoustic Mirror: The Female Voice in Psychoanalysis and Cinema.* Bloomington: Indiana UP.

2

Black and *Blue*: Kieslowski's melancholia

In *The Fragile Absolute*, Slavoj Žižek explicates Pauline love or *agape* as entirely distinct from "love *within the confines of the Law*." The "true agape," Žižek informs us, is "closer to the modest dispensing of spontaneous goodness" (Žižek, 2000, 100); and it is cinematically given its ultimate expression, in Žižek's mind, in Krzysztof Kieslowski's *Blue* (1993)—the first film in Kieslowski's exquisite *Three Colours Trilogy* (1993–4). To convey this idea of *agape* or the dispensing of spontaneous goodness in *Blue*, Žižek seizes on the final scene of the film in which the camera presents four figures who played intimate roles in Julie's life in various settings (Žižek seems to have missed a tiny, curled-up, naked figure of Olivier, who appears at the center of Julie's eye, as the fifth member of the series):

> Antoine, the boy who witnessed the fatal car crash in which her husband and children [sic] died; Julie's mother, sitting silent in her room in an old people's home; Lucille, her young striptease dancer friend, at work on the stage in a nightclub; Sandrine, her dead husband's mistress, touching her naked belly in the last phase of pregnancy, bearing the unborn child of her deceased lover. ... The continuous drift from one set to another (they are separated only by a dark blurred background across which the camera pans) creates the effect of mysterious synchronicity.
>
> (Žižek, 2000, 101)

Žižek takes his cue on how to read this final scene from an earlier shot, of Julie in her hospital bed after the traumatic car accident that kills her husband and five-year-old daughter. Atavistically frozen in shock, Julie lends her eye to the camera in a close-up that allows us to observe "objects in the hospital room reflected in this eye as derealized spectral apparitions." Encapsulated in this shot, according to Žižek, is Hegel's "night of the world," especially given that Hegel wrote that "one catches sight of this night when one looks human beings in the eye—into a night that becomes awful" (Žižek, 2000, 102). Julie's eye may be read as indicating Julie's symbolic death, her withdrawal from her symbolic bearings.

In a move that is too black and white rather than black and blue, Žižek contrasts this night of symbolic death with the final scene of what is to him symbolic daylight: "the final shot stands for the reassertion of life" (Žižek, 2000, 102). Žižek even reads the second or final drifting of camera shots (despite the "dark blurred background") as characterized by "ethereal lightness" (Žižek, 2000, 103). But does *Blue* veer in this way from night to day, or is the film more like Julie's sugar cube that soaks in her coffee, liquid of trauma, depression, grief—an absorbent object that receives special, prolonged attention? I read *Blue* as a meditation on a black sun that refuses, all the way to the end, to be bright, that resists losing contact with the rich darkness of depression. This stress on pervasive blueness turns out, moreover, to support a political reading of the film that Kristeva's book *Crisis of the Euro/pean Subject* (2000), Cathy Caruth's *Unclaimed Experience* (1996), and Ewa Ziarek's *An Ethics of Dissensus* (2001) can help us to flesh out.

Melancholic sublimation

In this endless mourning, in which language and the body revive in the heartbeat of a grafted French, I examine the still warm corpse of my maternal memory ... what I say is 'maternal,' because at the outer edge of words set to music and of unnamable urges, in the neighborhood of the senses and the biology that my imagination has the good fortune to bring into existence in French—suffering comes back to me, Bulgaria, my suffering.

JULIA KRISTEVA, *CRISIS OF THE EURO/PEAN SUBJECT*

Žižek interprets the opening (night) and closing (day) shots (as he sees them) in *Blue* as staging

the two opposed aspects of freedom: the 'abstract' freedom of pure self-relating negativity, withdrawal-into-self, cutting of the links with reality; and the 'concrete' freedom of the loving acceptance of others, of experiencing oneself as free, as finding full realization in relating to others.

In *The Fragile Absolute*, Julie swings from Schelling's "ego-tistic *contraction* to boundless *expansion*" (Žižek, 2000, 103).

In *Crisis of the Euro/pean Subject*, Kristeva outlines her own sense of two dominant modes of freedom. The former lies within the European tradition of philosophy, religion, and democracy, a subjective freedom that she mainly associates with Kant's "absolute autoactivity, a spontaneity and a power of man to determine himself on his own" (Kristeva, 2000, 119). Kristeva regards "the Western valorization of questioning," from Plato's dialogues to Augustine's sense of the ego, as culminating "in the Kantian affirmation of a spontaneous, sovereign, and in this sense liberatory understanding." This notion of freedom foregrounds the "power of autocommencement on the part of universal Reason" (Kristeva, 2000, 120). And it is this conception of freedom that, unfortunately, to Kristeva, has deteriorated into our current preoccupation with production, with the power to mass-produce objects of consumption.

At the opposite end of the spectrum from Kant's freedom of "autoactive understanding" or the Western glorification of questioning and critique, the latter idea of freedom that Kristeva identifies is that of Orthodoxy. It exalts "an ineffable religious inwardness" as well as "the ecclesiastical community in which it flourishes," in other words, mysticism (Kristeva, 2000, 134). Kristeva mainly derives her sense of such a freedom from her interpretation of the Orthodox Trinity. Here the Holy Spirit proceeds from the Father *through* the Son rather than (as in Catholicism) from the Father *and* the Son. As Kristeva writes, "the Orthodox 'through' suggests a delicious but deadly annihilation of the Son and of the believer"; "the Son (and with him the believer) is caught in an exquisite logic of submission and exaltation that offers him the joys and sorrows intrinsic to the master-slave dialectic" (Kristeva, 2000, 139). Man is thereby called to unite *freely* with God. Pleasure in pain is explored; masochism and the depressive position are eroticized. Kristeva celebrates the "sublinguistic, suboedipal, and supersensory adoration" of the Orthodox faith, tying it to a freedom to exceed the boundary, to inhabit a subjectivity that does not shut out passion, lament, or death. Herein are endless delights: silence, tenderness, love of beauty, a feeling of an inaccessible God; "thick sensory texture" that accompanies an "overabundance of soul" (Kristeva, 2000, 148, 150, 151).

Kristeva's Orthodox freedom seems to be more akin to Žižek's Hegelian sense of symbolic death than to his notion of Pauline *agape*, even though Žižek refers to the latter as mysticism. In other words, what Julie starts out from in *Blue* might be seen as a form of freedom that Kristeva would hope Julie would not lose altogether. Yet Žižek's interpretation of the film has Julie moving to an exclamatory affirmation, "a Yes! to life in its mysterious synchronic multitude" (Kristeva, 2000, 103), that surpasses sadness and pain. The work of mourning that Julie accomplishes, in Žižek's non-Hegelian eyes, leaves melancholia behind. Moreover, Julie's supposed final dispensing of spontaneous goodness would be merely a continuation of her compulsion to be "good and generous," qualities her husband Patrice attributes to her, a debilitating need that only suppresses her desire. Instead, in *Blue*, Kieslowski participates in the spirit of Kristeva's masochistic brand of Orthodox freedom by sustaining the blueness of melancholia from start to finish. In fact, in *Kieslowski on Kieslowski*, we read: "Blue is liberty ... the film *Blue* is about liberty, the imperfections of human liberty. How far are we really free?" (Stok, 1993, 212). After the car accident, Julie is utterly traumatized, catapulted into a severe depression, whose roots lie, I contend, in her missed relation with her mother. She attempts initially to shut it all out, but she eventually collects pieces of her past to stay close to her psychic history. *Blue* insists on retaining a connection to the maternal Thing. But before we consider how the film effects such a lifeline, we need to observe its basis in melancholia in the first place.

In *Black Sun: Depression and Melancholia*, Kristeva identifies certain triggers of such despair: "A betrayal, a fatal illness, some *accident* or handicap that abruptly wrests me away from what seemed to me the normal category of normal people" (Kristeva, 1989, 3–4, my emphasis). The force of the events that produce depression, Kristeva elaborates, is apt to be "out of proportion to the disaster that overwhelms" the subject (Kristeva, 1989, 4). An old trauma is disturbed. A current breakdown hits harder because of an earlier loss of someone once loved:

> The disappearance of that essential being continues to deprive me of what is most worthwhile in me; ... my grief is but the deferment of the hatred or desire for ascendency that I nurture with respect to the one who betrayed or abandoned me. My depression points to my not knowing how to lose—I have perhaps been unable to find a valid compensation for the loss? It follows that any loss entails the loss of my being—and of Being itself.
>
> (Kristeva, 1989, 5)

In *Blue*, this pattern can be discerned. The film offers a more elemental explanation (than the car accident alone) of Julie's psychic trouble: her ruptured relation with her mother, now institutionalized in a home apparently for Alzheimer's patients. It is as though Kieslowski uses Alzheimer's disease as a metaphor for a lost maternal object, as a representation of the malfunctional mother-daughter relation, which activated in the first place Julie's "impossible mourning for the maternal object" (Kristeva, 1989, 9). Julie's pitiful visit to her institutionalized mother—during which her mother clings to memories that exclude Julie, addresses her more than once as Marie-France (the mother's dead sister), and is mainly transfixed by some bungee-jumping on television—painfully conveys Kristeva's idea that depression is based on a non-loving but loved, and therefore hated, mother. "According to classic psychoanalytic theory (Abraham, Freud, Melanie Klein), depression," Kristeva tells us,

> conceals an aggressiveness toward the lost object, thus revealing the ambivalence of the depressed person with respect to the object of mourning. "I love that object," is what that person seems to say about the lost object, "but even more so I hate it; because I love it and in order not to lose it, I imbed it in myself; but because I hate it, that other within myself is a bad self, I am bad, I am non-existent, I shall kill myself."
>
> (Kristeva, 1989, 11)

"The complaint against oneself is exposed as a complaint against another, and putting oneself to death but a tragic disguise for massacring an other" (Kristeva, 1989, 11). The film retrospectively suggests that, having missed out on a reciprocal originary bond, Julie attempts suicide at the beginning (she swallows pills), flirts with suicide later in the blue swimming pool, cuts her knuckles on a wall so that they bleed, and in general deprives herself of comfort and desire. Suicide is, for the melancholic, a "merging with sadness and, beyond it, with that impossible love, never reached, always elsewhere, such as the promises of nothingness, of death" (Kristeva, 1989, 12–13). As a classic melancholic, Julie also cannot access her desire, since no erotic object can replace the preobject, the lost, yet psychically retained, maternal object confining her libido. Julie exhibits desire neither for her dead husband, Patrice, nor (at least during most of *Blue*) for Olivier. Had Julie desired her husband even before his death, she certainly would have sensed his lengthy love affair with Sandrine. "The melancholy Thing interrupts desiring metonymy, just as it prevents working out the loss within the psyche" (Kristeva, 1989, 14).

On the surface, however, Julie's melancholic cannibalism seems to involve her daughter (rather than mother). "Better fragmented, torn, cut up, swallowed, digested ... than lost," writes Kristeva. "The melancholy cannibalistic imagination is a repudiation of the loss's reality and of death as well. It manifests the anguish of losing the other through the survival of self, surely a deserted self but not separated from what still and ever nourishes it and becomes transformed into the self—which also resuscitates—through such a devouring" (Kristeva, 1989, 12). Finding one of Anna's blue-wrapped lollipops in her purse, Julie chews it up almost viciously, taking (like an animal) quick, hard little bites, devouring it, as if in an effort to consume her daughter, to incorporate her so as not to lose her, to repossess her. After the accident "Anna?" is the first word Julie utters. News of Anna's death (rather than that of Patrice) at the beginning of *Blue* causes Julie to wince in unspeakable pain. It is also Anna whom the ubiquitous melancholic color blue associates with, mainly through the fetishistic blue beads Julie tears off a blue lamp in Anna's "blue room" and carries with her throughout the film. And Julie attaches at the end of the film to Patrice's unborn baby, in Sandrine's womb, as if to reunite thereby with her daughter. However, Julie's own status as a mother serves as a substitute for her lost, yet psychically clung to, maternal Thing, as if to become a mother is both to identify better with the maternal Thing and to produce an object (a child) to be in its place. To eat a lollipop is also to become a child, which necessarily calls up a mother. Anna, Julie's mother, and Julie are all part of the same melancholic psychic constellation.

In 1996, before he died, Kieslowski commented on ways in which structures of bereavement define human beings. He thought that people have a fundamental need to imagine that those they have loved and lost somehow still surround them:

> they exist within us as somebody who judges us ... we take their opinions into account even though they're not there any more, even though they're dead. I very often have the feeling that my father is somewhere near by. It doesn't matter if he's actually there or not, but I wonder what he'd say about what I've done or want to do, that means he's there. My mother, too .... It's some sort of ethical system which exists somewhere within.
>
> (Stok, 1993, 134–5)

We can expect from this statement about the need to imagine lost loves that Kieslowski's art would avoid neutralizing grief, even in some form of aesthetic redemption. Kieslowski's stress, instead, falls on lost objects that do not entirely disappear, that cannot be fully surpassed. And so he bestows upon the abandoned, grief-stricken victim a fetish, a reminder of the lost love, a material trace. Julie hangs on to her mother through Anna, on to both of them through music, and on to Anna, her best substitute for the maternal Thing, through in particular the sparkling blue chandelier.

Blue prefigures its dedication to non-assuagement from the outset when Julie extends her finger to touch Anna's miniature coffin, underscoring the palpable nature of her loss. *Blue* overflows with tangible reminders that seem to refuse to vanish. Anna herself seems to revive and multiply in an excruciating scene in which a gang of boisterous girls, shimmering with gaiety, plunges into the blue pool, next to Julie. Featured eerily as an emblem of disaster at the beginning of the film, as Anna holds it flapping in the wind outside the window of the ill-fated car, the wrapper of Anna's lollipop, a piece of silver-blue foil/trash, gets reincarnated when Julie finds another one in her purse. *Blue* is structured according to one piece of undisposed garbage after another, its sustained illustration that "the Thing" is "a waste with which, in [her] sadness," the melancholic merges (Kristeva, 1989, 15). The single leftover piece of furniture in Julie's home, a mattress on which she and Olivier make love, is retained by Olivier, even though Julie had requested that it be discarded along with everything else in the house. Much is made in the film of an old, hunched over woman, dressed in a blue coat, stuffing a bottle into the hole of a recycling bin, where it gets stuck. And Julie throws "Patrice's" concerto into the teeth of a garbage truck, watches it get chewed up, but copies seem magically to surface: a street musician, the flutist, appears easily to have been able to acquire one. The deliberately trashed music of the concerto cradles the entire film. The punchline of the vulgar joke that Patrice was telling to Anna and Julie before and after the accident—about a coughing woman whose doctor prescribes a laxative and then says to her, "Now try coughing"—conjures up an image of withheld waste.

Not only through her psychic attachment to Anna does Julie cultivate her melancholia, but she also clings to the maternal Thing via "melody, rhythm, semantic polyvalency ... poetic form" in the guise of classical music. It is pretty clearly Julie who has composed her famous musician husband's concerto. This is the "writing" that Julie produces to bear "witness to the hiatus, blank, or spacing that constitutes death for the [depressive's] unconscious" (Kristeva, 1989, 26). And, although it is true that Julie eventually collaborates on this musical piece with Olivier and completes it, I do not think we are compelled to read her artistic activity as culminating in completed mourning, if "completed" signifies total detachment from suffering. Julie's return to music underscores her immersion in the semiotic of melancholia. While she gradually moves beyond the asymbolia that we might regard as the opaque cavern of the melancholic in her purest state, Julie's later turn to music for solace secures for her, as art according to Kristeva secures for the artist and connoisseur, "a sublimatory hold over the lost Thing" (Kristeva, 1989, 97).

Through art, Julie accesses the Real of her losses in a way that keeps them from disappearing. This is not merely a proper channeling of psychic energy into a culturally celebrated form (i.e., an instance of what is at least taken to be Freudian sublimation) but a way, through beauty, "the admirable face of loss," of transforming loss "in order to make it live" (Kristeva, 1989, 99). Julie's composing, with its ecstatic quality appropriating the death drive that fuels it, enables Julie to grieve in a manner that refuses to relinquish loss. Her final revision of the concerto clinches this point. After Julie confronts Patrice's mistress, Sandrine, in the bathroom at the court house, she plunges into a sharp-blue pool, swimming under water for a long time, as if to drown herself. However, later Julie is able briskly to write musical notes in blue ink, with a blue pen, as if the glistening water of the potentially deadly pool has taken form in the musical notes. Julie slows down and lightens the concerto. She removes the trumpets and percussion instruments and replaces the piano with flutes. Flute music, in fact, then plays through to the very end of *Blue*, until the completion of the credits. It harks back to the figure of the flute player in the film who has perhaps the most explicit thematic line: "You always gotta hold on to something."

Although in *The Fright of Real Tears: Krzysztof Kieslowski Between Theory and Post-Theory*, Žižek reads Julie at the end as forging a link between sublimation and the death drive (a view I wholeheartedly agree with), his further emphasis on a "reconstitution of the fantasy that allows us access to reality" as well as his sense that through such a fantasy Julie tames the "raw Real" (Žižek, 2001, 176) misses the function and meaning of Julie's melancholic sublimation: that it enables her not to avoid the Thing but to stay tied to it. Julie's concerto for the Unification of Europe, with its lines on Pauline love from Corinthians, partakes of the Real rather than protects against it. "[A]t the outer edge of words set to music," Julie, like Kristeva, can examine the "still warm corpse of [her] maternal memory," where "suffering comes back to her" (Kristeva, 2000, 169). Even at the end blueness pervades *Blue*.

Before Julie leaves for Olivier's place, Anna's dazzling blue beads (only blurry now, like beads in an impressionist painting) fill the screen, as if to color the couple's subsequent lovemaking. We next get another close-up of Julie's face only now expressing the *jouissance* of melancholic desire (Julie has gone to Olivier this time). As the images of major figures in Julie's life drift by, we see Sandrine's fetus via ultrasound in the same bright-blue color; and when Julie cries unmistakably near the very end, blue color, in the form of what resembles flames, creeps up, higher and higher, around her face. Next the screen turns totally blue like an abstract expressionist painting, as the concerto rises up, so that we are overpowered finally by music and blueness, sucked into a semiotic space, in an act of melancholic sublimation and desire that indexes the Real. Julie's grief is not overcome but presented; her loss accessed. Julie as well as the film itself, cinematically, refuses not to hold on to something. The film's crawling pace, fragments, pauses, and lulls, its many silences, sparse dialogue, general feeling of blankness, and its preoccupation with close-ups of Julie's pained and eventually blissful face as well as its non-diegetic music convey her mental state in ways that hold on to the intensity of her excruciating past—as desire embryonically emerges through confrontation with loss.

Julie gives up on her attempt to flee from loss, her total erasure of her past, her act of throwing it all away; she cannot forcibly achieve a deliberate liberatory understanding, founded on reason—the cold reason of shutting out her multiple losses. *Blue* reveals that this would be a mere impasse to freedom. Julie comes around, instead, to embrace a life enriched by the "trash" of the film. The music that haunts Julie as well as the film, and through the film the spectator, only testifies to loss's profound persistence. Julie, the film, and in turn the spectator—all stare loss/death straight in the face only now to get a grip on it. In the final image of Julie's mother, in fact, the mother closes her eyes, and a nurse comes rushing up, suggesting the mother's demise.

What is especially strange and intriguing is that the very music employed to keep the film awash in melancholia, even during the faint emergence of desire, the music that fills the ellipses of the film signifying the impossibility of Symbolically representing loss but the need to index it otherwise, more semiotically, is the concerto commissioned by the European Council to celebrate the unification of Europe. Why is *this* music, with such a globally weighty purpose, not more conventionally celebratory rather than so overpoweringly sad? Kieslowski would seem to be making Kristeva's point about the virtues of including melancholia on the international level as well.

Is the concerto, then, as he morosely but exquisitely presents it, not Kieslowski's way of expressing Kristeva's notion that "the Orthodox experience of subjectivity and freedom might, even given its own downside, complete, stimulate, and enrich Western experience" (Kristeva, 2000, 117)? In *Crisis of the Euro/pean Subject*, Kristeva sings the praises of depressivity, the non-performative sensibility, and the lack of capacity for critical reason. Their positive side is "the value placed on dependence, participation, and the bond," an "invisible mystery scotomized by the economy of the image" (Kristeva, 2000, 155). Relinquishing the image, Kieslowski conveys this profound mystery by punctuating his film with an infusion of blackouts accompanied by Julie's concerto—a combination that has the power to offer the spectator the experience of Kristeva's Eastern Orthodox believer. He/She is pulled into the "exquisite logic of submission and exaltation that offers him [or her] the joys and sorrows" of melancholia (Kristeva, 2000, 139) to shape a passionate subjectivity founded on death as a stepping stone within "a global civilizing effort" (Kristeva, 2000, 114).

The politics of melancholic sublimation

[I]t is here, in the equally widespread and bewildering encounter with trauma ... that we can begin to recognize the possibility of a history that is no longer straightforwardly referential. ... Through the notion of trauma ... we can understand that a rethinking of reference is aimed not at eliminating

history but at resituating it in our understanding, that is, at precisely
permitting history to arise where immediate understanding may not.

CATHY CARUTH, *UNCLAIMED EXPERIENCE*

In *The Fright of Real Tears*, Žižek explains that, faced with the gap between a
drab social atmosphere and "the optimistic, bright image which pervaded the
heavily censored official media," Kieslowski's first response was to represent
Poland more adequately in all the ambiguity of its dullness. Kieslowski took
"an authentic documentary approach." Žižek quotes Kieslowski to this effect:

> There was a necessity, a need—which was very exciting for us—to
> describe the world. The Communist world had described how it should be
> and not how it really was ... . If something hasn't been described, then it
> doesn't officially exist. So that if we start describing it, we bring it to life.
> (Žižek, 2001,71; Stok, 1993, 54–5)

But, according to Žižek, eventually the invasive quality of documentary, the
obscenity of "unwarranted probing into the other's intimacy," took its toll
on Kieslowski. He felt the "fright of real tears," now preferring glycerine to
make tears. Worried about exceeding bounds of privacy, Kieslowski entered
a "domain of fantasmatic intimacy ... marked by a 'No trespass!' sign" that
"should be approached only via fiction, ... to avoid pornographic obscenity"
(Žižek, 2001, 72). It was "a fidelity to the Real that compelled Kieslowski to
abandon documentary realism"; he encountered "something more Real than
reality itself" (Žižek, 2001, 71).

However, Žižek observes Kieslowski's retreat from documentary realism,
which Žižek claims Kieslowski relinquishes to access something more "Real,"
only to bring Kieslowski back to an "optimistic, bright image" like that "which
pervaded the heavily censored official [Polish] media" (Žižek, 2001, 71). Žižek's
idea of Kieslowski's depiction of his characters' lives ends up dovetailing with
a Communist vision of dancers gliding in a circle, the kind of image sketched
parodically in the fiction of Milan Kundera to convey a weightless, politically
induced drunken joy. The affirmation of life, the "Yes!" that Žižek attributes to
Julie (despite its Christian source), has a way of seeming disturbingly similar
to the supposed Communist euphoria that Žižek himself acknowledges
Kieslowski was rejecting.

Instead, it is crucial to realize that Kieslowski's sustained melancholia
serves as a *political* antidote to such lightness of being (and to reject Žižek's
sense of Kieslowski's utopian promise of sunny social reconciliation). In *Blue*,
melancholy, then, counters both Western consumerism and Communism.

As we have seen, the film inserts a concerto celebrating the contemporary unification of Europe into the dark space of trauma, where it brings forth the meaning of melancholia. Likewise, it is the melancholic nature of Orthodoxy that enables Kristeva to argue for the indispensability of Eastern European values to globalization. She recommends that the process of globalization access Orthodoxy's "mysticism of contact," its "sublinguistic," "suboedipal," "supersensory" qualities, its "subverbal sensuality." Kristeva laments the surrender "to the new world order that wants to see only a single head—no, a single computer" (Kristeva, 2000, 175). To view Kieslowski (another Eastern European), as Žižek does, as celebrating a triumphant mourning even at the end of *Blue* is to place him in Kristeva's category of those who give up on the delicious and deadly annihilation of the Son and the believer, as the Holy Spirit proceeds in the Orthodox faith from the Father *through* the Son. While eroticism in the West has been banalized and commercialized, nullified in a permissive society, its vitality is preserved in the Orthodox Church as the Son in the Orthodox Trinity engages in a master-slave dialectic with the Father and as the believer is called on, as a result, to participate in "an unprecedented exploration of pleasure in pain" or erotic mysticism (Kristeva, 2000, 139).

The intensification of vision and feeling at the conclusion of *Blue* is by no means that of a light Christian joy but much more of a profound mystical recognition of myriad painful interrelations. Herein may lie a form of redemption; but depressive *jouissance* (a *jouissance* prior to the letter, to the Symbolic Order, and tied to the mOther) is not sacrificed. Blueness persists. Kieslowski is incapable of ending with a vision that would rob us, or his film, of density; he would seem to be as unwilling as Kristeva to forget past losses. Just as Hannah Arendt did not share Adorno's view that to write poetry after Auschwitz is barbaric because for Arendt the imagination is alone able to "think" horror, Kieslowski produces an ending, in *Blue*, that "thinks" the trauma that Julie has undergone, one whose agony gets woven into the concerto for the unification of Europe.

In *Unclaimed Experience: Trauma, Narrative, and History*, Cathy Caruth offers a similar "thinking through" of the Resnais/Duras film *Hiroshima mon amour* (1959). In the end, trauma here goes untranslated and untranscended, and as a result imperfectly mourned. The Japanese man and the French woman "communicate" "through what they do not directly comprehend." Their encounter relies on "what they do not fully know in their own traumatic pasts." In turn, Caruth proposes, the spectator him/herself is offered "a new mode of seeing and listening ... from *the site of trauma*," just as in *Blue*, as soon as we are made to peer through Julie's eyes at her doctor, Olivier coming to visit, and the funeral televised on a miniature TV, from that moment on, our outlook emanates from the locus of trauma. A witnessing of trauma is able to take place only through incomprehension and "our departure from sense and understanding" (Caruth, 1996, 56); to Caruth, such immediacy is "inextricably tied up with the belatedness and incomprehensibility that remain at the heart of [a] repetitive seeing" (Caruth, 1996, 92).

Likewise, the father in the famous burning corpse dream in Freud's *Interpretation of Dreams* can only face, or "think," the knowledge of his child's death as he is asleep—dreaming. The dream itself wakes the sleeper, paradoxically, so that "the dream confronts the reality of a death from which he cannot turn away." With such an "awakening," there is no "simple movement of knowledge or perception" (Caruth, 1996, 99). The dream shows the necessity and simultaneous impossibility of confronting death. It allows an apprehension of that impossibility and in this way facilitates the (impossible) confrontation. Like Freud and Kristeva, Kieslowski also focuses on the parent-child bond—on Julie's similar awakening to a reality of her child's death from which she cannot turn away—to make the point of the inextricability of trauma and survival. Of course, Caruth too (like Kieslowski and Kristeva) is not just referring to individual catastrophes: she conceives of history itself as fundamentally predicated on trauma.

We can take this idea of the constitutive traumatic nature of history to a more practical level (as well as directly back to Kristeva) by engaging Ewa Ziarek's chapter, "The Libidinal Economy of Power, Democracy, and the Ethics of Psychoanalysis," in her book *An Ethics of Dissensus*. Ziarek can help us to understand more specifically what it means, and what it more ideally might mean, to carry the death drive—expressed in *Blue* as the passion to embrace the dead child as well as the "warm corpse" of "maternal memory"—to the political or civic sphere. Ziarek is completely Kristevan in her preoccupation with "an infinite responsibility for the Other." She ushers this concern into the political arena of democratic struggles, hoping that its ethics can serve as a supplement to hegemonic politics. Ziarek rethinks antagonisms constitutive of subjectivity in relation to the sociosymbolic order, taking into full consideration "the libidinal economy of drive" that subtends it. She brings to political theory, and mainly to the question of democracy, the issue of "the irreducible negativity within the subject at odds with its social positionality" (Ziarek, 2001, 118).

Borrowing from both Levinas and Kristeva, Ziarek proposes that a shift take place, a relocating of Imaginary Others—for example, Jews, blacks, women—who serve as a metaphor of a subject's own aggression. Instead, Ziarek would like to see "the acknowledgment of the internal alterity and antagonism within the subject be a condition of responsibility in intersubjective relations" (Ziarek, 2001, 127). Through the interplay of three psychoanalytic processes—traversal of fantasy, an encounter with the abject as one's own intimate yet inassimilable alterity, and sublimation of the death drive—the subject can come to terms with "the inassimilable otherness within herself and the exorbitant alterity of the Other," so that instead of violence (propelled by the death drive) toward the Other, the Symbolic Order may be restructured (Ziarek, 2001, 129). Ziarek looks to sublimation for a deflection of the aggressivity of the death drive, for satisfaction elsewhere. Instead of murderous destruction of the Other, in Ziarek's conception we have Symbolic transformation, as a result of an infusion of *jouissance* into the Symbolic. Confrontation with the drive, in all its "inassimilable negativity" (Ziarek, 2001, 134), can lead to ethical social relations. This is for Ziarek the heart of a feminist politics of radical democracy.

While Caruth posits the traumatic nature of history, Ziarek explains that it is a mischanneling of the subject's constitutive antagonism that has been, at least partly, responsible for certain racist traumas. This is the very reason why the structure of society and the method by which it is governed ought to take death into account. That is, history needs to acknowledge the constitutive traumatic nature of existence and subjectivity, to incorporate passion, lament, and death, to reconfigure itself as it evolves in relation to loss—in order to keep from producing specific traumatized victims. By recognizing the "foreigner" within ourselves, as Kristeva asserts on the first page of *Strangers to Ourselves*, "we are spared detesting him in himself" (Kristeva, 1991, 1). Racism and social conflict must stop bearing the burden of the trauma underlying history. That trauma, instead, needs to be articulated as the core of Being itself, in relation to which all existence, including that of history, necessarily forms, and to which a dose of melancholia keeps the subject tied. The process of globalization devoid of a melancholic link to loss and death will only sustain a demeaning, destructive, racist conception of the Other. A melancholic encounter with trauma, like Julie's in *Blue*, that is, with one's inassimilable intimate alterity, *das Ding*, maternal Thing, leading to a semioticization of the Symbolic, will cut down on social division, instead spreading *jouissance,* affect, and the drive democratically across the social, global arena.

To conclude, again in disagreement with Žižek, *Blue* does not progress from trauma to a kind, humanitarian gesture of reaching out nor does it provide a fantasy screen that offers protection from trauma. Neither does the film offer a compensatory aesthetics that would serve the same purpose. Instead, *Blue* immerses itself in unspeakable loss, allowing the viewer to swim in Julie's bright blue pool, to make as real as possible the Real of her grief. Especially through its many blackouts, *Blue* pulls the viewer into Nothing, escorting him or her to disarray.

"Nothing" plays a key role in this film. When the man who rents Julie's apartment to her inquires, "What do you do?" she replies, "Nothing. Nothing at all." Julie asserts to Antoine that "Nothing's important." And she mentions to her mother that she has one thing now to do—"nothing." Neither *Blue* nor this chapter, then, is ultimately a panegyric to fetishism, which gives way in the course of the film to Nothing. Fetishes such as Anna's blue lamp serve a purpose, ironically, in delimiting a space for loss that can metamorphose into blankness. Ultimately, there is nothing more important than Nothing in this film. The various ellipses in *Blue* are powerful: they lure the viewer into Julie's mental state so that the viewer too can temporarily lose his/her bearings. Through the film's indexing of loss, pain, and sadness, as well as the *jouissance* of melancholia, Julie and the spectator can begin to make a transition from a fixation on an object that fills in the blank to blankness itself, but a blankness or Nothingness fringed with blue. Toward the end of *Blue*, Olivier suggests that Julie identify herself, this time around, as the composer of the concerto. Now she is in a position to be acknowledged as the creator of a concerto that includes untranslated Greek lyrics. Now Julie can receive recognition as the maker (not of a fetish but) of a piece of art with a mystery at its center.

Kieslowski as well as Kristeva promotes a form of globalization cognizant of Caruth's sense of history, one that takes trauma into account, by conceiving of a subjectivity and society that retain, and are even willing to descend into, a memory of death, thus avoiding the unethical racist and chauvinistic pitfalls that Ziarek exposes. Kristeva favors the discovery of a traumatic/mystical dimension in the modern psyche, which will only come about once freedom is no longer confused with "the search for the best causes producing the best effects," "the unbridled pursuit of objects of desire," the media, production, atomization (Kristeva, 2000, 151, 160). The subject and the social, instead, require dependence—bonds—to be free, to have the opportunity of submission and exaltation, to exceed the boundary of convention that excludes Kristeva's "endless delights." One bond, then, that Kristeva clearly promotes is between Eastern and Western Europe. Through film, Kieslowski expresses Kristeva's sense of the need for a counterforce to this new world order of the accumulation of capital goods by featuring a profoundly sad concerto to celebrate a major step in the process of globalization—European unification. It is this politicized classical music, being the only thing remaining in Kieslowski's *Blue* during the evacuating gaps in the film's visual continuity, the blackouts, that keeps the incomprehensibility of trauma alive and the maternal corpse warm—which is why it is necessary to regard Kieslowski's film as both black and blue.

Works cited

Caruth, Cathy (1996) *Unclaimed Experience: Trauma, Narrative, and History.* Baltimore: The Johns Hopkins UP.

Kristeva, Julia (1989) *Black Sun: Depression and Melancholia.* Trans. Leon S. Roudiez. New York: Columbia UP.

—(1991) *Strangers to Ourselves.* Trans. Leon S. Roudiez. New York: Columba UP.

—(2000) *Crisis of the Euro/pean Subject.* Trans. Susan Fairfield. New York: Other Press.

Stok, Danusia, Ed. (1993) *Kieslowski on Kieslowski.* London: Faber and Faber.

Ziarek, Ewa Pronowska (2001) An *Ethics of Dissensus: Postmodemity, Feminism, and the Politics of Radical Democracy.* Palo Alto, CA: Stanford UP.

Žižek, Slavoj (2000) *The Fragile Absolute: Or, Why is the Christian Legacy Worth Fighting For?* London: Verso.

—(2001) *The Fright of Real Tears: Krzysztof Kieslowski between Theory and Post-Theory.* London: British Film Institute.

Filmography

Trois Couleurs (Three Colours), 1993–4*: Bleu (Blue),* 1993. Krzysztof Kieslowski (writer and director). Miramax Films. France.

3

"The void of another enjoyment": *Breaking the Waves*

The cinema substitutes for our gaze—a world more in harmony with our desires.

ANDRÉ BAZIN, QUOTED IN GODARD'S *CONTEMPT*

This chapter focuses on hysteria. In Chapter 4, through an analysis of Shainberg's *Secretary* and Haneke's *The Piano Teacher*, perversion will be added to our array of psychic structures; obsessional neurosis also will be taken up, in both Chapters 4 and 5. These opening chapters concentrate on films that expose certain psychic patterns as they position the subject in relation to Love. Clinging to the maternal object, *das Ding*, and Thanatos, the melancholic avoids Eros, whereas the hysteric frantically breathes life into Eros by remaining in the place of *objet a*. As a result of this quest, however—to become the *objet a*, for a lover whose desire she is desperate to sustain, with her as his unattainable goal—the hysteric can end up falling into the aporia of Love, the site of Lacan's impossible sexual relation.

Whereas Kristeva provides a compelling theory of melancholia, Lacan's theory of hysteria underpins this chapter.[1] Lacan explains that the hysteric turns to Love to compensate for her lack of feminine identification. Lars von Trier's *Breaking the Waves* (1996) invites an examination of such hysteria just as it moves us deeply into Lacan's concept of Love, Love beyond the Law,

Love in the Real, unsignifiable Love. Rather than negotiating a distant relation to the gaze (the tendency of desire), being a "love film," *Breaking the Waves* crosses the border between the Symbolic and the Real to an extent that risks provoking psychotic collapse.

Indeed, it might be said, in general, that as film attempts to exceed the limits of signification—especially as it responds to the challenge of presenting Love—a shift takes place in the direction of *jouissance* as the visual displaces language. As Juliet Flower MacCannell proposes in a chapter titled "Love outside the Limits of the Law," in her book *The Hysteric's Guide to the Future Female Subject*, Lacanian Love edges over into "the same unspeakable *jouissance* Lacan designated as the 'feminine' one" and opens "where the Symbolic chain is broken down, revealing something unsayable, even transcendent that escapes its range." An "impossible quest," it puts one "eyeball to eyeball with the Thing" (MacCannell, 2000, 236). We might think of contemporary film, then, as the exemplum *par excellence* of postmodernism, as it makes a more determined raid on the beyond of the Symbolic—as it puts the spectator "eyeball to eyeball with the Thing." Because the artist attempting to express Love is trying to convey what is by definition beyond words, filmmakers have the advantage. Unlike writers, they can avoid the contradiction in using language to access what exceeds it. Film can give us a better purchase on desubjectification as well as on the impossibility of Love that produces that shattered condition. Through film, one can more easily catch a glimpse of the inarticulable.

In *Intimate Revolt*, Kristeva offers a psychoanalytic explanation for such a rare achievement through her emphasis on the close relation of the visible and the drives. Why, she asks rhetorically, is the visible prone to synthesizing our most fundamental drives and to exposing the riskiest games we play with love and death? Kristeva in fact puts what I am suggesting about the intimate connection between film and the impossibility of Love in the extreme terms of psychosis, as she regards cinema as constantly offering an exploration of other uninhabitable identities to the extreme point of psychosis. She is thinking in particular of a certain type of cinema, the "thought specular," that "explores the specular, that reproduces it most closely to its untenable logic, or that preserves only its strident, discordant, ironic logic: Eisenstein, Hitchcock, Pasolini..." (Kristeva, 2002, 73). While the thought specular *per se* is not yet our focus, Kristeva's stress on the fascination of the specular seems worth mentioning here since the specular has the capacity to embody an unsymbolized, unverbalized, raw drive, drive being intimately tied to *jouissance* as well as the force propelling Love. Moreover, film's propensity to express *jouissance,* to face the Thing, touch the Real, capture the drive, indicate the not-all, and convey unsignifiable, desubjectifying Love dovetails with its ability to offer its spectator a psychoanalytic experience, with its capacity, in other words, to serve as Kristeva's thought specular or the type of film that can summon the viewer to explore psychic depths that have the potency to revive subjectivity.

The first section of this chapter initially spells out my conception of Lacan's three orders of Love and then proceeds to elaborate his theory of hysteria. For *Breaking the Waves* depicts an "hysterical" Woman in Love, a "masochistic," mystical Wom/an—that is, a Woman who doesn't exist—in Lacanian Love, in a way with God. As Stephen Heath proposes, in "God, Faith and Film: *Breaking the Waves*," "Love is the very substance of von Trier's film, not just in the sense that, like the mass of fiction films, it is indeed a love story but, more fundamentally, in that love is the film's topic and very purpose, is the binding expression of its conjunction of religion, eroticism and possession" (Heath, 1998, 93–4).

I am interested in comprehending *Breaking the Waves* as an attempt at presenting this unrepresentable, impossible Love. Heath picks up on this latter aspect of the film as well: "The wager ... is thus one of representation: [*Breaking the Waves*] seeks to depict and urge something about love at the same time that it wants to stand for—indeed *be*—it; a love story, but also a 'love film,' itself as *film* guaranteeing love, truly representing its truth" (Heath, 1998, 94). The heroine of *Breaking the Waves* gets mired in the internal contradiction of her hysterical logic and as a result falls into the pit of Love. Bess thereby enables the desire of the Other at the price of her subjectivity, as she coalesces with, rather than simply pretends to be, *objet a*. This is the cost that an hysterical spectator—driven to elicit the desire of the Other or in other words to become its cause—might avoid by engaging von Trier's film at the level of her unconscious.

Lacanian Love: giving what one does not have

The epithalamion, the duet (*duo*)—one must distinguish the two of them— the alternation, the love letter, they're not the sexual relationship. They revolve around the fact that there's no such thing as a sexual relationship.

JACQUES LACAN, *ENCORE*

There is a "radical distinction," in Lacan's view, "between *loving oneself through the other*—which, in the narcissistic field of the object, allows no transcendence to the object," what we might call narcissistic or first-order love, and love produced via "the circularity of the drive, in which the heterogeneity of the movement out and back shows a gap in its interval" (Lacan, 1981/1973, 194). In the latter case, what I call second-order love—tantamount to desire—the true, compelling, ultimate love-object is more than, exceeds, the person beloved. The love-object is someone who is—or something that is—in a way, *not*—not there, but whose present absence is absolutely, paradoxically, necessary for the love. In second-order love—i.e., the "love" that compensates for the lack of a sexual relation—the object of desire is sewn together with the object of the drive, the latter of which (that is, the drive) serves as a basis of one's love pursuit. Drive encircles *objet a*. We fall in love with (unconsciously) the *objet a*, that is, with what the beloved, magically invested with the *objet a*, does *not* possess, the never-attainable "object" of desire. Hence Lacan asserts that the beloved is able to give what he/she does not possess.

In theorizing Love, Lacan proposes that it is in the field of the Other that the subject must engage in "pure activity," one example of which, he writes, is the exercise of any drive—a masochistic drive, for example—which "requires that the masochist give himself...a devil of a job" (Lacan, 1981/1973, 200). A central question, therefore, is whether masochism is integral to Lacan's paradigm of Love. It would seem that "the mystery of love" entails the devilish job of searching, in the field of the Other, for a lost part of oneself (Lacan, 1981/1973, 205). Mediated by love, the object of the drive gets appropriated as the object of desire. But what, more fully, is the devilish job given to the subject by such a transfer?

This is indeed a risky maneuver. My answer is that in negotiating the move from drive to desire, the subject must beware of falling into the chasm of Love in-between. That is: since a gap necessarily exists between the ostensible object and the object-cause of desire (*objet a*), there really is no object of love, only its semblance. There is an object-cause of desire located in a false object (the beloved), and therefore, as Bruce Fink stresses, in *A Clinical Introduction to Lacanian Psychoanalysis*, "*Human desire, strictly speaking, has no object*" (Fink, 1997, 51). Moreover, since the true object of love would have to *be* the missing part, encountering it would be, if it could happen, an encounter with the gaze. In other words, if the subject were to recognize his/her absent self at this point of lack, at the point of the *objet a*, he/she would encounter the constitutive absent love object, the gaze. But how can the subject sustain itself upon coalescing with what he/she is not?

The final two paragraphs of *The Four Fundamental Concepts of Psychoanalysis* clinch this idea of what I call third-order Love—a Love beyond narcissistic love as well as beyond desire—as more than dangerous, as potentially annihilating, as is the gaze. Lacan posits Love in a "beyond" (Lacan, 1981/1973, 276). It is only the *signification* of a limitless love that may emerge, within the limits of the law, in the realm of desire: desire being the movement toward a love object; and Love being psychic consummation with the *objet a*. To be in Love in this latter sense is to head toward dissolution, the loss of what we call sanity, for it is to cross into the "beyond" (meaning beyond the Symbolic Order, rather than a transcendent celestial sphere), to defy the limit of the Law; and so it gives one the devil of a job. It is to annex to oneself that missing part that one *must* lack to maintain subjectivity. Therefore it is impossible—as Lacan proposes in *Encore*, "love is impossible"—providing entry into the impossible Real (Lacan, 1998/1975, 87). Being limitless, "outside the limits of the law," such a Love may "live," Lacan writes—and I add, can "be lived"—only "[t]here" (Lacan, 1981/1973, 276). Achieving Love, therefore, might be regarded as the ultimate masochistic act, requiring one's own blissful obliteration.

Lacan's eleventh seminar, *The Four Fundamental Concepts*, gives the impression that all these matters pertain similarly to men and women. But in *Encore*, Lacan describes two forms of *jouissance*—phallic *jouissance* and Other *jouissance*—that situate "man" on the side of desire (or phallic *jouissance*) and "Wom/an" on the side of Love (or Other *jouissance*). Here, the problem of Love is put more specifically in terms of the impossibility of a sexual relation between a man and a Wom/an. Whereas in *The Four Fundamental Concepts* all subjects seem to risk devastation upon achieving Love, in *Encore* it is the unfeasibility of the sexual relation—because of the incommensurability of the "man" and th/e "Woman"—that makes Love impossible. And it is impossible for the "man" and th/e "Woman" in different ways.

Lacan regards Eros as "a tension toward the One" (Lacan, 1998/1975, 5). Desire (or phallic *jouissance*) merely leads one to aim at the gap between oneself and the Other, while Love is at the place of Being, adhering to what slips away in language. Love itself therefore cannot be articulated. The stumbling block is the inadequacy of a *relation* between the One and the Other. And so the "man" through fantasy places an "object" in the position of what cannot be glimpsed of the Other. But for th/e Woman, something beyond *objet a* is at stake in what comes to compensate for the sexual relation that does not exist. A Wom/an enters into a *ménage à trois*, making God the third party in the business of love. For a man, the act of love entails approaching the cause of his desire, *objet a*. But a Wom/an exceeds the phallic function; she is something more, acting on a *jouissance* of the body surpassing the phallus. Hers is a *jouissance* that belongs to th/e Woman, that is, to th/e Woman who doesn't exist. Hence she is a mystic, one who has a sense that there is "a *jouissance* that is beyond" (Lacan, 1998/1975, 76).

In "A love letter," in *Encore*, Lacan describes th/e Woman as fundamentally related to the Other. She is the Other in the sexual relationship, the Other being what is missing, what cannot be added to the One. And it is insofar as her *jouissance* is radically Other that th/e Woman has more of a relationship to God. Her *jouissance* is "in the realm of the infinite" (Lacan, 1998/1975, 103), in the realm of the not-whole, or "not-all." On the male side, there is the reduction of the *jouissance* of the Other to *objet a*; on the female side, there is the enigmatic. All love is attached to the illusion that the sexual relation may stop not being written. Yet true Love resides, not in writing but, in Being.

In *What Does A Woman Want?*, Serge André poses the question of whether it is possible to know *anything* about Other *jouissance*. In response, he makes a suggestion that returns us to the topic of masochism—that through suffering one might access *jouissance*. Would such suffering include, or even be, the desubjectification that th/e Woman undergoes when she is in Love? If this is the case, it may appear that there are two dominant forms of masochism operating in Lacan, one aligned with "man," in the form of perversion, and the other with "Wom/an," in the form of desubjectification. In fact, André believes that the only way we (or perhaps I should say men) can begin to approach th/e Woman who doesn't exist is through perversion, for

> [t]he man who gets himself humiliated, insulted, whipped by his confederate is really seeking to take her place as the woman. He offers himself as object in a typical masculine fantasy scenario only in order to experience the remaining *jouissance* not mastered by that fantasy.

Perversion offers "a kind of mimetic caricature of feminine *jouissance*." In fact, the first time Lacan dealt with the question of the *jouissance* of the body, "he framed it in terms of the *jouissance* of the slave" (André, 1999, 270).

Although there is a fine line here, what André wishes to stress is that, while the masochistic position may share an aim with the feminine position, they are distinct, one the caricature of the other. While the masochist posits the Other, th/e Woman is in the place of the Other. While the pervert "slip[s] into the skin of this Other body, like a hand into a glove," th/e Woman attests to the "*impossible subjectivation of the body as Other*" (André, 1999, 272). So, technically, we must consider St. Teresa of Avila, for example, a mystic rather than a masochist, or a suffering mystic rather than a masochistic pervert. But beyond what we call her is the question of her representation. André even comments about St. Teresa that her self-description of being "carried away," "ravished," "seized" irresistibly makes her as much of a caricature as the masochistic pervert. Can Wom/an's *jouissance* or a Woman in Love be represented? Is all such signification ridiculously inadequate to what cannot be written? A "love film" (as Heath calls it), Lars von Trier's *Breaking the Waves* seizes on that question and in so doing points to film's capacity to summon the unconscious of its viewer.

A "love film"

I situate—and why shouldn't I—God as the third party in this business of human love[.] Even materialists sometimes know a bit about the *ménage à trois*, don't they?

JACQUES LACAN, *ENCORE*

Now to touch on the rudiments of hysteria. For it is the hysteric who often finds herself, or I should say loses herself, in the realm of Love in an effort to solve her problem of femininity. And it is the case that the heroine of the film I want to examine, *Breaking the Waves*—because it attempts to represent a Woman in Love—exhibits hysterical symptoms, as she emerges from a family apt to generate such symptoms, with its missing father, recently dead brother, and cold, stern mother. It is Bess's mother who accuses Bess of having "a fit of hysterics" even as the mother exudes an abject *jouissance* especially threatening to her daughter desperately seeking feminine identification.

To Lacan, hysteria is a failure of repression that results in the obliteration of the boundary between the sexual and non-sexual. But there is another failure prior to this one. The hysteric's father typically fails her by not offering the support she counted on. Being structurally impotent, the father was not able to grant her what she needed to establish her femininity. Because she lacks such a signifier, the hysteric's body image cannot entirely clothe and eroticize the Real of her body. She can, in fact, go so extravagantly far as to become ill due to the father's deficiency. She may devote herself to repairing him, sometimes sacrificing her entire life, in particular her love life, in the process. For she may denounce phallic impotence only "in the name of a more powerful phallus; she [consequently] wants more and more" (André, 1999, 125).

The hysteric, therefore, is inclined to remain contentedly *unsatisfied* in the pursuit of one master after another, exposing their insufficiencies one by one in an ongoing, persistent effort to flaunt—and thereby convince herself of—her own desirability as well as to avoid "the danger of experiencing the satisfaction of utmost pleasure, a pleasure that, were [s]he to experience it, would make [her] crazy, ... dissolve or disappear" (Nasio, 1998, 5). The trouble comes when her unrelenting pursuit of a feminine identification leads to the creation of a "fantasy of a monster whom we call the other, now strong and all-powerful, now weak and ill, always immense" (Nasio, 1998, 5). She finds herself *confronted* with the a-sexuated Real of the body in some form of phallic potency, which she cannot manage as it would be an excess on top of her own constitutive, unrepressed excess.

That is: we would expect the hysteric to flee in the opposite direction of the Real (as hysterics are wont to do), forever pretending to wish to plug the lack in the Other, which pretense keeps her, as well as the Other, in a state of perpetual unsatisfied desire. Yet, it is in pursuing phallic potency—at first in ordinary men who inevitably fail her and then in superhuman sources—that she can come apart. This is the potential pitfall in hysteria. A woman's demand that tribute be paid to her femininity may lead her exactly where she does *not* want to be. Wanting more than the ordinary phallus, she can get entangled in the internal contradiction of her logic, both wanting and really not wanting to plug the lack in the Master or Other. Looking to seal over the breakdown of her body image through her dream of an all-powerful phallus, she may be drawn into an ever greater devotion to the Other, where she ends up sacrificing everything for Him. In this scenario, she shifts from having a textbook hysterical reaction to her lack of feminine identification—from, in other words, her game of offering and not offering herself to the Other, in which her expectation is to receive "a frustrating non-response" (Nasio, 1998, 3)—to seeking and finding Love to solve the problem of this inadequacy, that is, to becoming a Woman who doesn't exist, paired with a Man beyond castration. What the hysteric only pretends to want to do—to "constitut[e] herself as the object that makes the Other desire, since as long as the Other desires, her position as object is assured" (Fink, 1997, 120)—the Woman who does not exist carries out.

This is the trajectory in *Breaking the Waves*. The heroine, Bess, a young, apparently half-witted, fatherless, Scottish woman, turns to Love as the surest way, in Lacanian terms, to repair the Other, since (third-order) Love (were it to exist) would more than compensate for the genital drive that fails to unite the subject with the Other. Bess chooses as a partner an Englishman (Jan), a stranger working on a North Sea oil-rig. Yet, as Lacan indicates in *Encore*, the feminine position is ultimately addressed to God, with the man as the phantasmatic place-holder.

It is interesting in this connection, though, that once Jan has been paralyzed from the neck down so that Bess and Jan can no longer enjoy sex, and therefore are in a sense able to have a "sexual relation" as Lacan conceives of it—as having nothing to do with physical relations or even with the impasses of sexuation (the "man" and th/e "Woman")—Bess has trouble accessing God in her periodic prayer sessions. Bess seems to progress in the film from attempting to meet the demands of a strict, chastising God, to a Lacanian "sexual relation" with Jan, which in turn ("Jan and me, we have a spiritual contact," Bess quietly boasts) paves the way to a supreme being who can make her all Wom/an. After the accident on the rig, Bess and Jan's relationship would seem to exemplify the sort of rare "encounter" that Lacan briefly alludes to at the end of *Encore* as

> what momentarily gives the illusion that the sexual relationship stops not being written—an illusion that something is not only articulated but inscribed, inscribed in each of our destinies, by which, for a while—a time during which things are suspended—what would constitute the sexual relationship finds its trace and its mirage-like path in the being who speaks.
> (Lacan, 1998/1975, 145)

Is theirs not a Love "that approaches being as such in the encounter" (Lacan, 1998/1975, 145)? Is film the site where Love that cannot stop *not* being written can thrive? And is the muteness of *Breaking the Waves* especially conducive to this brief encounter achieving an elusive expression? Lacan's assertion that "no relationship gets constituted between the sexes in the case of speaking beings, for it is on that basis alone that what makes up for that relationship can be enunciated" (Lacan, 1998/1975, 66) would seem to imply a "relation" between non-speaking beings. Reading the film through this same Lacanian lens, Stephen Heath too notices Bess's eventual status as a Wom/an beyond the phallic law as well as the film's consequent "holding at all costs to a truth of relation set beyond the banality of phallic separateness" (Heath, 1998, 98).

Paralyzed, Jan offers the hystericized Bess a provisional feminine identification. His "prick" (a term Bess seems both embarrassed and delighted to use) can in her verbal fantasies always be "huge," filling her up as a successful substitute for the impotent father/Other whom she is dedicated to repair through such replacement. Jan's now rigid body almost seems to be the space into which his phallus has expanded—the corpse-like site where Bess confronts the asexuated Real of the body. By encountering the phallus in full like this, she is catapulted beyond the phallic function, predicated on lack. Bess lights up upon hearing that Jan, although severely paralyzed, will live, curiously seeming to have no regret about their lost sex life. She is devastated when Jan, much more attuned to such a loss, urges her to take a lover. "It often happens," writes Nasio about hysteria, "that love is transformed into devotion to a sexless other (an invalid, a priest, or a psychoanalyst)" (Nasio, 1998, 105). And as Jan wants Bess to have sex with other men and subsequently to narrate to him the juicy details, her *jouissance* of being gets further generated and manifested in her suffering sex and violence at the hands of strange men, enhancing a kind of "impossible" sexual relation between the two of them, Jan and Bess.

Having filled Jan's lack to the point of rendering him a fully phallic Man beyond castration (Bess feels absolutely responsible for Jan's accident on the rig), she sacrifices her subjectivity for Jan as she collapses into the asexuated Real of her tortured body. She enacts Lacan's proposition that "being is the jouissance of the body as such, that is, as asexual" (Lacan, 1998/1975, 6). In turn, Bess sacrifices for God as well. On the boat the fatal second time, sailing out to put herself at the mercy of exceedingly brutal, knife-happy sadists, Bess prays, accesses God, and offers one of her crazed smiles, her face completely aglow as if made radiant by her connection to (Lacan's) God, a God beyond the Law. Challenging the Presbyterian Elders, toward the end of the film, Bess cries out her incomprehension over how one could unconditionally love a Word, or a Law, even of God. Instead, to Bess, unconditionally to love a human being, and through him to love God, to participate in such a *ménage à trois,* beyond language and the Law, is divine "perfection."

To achieve such perfection, Bess desubjectifies herself, in an experience of the *jouissance* of Being, to the extent that eventually "she comes up against the limit of the 'nothing' to which she is [apparently] condemned" (André, 1999, 128), to borrow André's description of a possible vanishing point of the hysteric's story. In the end Bess experiences the fatal nature of "perfect" Love and thereby demonstrates the relation of Love to the death drive. In encountering her lover as a (capital M) Man and as God, vicariously through men who violate her, Bess destroys herself, as she *must* be destroyed by such a "limitless love," beyond the Law. When Bess's sister-in-law tries to explain to Jan that Bess "isn't right in the head," Jan replies, cryptically but knowingly, "she just wants it all"—which puts Bess in the place of Other *jouissance*, that is, ironically in the place of not-all (since "all" would imply an exclusion and therefore leave something out, hence not be "all"), in the place of th/e Woman who is "there in full" at the same time as "there is something more" (Lacan, 1998/1975, 74).

Clinching the idea that she is a postmodern Antigone driven by "radical desire," the "sublime desire" of the saint or mystic, Bess, enacting the ethics of the saint, enables the miraculous resurrection of Jan at the end.[2] Noting that Bess is "the core around which the film pulsates," Stephen Heath is again on my "wavelength":

> the end of the film is...with [Bess] only in as much as it allows the men to be content in her goodness, the miracle *of her:* it depends after all on her death, the disposal of her body, the breaking the wave of *her* enjoyment.
> (Heath, 1998, 105)

Bess, who so poignantly at the start of the film wanted Jan to want her, wanted, in other words, to convince him that she could fill his lack—"Have me now?" Bess asks coyly in the public bathroom at her wedding party, only minutes after being married—now has "successfully" become his *objet a*, the object-cause of his desire, just what every hysteric seems to want to be.

> Rather than taking the object for herself, as in obsession, the hysteric seeks to divine the Other's desire and to become the particular object that, when missing, makes the Other desire. She constitutes herself on the subject side of the 'equation' as object *a*.
>
> (Fink, 1997, 120)

Bess follows to the end her intuition that by obeying Jan's wishes she will revive him. He asks her to take lovers and to narrate the details of her sexual experiences to him, to turn herself in this way into a sexual object-cause of desire. Bess takes Jan's request to an extreme, and it works. She kills herself to please him.

Having sought throughout the film ways of satisfying the Other (her sister-in-law comments to Bess, "you'd give anything to anybody," and she informs Jan that he could get Bess to do anything he wants her to), in the end Bess coalesces with the Real absence of *objet a*. She thereby fulfills the hysteric's fantasy, the fantasy the hysteric wants to remain a fantasy, although it is the case that *objet a* is in the position of truth for the hysteric—as Fink puts it, "the truth of the hysteric's discourse, its hidden motor force, is the real" (Fink, 1995, 134)—and so in a way it makes sense that *objet a* is her destination. Having taken on "the devil of a job," having been stabbed to death, Bess desubjectifies herself, having apparently sought out such sacrifice through her pursuit and, one might say, achievement of Love, which gift of Love, Love in the "beyond," the infinite realm of not-all—having put Jan into relation with the Real—inspires Jan's unconscious desire to resist his paralysis, to rise up from his deathbed and live.

It would seem that ultimately Love entails the destruction of one's existence—which is, I propose, another variation on what Lacan means when he claims that Love is giving what one lacks, insofar as lack is the basis of subjectivity—even as it blows vitality into the beloved. This is perhaps why Lacan regarded the analyst, engaging in transference love, as a saint—"there is no better way of placing [the psychoanalyst] objectively than in relation to what was in the past called: being a saint" (Lacan, 1990/1974, 15). It would seem too that while Love may be mutual, being impossible, it cannot last for long and that inevitably it breaks apart into desire, on the one side, and either suicide or dejection, on the other. But a "love film" can serve in a way as a more lasting encounter with Love beyond the Law, as it conveys the incomprehensibility of Love, God, and "marriage" as the loving union of two people "in God" (that *ménage à trois*), and thereby manages to gesture toward the "not-all" even beyond its own cinematic borders. The bells at the end of *Breaking the*

Waves are internal (material objects) only to signal the beyond of the film: Jan's friend proves to him the impossibility of the bells actually being there. The final unlocalizable but material/mystical bells are an included exclusion, indexing Wom/an's *jouissance* and the idea that Love is not-all—a "mighty power."

In *Breaking the Waves*, Lacan's inhuman Love is shared appropriately by a mystical Wom/an and God.[3] After Jan is paralyzed, he graduates from phallic *jouissance* to something more but is soon revealed to be merely a stand-in for a much more formidable lover, God. The sexual relation is dehumanized. It is shown finally to fail on the human level, to be humanly impossible and divinely possible. In *Breaking the Waves*, the supreme emotional challenge to the Symbolic—Love—is ultimately revealed to be outside the domain of Lacan's "man." But Bess advances beyond the psychic state of the hysteric to "what the representational terms of the film compulsively cannot grasp," a certain "surplus that has no containable limit, that is over and above phallic representation—the void of another enjoyment" (Health, 1998, 105).

Contemporary film's compatibility with the Real would seem to facilitate such a presentation. As Todd McGowan writes in the introduction to the collection *Lacan and Contemporary Film*, "One of the salient features of recent cinema is its proclivity for staging an encounter with the traumatic Real" (McGowan, 2004, xviii). Psychoanalytic readings of contemporary film can expose and foster this postmodern genre's unusual capacity to fathom the lack in meaning, the beyond of the signifier, and the Nothing of Love. And insofar as the hysterical spectator is able to lose him/herself in that abyss, he/she has the potential to traverse a fundamental fantasy capturing that spectator in the nightmare of hysteria. Such potential on the part of the spectator to experience a psychic shift and in turn to gain relief from the grip of a misery-producing psychic structure or trauma will be explored much more extensively in later chapters, as our spotlight expands beyond the inner workings of films to their mode of seduction and its impact on the viewer through a full engagement with Kristeva's genre of the thought-specular film.

Notes

1 Technically, in psychoanalytic theory, melancholia is not considered a "psychic structure." One might be a melancholic obsessional or suffer from melancholic perversion, and so forth.

2 For an elaboration on the sublime desire of the saint in connection with the ethics of psychoanalysis, all in relation to Antigone/*Antigone*, see my "Ethical Erogenous Zones," *JPCS: Journal for the Psychoanalysis of Culture & Society* 3, (2) (Fall, 1998): 109–21.

3 In *New Maladies of the Soul*, Kristeva presents Jeanne Guyon (1649–1717), "one of the last great French mystics," as her first example of an hysteric. Guyon, not surprisingly, "took pleasure in pain," in her pursuit of love that entailed submission to God (Kristeva, 1995, 64–5). Kristeva highlights the hysteric's quest for "a maximal symbolic and psychic jouissance," as the hysteric postulates the futility of her desire (Kristeva, 1995, 70). The paradox would seem to be that while the hysteric refuses to obtain satisfaction by consummating desire, she obtains dissatisfaction, a variation on the very satisfaction/*jouissance* she desperately avoids.

Works cited

André, Serge (1999) *What Does A Woman Want?* Ed. Judith Feher Gurewich. Trans. Susan Fairfield. New York: Other Press.
Fink, Bruce (1995) *The Lacanian Subject: Between Language and Jouissance.* Princeton: Princeton UP.
—(1997) *A Clinical Introduction to Lacanian Psychoanalysis: Theory and Technique.* Cambridge: Harvard UP.
Heath, Stephen (1998) "God, Faith and Film: *Breaking the Waves.*" *Literature & Theology*, 12 (1): 93–107.
Kristeva, Julia (1995) *New Maladies of the Soul.* Ed. Laurence D. Kritzman. Trans. Ross Guberman. New York: Columbia UP.
—(2002) *Intimate Revolt: The Power and Limits of Psychoanalysis.* Trans. Jeanine Herman. New York: Columbia UP.
Lacan, Jacques (1981/1973) *The Four Fundamental Concepts of Psycho-Analysis: Book XI.* Ed. Jacques-Alain Miller. Trans. Alan Sheridan. New York: Norton.
—(1990/1974) *Television: A Challenge to the Psychoanalytic Establishment.* Ed. Joan Copjec. Trans. Jeffrey Mehlman. New York: Norton.
—(1998/1975) *Encore 1972–1973: On Feminine Sexuality/The Limits of Love and Knowledge: Book XX.* Ed. Jacques-Alain Miller. Trans. Bruce Fink. New York: W. W. Norton & Co.
MacCannell, Juliet Flower (2000) *The Hysteric's Guide to the Future Female Subject.* Minneapolis: University of Minnesota Press.
McGowan, Todd (2004) *Lacan and Contemporary Film.* Ed. Todd McGowan & Sheila Kunkle. New York: Other Press.
Nasio, Juan-David (1998) *Hysteria from Freud to Lacan: The Splendid Child of Psychoanalysis.* Ed. Judith Feher Gurewich. Trans. Susan Fairfield. New York: Other Press.

Filmography

Breaking the Waves (1996) Lars von Trier. October Films. U.S.A.

4

The use of perversion: *Secretary* or *The Piano Teacher?*

One can say that S&M is the eroticization of power, the eroticization of strategic relations. What strikes me with regard to S&M is how it differs from social power. . . .
[T]he S&M game is very interesting because it is a strategic relation, but it is always fluid. . . . Or, even when the roles are stabilized, you know very well that it is always a game. Either the rules are transgressed, or there is an agreement, either explicit or tacit, that makes them aware of certain boundaries. This strategic game as a source of bodily pleasure is very interesting.
. . . It is an acting-out of power structures by a strategic game that is able to give sexual pleasure or bodily pleasure.

MICHEL FOUCAULT, *ETHICS*

Lesbian S/M has been touted as an effective means of coping with, if not curing, psychic trouble for some time now, especially by lesbian practitioners of the art. Performance of power, lending the performers control, allows a certain grip on the traumas being reenacted, as *Coming to Power: Writings and Graphics on Lesbian S/M* testifies. In "If I Ask You to Tie Me Up, Will You Still Want to Love Me?" Juicy Lucy values sexual S/M as "a healing tool"

(*Coming to Power*, 1987, 60). She was a battered woman for years and now claims "the right to release & transform the pain & fear of those experiences," any way she pleases (*Coming to Power*, 1987, 30). She describes S/M as "growthful," "trust building," "loving," "creative, spiritual, integrating, a development of inner power as strength" (*Coming to Power*, 1987, 61). Through lesbian S/M, Lucy faces what she calls her "inner side" and thereby reclaims herself, defusing in the process the terror and powerlessness she had experienced through former rapes and beatings. Jayne, in "Improptu S/M," describes submitting to the whip with immense relief and soaring "like a bird in flight, freed of the earth's pull" (*Coming to Power*, 1987, 193). And Susan Farr, in "The Art of Discipline: Creating Erotic Dramas of Play and Power," after complaining about the hypocrisy of our society, which "accepts systematic violence" but "issues stringent taboos against consenting adults exploring the complexities of power and sexuality," sings the praises of S/M exploration as a way of finding an outlet for frustration, anger, jealousy, and guilt as well as producing the obligation to give comfort and love (*Coming to Power*, 1987, 185). Perversion can have therapeutic effects. This chapter analyzes two fairly recent films that feature perverse acts not just to test this already well-examined thesis but also to foreground two dominant ideas within the contemporary psychoanalytic community about the optimal way of handling psychic trouble.

Speaking generally, the aim of psychoanalysis until recently was thought to be to treat symptoms, to excavate them by unveiling repressed material that renders them necessary. Ideally, symptoms were interpreted and thereby dissolved, paving the way for psychic health. A shift then took place, at least in Lacanian circles. As Lacan's later work gained prominence, in particular his *sinthome* seminar (1975–6) with its emphasis on James Joyce, the focus slid from curing a symptom to producing a *sinthome*. The symptom acquired an ontological status upon being conceived as a "*sinthome*," as "our only substance, the only positive support of our being, the only point that gives consistency to the subject" (Žižek, 1989, 75). To stick with film: in an essay called "Art as Prosthesis," Parveen Adams, for example, looks at Cronenberg's *Crash* as a work of art like *Finnegans Wake* insofar as it ties the knot of the Imaginary, Symbolic, and Real "in such a way that, as in the ecriture of Joyce, it bolts the subject in place" (Adams, 2003, 163). From this perspective, were the symptom to be dissolved, a psychotic catastrophe would ensue, which is just what Joyce's writing, according to Lacan, enabled him to bypass.

It is probably no accident that perverse works of art turn out to be the very texts often taken up by psychoanalytic critics to illustrate the function of the *sinthome*. Possibly there is something about a perverse work of art that pressures the reader or viewer to produce a *sinthome*, to secure the Real, Symbolic, Imaginary knot. Perhaps the perverse aesthetic object, immersed in *jouissance*—in negotiating its own tense, ambivalent relation with the absent big Other, in its effort to construct an evasive big Other—threatens the viewer's/reader's illusion of the Symbolic Order enough to cause him/her to generate a remedy to such a deficiency. Perversion may loosen the relation to the law for the viewer/reader, exposing its impotence. As Jacques-Alain Miller comments, although he may suffer over his ability to do so, "the pervert present[s] himself as able to reveal the truth of enjoyment to the non-pervert" (Miller, 1996, 306). The pervert struggles to prop up the ineffectual law, in various forms as well as to different degrees and for different purposes, perhaps depending on the extent of the disavowal, while the viewer/reader of a work featuring that exquisitely agonizing negotiation may become psychically destabilized enough to feel the urge to form and embrace a symptom raised to the status of a *sinthome*—a Real kernel of enjoyment through the signifier—that leaves the (absent) Other behind.

Clinicians too, for a while, have been thinking in terms of both perversion and the *sinthome* rather than in terms of cure. Bruce Fink asserts that the aim of analysis is "*to allow the analysand . . . to enjoy his or her enjoyment*," to permit the drives to "pursue their own course," even to facilitate "their perversion," insofar as the drives always seek satisfaction that might be considered perverse (Fink, 1997, 41). Likewise, Miller writes that the aim of the treatment is by no means normalization but "to give permission for perversion, permission for object *a*" (Miller, 1996, 314). And, in *Enjoy Your Symptom!*, Žižek offers his own philosophical/psychoanalytic explanation for these clinical conclusions, by stressing that the Real inheres not only in death but in life as well. "In other words, the Freudian duality of life and death drives is *not* a symbolic opposition but a tension, an antagonism . . . the very notion of life is alien to the symbolic order. And the name of this life substance that proves a traumatic shock for the symbolic universe is of course *enjoyment.*" The stain of enjoyment can never be expunged, since the very gesture of renouncing enjoyment produces a surplus enjoyment. One might as well, therefore, attach oneself to it or claim it, as opposed to attempting to eradicate it, since *jouissance* will inevitably resurface. Here what is at issue is "an *object* in the strict sense of materialized enjoyment— the stain," an "uncanny excess." In thinking about this dialectic of enjoyment and surplus enjoyment, Žižek is led, in fact, to invoke "primal masochism" (Žižek, 2001, 22).

But at the same time as the *sinthome* dominates the contemporary psychoanalytic scene, theoretically and clinically, the Lacanian notion of an "authentic act" has grabbed a great deal of attention. The authentic act is a profound way of effecting the original goal of psychoanalysis (to cure symptoms through an exposure of repressed material) by cutting across the fundamental fantasy, to obtain distance from it, to open up the empty place in the Other. How? Through an intervention of some sort that causes a total restructuring of the subject's Symbolic coordinates. Žižek, oddly enough, has raised this Lacanian concept to a high level of intensity. Whether or not Antigone, for example, commits an authentic act, whether or not an authentic act, insofar as it implies not ceding one's desire, is the Lacanian mode of being ethical, and where one ends up after such an act is committed are three key but unresolved issues that have been hotly debated. *Sinthome* or authentic act—for which, if one even has a choice, should one strive?

A juxtaposition of Steven Shainberg's *Secretary* (2002) with Michael Haneke's *The Piano Teacher* (2001) poses this same question. Both films present heroines whose self-mutilation occurs apropos psychic disturbances over a parental passionate attachment. In each case the heroine turns to a male sexual partner for an extension of or substitute for the neglectful or abusive parent in the form of S/M relations. And in both films, a contract becomes part of the deal. In *Secretary*, the two members of the S/M couple go contractless at the start, and for most of the duration of the film, and eventually bind themselves legally together. In *The Piano Teacher*, we have the reverse. Here hero and heroine more or less begin with a written S/M contract that they might be said subsequently to exceed. In one case (*Secretary*), an attempt is made to transform symptoms into enjoyment; in the other (*The Piano Teacher*), there is a move, facilitated by the initial contractual S/M relations, to revert to, and eventually tear through, the heroine's fundamental fantasy. The marital contract in *Secretary* might be regarded as binding up, as well as binding together, the obsessional, sadistic symptoms of Mr. Grey and the masochistic hysterical symptoms of Lee. But it is only when the boundaries of the written contract in *The Piano Teacher*, in the form of Professor Kohut's letter to her student, are surpassed, only when the piano professor loses control of her student's violence toward her, that she has a chance to overcome her psychic problems.

Secretary: A binding of enjoyment

Mr. Grey: We can't do this twenty-four hours a day, seven days a week.

Lee: Why not?

SECRETARY

In *The Sublime Object of Ideology*, Žižek elaborates on the view of Lacan's last pedagogical stage, in which the symptom was conceptualized as a "real kernel of enjoyment" that "persists as a surplus and returns through all attempts to domesticate it ... to dissolve it by means of explication" (Žižek, 1989, 69). In his typical pop style, Žižek offers the *Titanic* as an example of such "inert presence," "a Thing in the Lacanian sense: the material leftover, the materialization of the terrifying, impossible *jouissance*," "a sublime object" (Žižek, 1989, 71). This, Žižek proclaims, is the symptom as Real, the symptom that refuses to vanish. As Žižek writes:

> The symptom is not only a cyphered message, it is at the same time a way for the subject to organize his enjoyment—that is why, even after the completed interpretation, the subject is not prepared to renounce his symptom; that is why he "loves his symptom more than himself."
>
> (Žižek, 1989, 74)

Lacan met the challenge of this conception of the symptom with his neologism "*sinthome*," which Žižek defines perfectly as "a certain signifying formation penetrated with enjoyment: it is a signifier as bearer of *jouis-sense*, enjoyment-in-sense." This symptom/*sinthome* enables us to opt for something, the symptom-formation, rather than nothing, as we *bind* "our enjoyment to a certain signifying, symbolic formation" that "assures a minimum of consistency to our being-in-the-world." From this perspective, to lose the symptom/*sinthome* is to greet the end of the world, to yield to the death drive. Identification with the symptom is therefore considered to be desirable. The patient must recognize and embrace "the Real of his symptom, the only support of his being. That is how we must read Freud's *wo es war, soll ich warden* ["Where id was, there ego shall be"]: you, the subject, must identify yourself with the place where your symptom already was; in its 'pathological' particularity you must recognize the element which gives consistency to your being." Such a symptom/*sinthome*, Žižek states, is "a binding of enjoyment": a "positive condition" of a "stain" that "cannot be included in the circuit of discourse" (Žižek, 1989, 75).

A binding of enjoyment, a strategic situating of a "stain"—or two "stains," his and hers—that challenges the normal network of social bonds is what the film *Secretary* is all about. On this reading the odd S/M couple at the center of this film, Mr. Grey and Lee, might be regarded as "queer" and thus as resignifying marriage as queer by bringing their "abnormality" into the institution of marriage and thereby altering that legal arena in a way that Judith Butler typically imagines. For the sake of social transformation, Butler almost always favors the rearticulation of mundane social relations by deviant or subversive practices. In *Secretary*, we have just that: transformation through performativity, a perverse reiteration of a conventional and exclusionary norm, the S/M couple now married and living happily in the suburbs, soon no doubt to have kids. In the film Mr. Grey asks Lee twice, in relation to her application for the secretary job, "Are you pregnant?" While it is Lee's "normal" boyfriend Peter who explicitly characterizes himself as the kind of guy who wants to be married with kids, it is the fastidious, meticulous, sadistic, obsessional Mr. Grey who, at the end of the film, is in the position to fulfill Peter's banal dream. Baffled by Lee's bizarre behavior—her wish to have him spank her; the firm planting of her hands on Mr. Grey's desk; her determination to remain at Mr. Grey's desk until Mr. Grey returns (which requires urinating at his desk and becoming extremely hungry)—Peter is displaced by Mr. Grey. It is not exactly that Peter loses and Mr. Grey wins Lee but that Mr. Grey usurps Peter's social place. At the end we are told that Mr. Grey and Lee "looked like any other couple you might see."

I ought to add parenthetically, however, that in *Contingency, Hegemony, Universality* Butler curiously singles out gay/queer marriage as one act of resignification she does not promote. Butler states unequivocally that, with regard to the issue of gay marriage, she refuses to argue for a "view of political performativity which holds that it is necessary to occupy the dominant norm in order to produce an internal subversion of its terms," because, as she states in an uncharacteristically gothic style, "sometimes it is important to refuse its terms, to let the term itself wither, to starve it of its strength" (Butler, 2000, 177). Nevertheless, if we can accept a metonymic slide from "gay" to "queer" marriage here and in turn embrace the idea that the couple formed by sadistic Mr. Gray and masochistic Lee is "queer," then Butler's typical strategy (rejected in this single case) of occupying the dominant norm to resignify its terms is just what happens in *Secretary*.[1]

Resignification in the political realm might even be seen as analogous to the *sinthome* in the psychoanalytic realm, in that something sick and in need of political change—the conventional, heterosexist attitude that excludes queerness—is *transformed* into "a certain signifying formation penetrated with enjoyment," i.e., with the queerness previously walled off in the periphery of the Symbolic. Read as a *sinthome*, *Secretary*'s ending—in which sadomasochistic acts, such as the husband tying his wife up to a tree and having sex with her there on their "honeymoon" (after the June wedding) or the wife dropping a dead bug onto their impeccably made marital bed, as part of their new suburban lifestyle— emerges as a means of enjoying social symptoms, heterosexist marriage being symptomatic of an ill society. Politically speaking, the reiteration of such a new norm, S/M practitioners on the block, would have the benefit of maintaining the symptom—the institution of marriage—in a form that redeems it: *sinthome*.

This idea can be elaborated psychoanalytically in Deleuzean terms. In *Secretary*, Mr. Gray and Lee would seem to be suffering from a pathological condition (Mr. Grey himself at one point comes to the stark realization that their "disgusting" S/M routine must not persist), even as (especially at the end) they experience punishment (the reception and infliction of it) as though it justifies their satisfaction. By appropriating the legal system—the institution of marriage—by infusing such a form with the perverse contents of their own S/M activities, Mr. Grey and Lee act on the Deleuzean model of masochism whereby the pervert, hardly a victim, is a shrewd manager scheming to usurp the power of the lawgiver by shifting his authority to punish onto someone whose enactment of it will result in satisfaction. In this way *Secretary* performs a sadomasochistic caricature of Symbolic prohibition. As Deleuze writes, "The element of contempt in the submission of the masochist has often been emphasized: his apparent obedience conceals a criticism and provocation. He simply attacks the law on a different flank" (Deleuze, 1971, 77). Obeying the law (getting married and so forth) in order to break it (continue S/M relations within this legal norm) is a perverse way of generating *jouissance*: the pervert requires the law to enjoy it. Pseudo-limits that the pervert brings to bear on himself become something with which to play, because "the pervert gets off on the very attempt to draw the limits to his *jouissance*" (Fink, 1997, 193).

The film *Secretary* is unquestionably self-conscious about its transmission of "illegal" pain to legal play. Midway through, Lee listens to a tape called *How to Come Out as a Dominant/Submissive* that dissuades its listener from running from pain and urges her instead to embrace the entire spectrum of feeling. Having internalized the lesson of the tape, Lee later pronounces that she has always suffered somehow, but now her fear of suffering is gone because she has found someone to feel and play with, in a way that feels "right" to her. Read along these lines, the marriage of Lee and Mr. Grey at the end serves as a kind of writing in the Real, where writing is represented by the institution of marriage. Just as Joyce in *Finnegans Wake* arrived at the *sinthome* as a way of having his *jouissance* through the letter, here we have a perverse "marriage in the Real." Rather than being cured, or even needing to be cured, two symptoms— the institution of marriage in the political reading and sadomasochism in the psychoanalytic reading—are resignified. Marriage is queered; S/M is legalized, although the legitimating of perversion only parodies (rather than upholds) the law.

The final shot in *Secretary* is of Lee staring penetratingly at the viewer. She seems to be sending a message, as her stare lingers. Given that Lee looks so long and hard, one might be tempted to interpret her stare as a Lacanian gaze, as located in the constitutive lack of the viewer's subjectivity. But the message that such a gaze would relay—"You, too, can traverse your fundamental fantasy leading to self-mutilation"—is inconsistent with the film's psychoanalytic implications. Having illustrated a clear transferal of self-inflicted pain—enacted in response to an alcoholic, unemployed, domestically abusive, troubled and therefore neglectful father—to pain/enjoyment inflicted by a lover, *Secretary* through its final shot of Lee's stare seems to encourage the enjoyment of symptoms rather than their dissolution.

Or, on the contrary, does the specific contractual nature of the ending of *Secretary* eradicate the erotic tension of the film—tension that becomes excruciatingly pleasurable especially in the scenes of Mr. Grey spanking Lee and then perhaps most acute in the scene in which he has her bend over and lower her panty hose and panties while he proceeds to masturbate? Are the S/M antics at the end, in other words, comparatively silly and sensuously flat? (One critic refers to the "too tidy and 'cutesy' coda.") Is the glaze of soft-porn that gets laid over the bath and bedroom scenes, too, part of the film's *challenge* to the idea that symptoms can metamorphose into daily doses of *jouissance*? Another way of putting this is to ask Žižek's question of Butler's idea of resignification: Is it not merely "cosmetic surgery"? In *Contingency, Hegemony, Universality*, Žižek charges Butler with limiting "the subject's intervention to multiple resignifications/displacements of the basic 'passionate attachment', which therefore persists as the very limit/condition of subjectivity." He wonders how something new is produced through "*performative displacements or resignifications*" (Žižek et al., 2000, 221). (Hence, *if* my analogy between resignification and the *sinthome* is acceptable, this puts Žižek in conflict, or at least in conversation, with himself, since he is on the side of the *sinthome* but also challenges Butler's resignification. Championing Antigone, however, Žižek is also on the side of the authentic act, and so he can appear to be on all sides.)

Extending this reasoning, which questions the production of something new through resignification or even the *sinthome*, to my reading of *Secretary* thus far, we might ask how the substitution of Mr. Grey for Lee inflicting pain on herself really alters Lee's damaged passionate attachment to her distant father? Is not the S/M relation with Mr. Grey a veneer covering real wounds that are sustained by Lee's marriage as they were by her self-punishment? Does not preserving one's symptom, no matter what form it takes, keep alive one's pathology? And does the film *Secretary* itself come to this realization by exposing at the end a certain dopey, saccharine quality to the now legalized S/M relationship?

The Piano Teacher: radical subjective intervention

In *Contingency, Hegemony, Universality* (a series of electrifying debates among Judith Butler, Ernesto Laclau, and Slavoj Žižek), Žižek argues for radical transformation that exceeds "mere displacement/resignification of the symbolic coordinates that confer on the subject his or her identity" (Žižek et al., 2000, 220). Here Žižek favors the Lacanian "act" in its capacity of, rather than enjoying, traversing the fundamental fantasy to disrupt the passionate attachment (which serves for Butler as the ineluctable background of her concept of resignification). This Lacan, the "Lacan of the Real," Žižek points out, exposes paternal authority as "one among the possible 'sinthoms' which allow us temporarily to stabilize and co-ordinate the inconsistent/nonexistent 'big Other'" (Žižek et al., 2000, 221). The *sinthome* now seems to be a provisional, if not flimsy, solution.

Following Lacan's idea that the purpose of psychoanalytic treatment is to touch the impossible Real, Žižek in *Contingency, Hegemony, Universality* advocates the psychoanalytic *act*. An act "redefines the very contours of what is possible" by accomplishing what appears to be "impossible" (Žižek et al., 2000, 121). For Žižek, the act is not tantamount to impotent, self-directed aggression but involves striking at oneself by stabbing what one deems most precious. In this way "the subject gains the space of free action" "by cutting himself loose from the precious object" (Žižek et al., 2000, 122). An authentic act redefines the subject by changing the coordinates of the subject's "disavowed phantasmic foundation." The "spectral dimension" that constitutes us, the "undead ghosts" that haunt us—these are ultimately what get disturbed and disempowered through an authentic act, since this is the stuff that fundamental fantasies are made of (Žižek et al., 2000, 124).

Žižek sustains his emphasis on the authentic act in his predominantly political text *Welcome to the Desert of the Real*. Here he reads the terrorism of September 11, especially the attack on the World Trade Center, as the entry of what had "existed (for us) as a spectral apparition on the (TV) screen" into our reality, thus shifting or having the potential to shift "the symbolic coordinates which determine what we experience as reality" (Žižek, 2002,

16). Žižek regards the terrorist attacks as the domain of psychoanalysis since psychoanalysis is preoccupied with explaining why "nightmarish visions of catastrophes" erupt within well-being. September 11, to Žižek, had the potential to demonstrate Lacan's notion of "traversing the fantasy" that entails first identifying with the fantasy that "structures the excess that resists our immersion in daily reality" (Žižek, 2002, 17). This process is ultimately not to enjoy one's symptom, however, since the symptom is the clue and counter to the existence of the repressed level of our psyche. Symptoms defend against or fill voids that an authentic act allows one to penetrate, for the sake of extinguishing the fundamental fantasy that keeps us stuck.

But unlike Antigone who "assumes the limit-position...of the impossible zero-level of symbolization" (Žižek, 2002, 99), the United States missed the opportunity given to it. On and after September 11, the United States refused "to realize what kind of world it was part of" (Žižek, 2002, 47), to participate in an authentic or ethical act, the spectacle of which the terrorists "openly displayed" (Žižek, 2002, 136). (Žižek means here that the terrorists displayed to us the possibility of our own authentic act.) Well aware of how "sacrilegious" it might sound, Žižek nevertheless sticks to his comparison between Antigone's act and the World Trade Center attacks: "they both undermine the 'servicing of goods', the reign of the pleasure-reality principle" (Žižek, 2002, 142). They both open up the possibility of taking an invaluable risk that, in the case of the United States, would shatter "our liberal-democratic consensus" (Žižek, 2002, 154). (Antigone occupies two positions in Žižek's analogy: she is the United States only receptive to the authentic act; and she parallels the terrorists who offer this opportunity to the United States to traverse its fundamental capitalist fantasy.)

As a further illustration of the "passion for the Real" (which Alain Badiou has singled out as the primary feature of the twentieth century), and just prior to his discussion of Haneke's film *The Piano Teacher*, Žižek addresses the phenomenon of cutters (mostly women "who experience an irresistible urge to cut themselves with razors or otherwise hurt themselves"). He speculates that such self-mutilation demonstrates a passion for the Real through a "desperate strategy to return to the Real of the body." Cutters are not suicidal, however, but in pursuit of "a hold on reality." Žižek's point, at least initially, seems to be that cutters attempt to access the Real in order to root themselves in reality, as opposed to "tattooers" who inscribe their bodies to guarantee their "inclusion in the (virtual) symbolic order" (Žižek, 2002, 10). But when Žižek returns a few pages later to this topic, he entertains a twist: that cutters are escaping from "not simply the feeling of unreality, of the artificial virtuality of our lifeworld, but the Real itself which explodes in the guise of uncontrolled hallucinations which start to haunt us once we lose our anchoring in reality" (Žižek, 2002, 20). Which is it? Do cutters access the Real of the body to anchor a reality threatening to turn virtual? Or do they flee the Real that threatens them when reality is lost? Žižek slides from these speculations directly into an analysis of *The Piano Teacher*—in which the piano teacher and cutter Erika Kohut has an S/M affair with her putatively normal piano student Walter—because Žižek reads the film as speaking to "this conundrum" (Žižek, 2002, 20).

However, when Žižek gets down to analyzing Erika's masochistic demands as well as Walter's "rape" of Erika, he misses the implications of their affair that Žižek's own emphasis on the notion of the authentic act driven by the passion of the Real should have primed him to discern. Erika's letter to Walter Klemmer (her quite enamored piano student) requesting various sadomaso-chistic acts is to Žižek a laying bare of her fantasy. So far, so good. But Žižek concentrates on how repulsive such an unveiling of her desire is to Klemmer, as though Klemmer were the "Other" whose anxiety Erika's masochism provokes and therefore as though Klemmer were our main concern. The "rape" scene is to Žižek "performed in reality" nevertheless "deprived of its fantasmatic support" and hence "turns into a disgusting experience which leaves [Erika] completely cold, pushing her toward suicide" (Žižek, 2002, 21). I fail to see how this reading resolves the cutting conundrum; but my own sense of Erika's traversal of her fundamental fantasy certainly speaks to it.

The Piano Teacher is saturated with the blood of cutting. Early on, after the first fight between Erika and her mother (over Erika's surreptitiously purchased, elegant frock that itself gets torn), the mother asserts, to her brilliant pianist daughter, "I should cut off your hands." This line is echoed later when another pianist's mother, also hyper-active over her daugh-ter's musical success, comments that whoever cut her daughter's hands should have his hands chopped off. Since it was Erika herself who planted shards of glass in Anna's coat pocket, this line too pertains to Erika. Erika's cutting of her student's hands might be taken, then, as vicarious fulfillment of the threat/wish of her own mother toward her (although one can certainly point to the more overt motive of jealousy over Walter Klemmer's charming attention to Anna). However, given that Anna (like Erika) occupies a position of submission to maternal pressure and control, Erika's cruel act could also be read as offering a long, if not final, benevolent respite to Anna from *her* mother's overbearing influence. Similarly, Erika's bathtub act of genital mutilation can seem like an attempt at removal from the mother if read as a symbolic triggering of menstruation, implying maturation from girlhood to womanhood. (The first words of the film are the mother's "Good evening, child.") When Erika has finished cutting herself, she takes a sanitary pad (rather than, say, a large band-aid) to contain the blood, and when her mother notices that blood is dripping down Erika's leg, the mother remarks that now she knows why Erika is in such a bad mood, clearly indicating that she thinks Erika is menstruating. The mother proceeds to announce how unappetizing Erika's blood is, revealing her unease with this supposed sign of her daughter's sexual maturity. And yet, immediately after Erika has sliced her genitals with a razor, her mother calls her for dinner, and Erika instantly responds "Coming Mama," as though her cutting is a source of *jouissance* in relation to the mother. Likewise, after Walter rejects Erika's requests early on, finding her repulsive upon reading her letter to him, she relapses into the *jouissance* she shares with her mother. Erika's impassioned embrace and kissing of her mother in bed, where she proclaims repeatedly "Je t'aime," as well as her awe over viewing "the hairs of [her mother's] sex," clinch the idea that a melancholic Erika exhibits a perverse psychic structure, constituting herself as the struggling object of her mother's *jouissance*.

Up to the "rape" scene, then, we can take cutting to signify the play of intimacy with and rebellion against the mother, a form of self-punishment sustaining and resisting the mother's control, abuse, and punishment of Erika, a perverse way of offering herself as an object of her mOther's *jouissance*, which brings bliss to Erika even as it inflicts pain. The pervert (as we know) notoriously flirts with the law, seeming to wish to install it. The deliberate situating of a masochist and a punisher again calls up the strategy of Deleuzean masochism modeled on what transpires in Leopold von Sacher-Masoch's *Venus in Furs*, although in *The Piano Teacher* we have a gender reversal. The Masochian/Deleuzean masochist positions the mother to punish him, now pleasurably, to eliminate the threatening father from the Symbolic Order. As Theodor Reik states in *Masochism in Modern Man*, the masochist "submits voluntarily to punishment, suffering and humiliation, and thus has defiantly purchased the right to enjoy the gratification denied before" (Reik, 1941, 428).

Deleuze's masochist is essentially his own torturer. Based on his interpretation of Masoch's writings, Deleuze stresses a love affair often initiated by a letter and regulated by a contract: the masochist fashions his female tormentor into a despot, who must cooperate and "sign." As Deleuze elaborates:

[T]he masochistic hero appears to be educated and fashioned by the authoritarian woman whereas basically it is he who forms her, dresses her for the part and prompts the harsh words she addresses to him. It is the victim who speaks through the mouth of his torturer, without sparing himself.

(Deleuze, 1971, 21)

Through this scheme the Deleuzean masochist atones for his resemblance to the father and the father's likeness in him. The father is being beaten, cancelled out, abolished, through an idealization of the functions of the "bad mother" that are transferred onto the "good mother." Now the mother stands for the law under the newly prescribed conditions.

Deleuzean masochism is ultimately formal. It entails fantasy, delay, and provocation: the masochist demands punishment that alleviates his castration anxiety by allowing him to enjoy the forbidden fruit. Incest becomes possible. Whereas castration precludes incest, in Deleuzean masochism its enactment by the mother produces it. Hence the masochist can enjoy incest now assimilated by displacement "to a second birth which dispenses with the father's role" (Deleuze, 1971, 81). Fetishism (or disavowal) and suspension are the key psychic components of this process. Disavowal moves the ownership and privileges of the phallus to the mother; the masochist disavows her lack. And suspense establishes the ideal, suspended "above" reality, that enables the masochist to be resexualized as a "new man."

In general, Deleuze insists on the difference between sadism and masochism, clarifying that sadism provides roles for fathers and daughters and masochism for mothers and sons. However, he opens up another theoretical possibility for daughters in pointing out that "*in masochism a girl has no difficulty in assuming the role of son in relation to the beating mother who possesses the ideal phallus and on whom rebirth depends*" (Deleuze, 1971, 59–60, my emphasis). Yet we don't quite have that scenario in *The Piano Teacher*, either. Her mother being already in the place of authority, Erika's pre-Oedipal union would actually appear to be with her father. Imaginary father and daughter merge through parallels made between them throughout the film: Erika's mother pronounces her "mad," and Erika's father dies "completely mad"; Erika tells Klemmer that she can relate to Schumann's condition of "the twilight of the mind," his state of being just prior to, "a fraction before," losing his sanity, as Adorno explains it, since her father died in the Steinhof Asylum. And Erika sleeps in the father's place, kisses the mother, and seems to be in love with her. (Erika is male-identified too in viewing pornography; the film plays up this gender crossing by having men who surround the booths notice Erika as though she sticks out.) It is Erika's *mother* (like the father in Deleuze's theory), then, who needs replacement, and her father whose pleasurable punishment might facilitate that circumvention. Ergo: Erika seizes on Walter Klemmer as the agent of the punishment she wants inflicted on her—as a fatherly substitute for the punishment-wielding mother. It is therefore no accident that when Walter links himself to Schubert and Schumann (associated in the film with Erika's father through the father's troubled psyche) Erika "falls in love" with him.

Walter thereby enters the place of the Imaginary father. But, eventually, rather than sustaining perverse impulses, Erika's masochistic urges seem meant to supplant the mother, to put a partner (Walter Klemmer) in her place, to usurp her matriarchal power by installing the Law-of-the-Father insofar as he lodges a wedge between Erika and her suffocating mother. Walter therefore plays two fatherly roles in Erika's psychic drama: one Imaginary, to give Erika pleasure like that of the male masochist incestuously entangled with his mother, and another Symbolic, insofar as he enforces the incest taboo.

Erika wants Klemmer to draw her blood, to slap and hit her, so that she—in relation to her mother—no longer has to punish herself. She specifically requests that he tie her up and hurt her in the proximity of her mother, as if to stage a scene for her mother of Erika reaping the *jouissance* of such blows at the hands of another, to advertise to her mother that mommy has been usurped. "The urge to be beaten has been in me for years," Erika tells Klemmer. And then, she issues a command that reflects the paradoxical core of Deleuzean masochism: "From now on you give the orders." As we also read in Elfriede Jelinek's novel *The Piano Teacher* (on which the film was based), Erika Kohut deploys her love to make this boy her master, but "The more power he attains over her, the more he will become Erika's pliant creature....Yet Klemmer will think of himself as Erika's master" (Jelinek, 1983/1989, 207). This paradox of the slave's control, or the master's pliancy, is spelled out again a few pages later in the Jelinek novel: "He should be free, and she in fetters. But Erika will choose the fetters herself. She makes up her mind to become an object, a tool" (Jelinek, 1983/1989, 213). Klemmer's suspicion is that Erika is "sick" and in need of "treatment"; he fails to realize that the "sadism" he has been set up to perform constitutes the treatment.

Once Klemmer becomes frustrated, provoked, and roused enough to enter Erika's S/M strategic theater, he performs most effectively. (I have thus far put the term "rape" in quotation marks because whether Klemmer rapes or, on the contrary, loves/cures Erika or does both is an issue.) When Klemmer barges into Erika and her mother's flat overcome with rage and proceeds to violate Erika, he keeps reminding her of snippets from her letter. This late scene in which Klemmer slaps, punches, kicks, and then has intercourse with Erika, just outside her mother's bedroom door, drawing serious blood and planting serious bruises, would seem to be a real/Real fulfillment of Erika's initial masochistic script. (It really happens, and it happens in the Real.) Klemmer now gives the orders, as she had commanded him to do. But Walter Klemmer must exceed Erika's control, her demands, to please her: part of the contract is that when Erika pleads with him to stop, he shall ignore her. He must become more than her puppet, as he does. And yet, insofar as Walter exceeds Erika's control, he is only governed by it since that is precisely what she wanted him to do. However, although this is an unending cycle, it is by no means a frivolous game, as it would have been had Klemmer played the role immediately with none of his eventual fury.

Therefore, in no way is their final S/M scene unadulterated male violence against an unconsenting woman. Rather, she eggs him on to reap the *jouissance* of his violence. As Walter rather viciously hurts Erika, Klemmer reminds her that she is partly responsible, and in response Erika twice speaks the word "yes." During the course of the *act*, he asks, "Are you trying to tell me I should go?" No response. About to depart, his brutality completed, the contract fulfilled, he asks if she is all right, and she nods. Injecting into the scene key fragments from Erika's letter, Klemmer repeats: "As for my mother, forget her." His reverse injunction to Erika to "Forget your mother" foregrounds the point that Klemmer's role is to assist Erika in bypassing the mother. In the Jelinek novel, Klemmer is conscious that "Mother drove in the stakes. But Erika is not afraid to pull those stakes out...and to hammer new ones in. Klemmer is proud that she is making this effort with him of all men" (Jelinek, 1983/1989, 235). Klemmer serves as the male Wanda, the male dominatrix, in this Venus-in-Furs drama. Here the daughter uses fantasy to cancel out the mother by staging her relation with the "father."

To return to Žižek's cutting conundrum: cutting, as we have seen, reflects Erika's internal battle between remaining close to her mother by meeting the mother's demands and separating from her. Caught in disavowal (of the mother's lack), Erika wields her razor as both the mother's phallus and its demise, as a threat to the existence of that phallus. By positioning Klemmer to cut her, Erika attempts to shift out of her role as the object of her mother's *jouissance* into the feminine role of object of Klemmer's desire. (She insists that she wants everything he wants but indicates that first they need to abide by the terms of her letter or masochistic contract.) She sets him up to offer her this new object position especially in the Vienna Conservatory bathroom when she stimulates Klemmer but leaves him in his tumescent state, ordering him to *face her*. (Erika orders him to look not at his penis but at her.) Her performing fellatio on Walter on the hockey-rink premises enables Erika to vomit up the abject (the incorporated maternal body/object/Thing), so that she can feel cleansed. "I'm clean," she explains with pride: "Inside as well as out." Cutting, or Klemmer's blood-drawing violence against Erika, now provides a way to escape the confines of her bondage to the mother. At this stage Erika moves from bearing a melancholic perverse psychic structure to *using* perversion strategically to effect a psychic transformation.

The culminating scene of Klemmer's violence at the end of *The Piano Teacher* allows Erika to sever her passionate attachment to her mother, to traverse her fundamental fantasy, giving *her* the chance to define the contours of her subjectivity. Through Klemmer, she strikes at herself no longer through impotent acts of self-directed aggression but through an "authentic act" that cuts her loose from her most precious object. The undead ghost of Erika's mother who more than haunts Erika is exorcised through Erika's excursion into the Real excess of her former perverse identity. The "rape" is indeed ultimately "deprived of [any] fantasmatic support" (Žižek's words), since its very purpose is to reduce Erika to zero by depositing her fully in the ungirded Real. Just as the Islamic terrorists' September 11 attack, in Žižek's conception, gave the United States a chance to remake itself, Klemmer's "rape" of Erika gives her an opportunity to transform herself. Erika's blankness during the "rape," her corpse-like position and ashen facial expression, only enhance the point that she is entering absence, an abyss, an empty psychic space that will enable her to configure herself. Were Erika to experience the vitality and pleasure that Klemmer urges her to show, she would risk evading or perhaps even extending the fusion with her mother, the trauma of that attachment. But *The Piano Teacher* refuses to banalize perversion. Instead, it surpasses enjoyment of one's symptom and, by shifting Erika's traumatic relation to the mother to her piano student's violent lovemaking, offers a Kristevan moment of grace, an interweaving of death and life or the timeless and time, a moment in which death is inscribed within lived actuality, signaling the potential of rebirth.

A third type of cutting closes the film, a puncturing that features Erika's striking at herself quite literally and histrionically, announcing Erika's desubjectification. In the foyer of the Vienna Conservatory, Erika stabs herself. The former submissive Erika is now dead, her fundamental melancholic fantasy gluing her to the demanding mother traversed. But, unlike Antigone, Erika walks steadfastly away. Clutching her bag, Erika almost seems "on the go," heading at a swift pace toward a destination. Whereas Antigone cedes her desire in dying (my view differs from Žižek's here), Erika has a chance for a new life of desire. Erika stabs herself in her upper chest (above her heart), implying that her knife strikes a muscle that would impair Erika's piano playing for good and that therefore Erika has also broken the union with her Schubert- and Schumann-identified father. As a Deleuzean masochist, Erika has used Klemmer to secure pleasure in the realm of the Imaginary father unhampered by the mother's interference. But her authentic acts—both the "rape" and the stabbing—have positioned her to start doubly anew. While the earlier masochistic engagement with Walter seems specifically to target the mother, with this final act of cutting, Erika detaches from her lost, dead, Imaginary father as well. Now she cuts all ties. Is *The Piano Teacher* not a film about a woman's multiple perverse psychic enthrallments—with a happy ending?

That is: the Deleuzean masochist gives primacy to idealization; he enjoys and ends up in the Imaginary. His resexualization proceeds as his narcissistic ego contemplates itself through an ideal ego effected by the agency of the oral mother. Although in the case of Erika strategic masochism serves as a progressive move beyond her earlier position as object of her mother's *jouissance*, insofar as she remains comforted by the Imaginary father, she too is "psychically stuck" (from a non-Deleuzean perspective). Deleuzean masochism, I am suggesting, functions differently for a woman than a man, who is stranded in an incestuous bath with the mother, since she can deploy it to move *through* the Imaginary, via the Nothing of the Real, to the destination of the Symbolic. Perhaps, through a masochistic authentic act, achieved within the Deleuzean masochistic strategy of setting up a surrogate sadist to overthrow the power of the mother, a woman suffering from maternal domination can achieve desiring subjectivity beyond all Imaginary attachments.

In masochism, the pervert plays with the law; he experiences perverse *jouissance* by doing so. Situating the mother through a dominatrix to punish him pleasurably, the pervert continues to enjoy, now incestuously. In the role of the Deleuzean masochist, Erika continues her perverse behavior, though we might regard her as having "graduated," through Klemmer, from being the object of her mother's *jouissance* to deliberately toying with the Imaginary father. However, Erika, I am arguing, playing but losing the game, lets it reduce her to a pulp. And by the end Erika leaves behind the sly strategies of Deleuzean masochism altogether, as she moves beyond Mommy *and* Daddy in striking at herself in a second and much more deliberate authentic act. First, Erika leaves behind the *jouissance* of her initial Imaginary melancholic dyad with the mother, by shifting to a father figure who revels with her in the *jouissance* of violence. Second, she gives up the incestuous bliss experienced with the Imaginary father, who, *insofar as he inserts a wedge between Erika and her mother*, functions as the Law of the Father. While Klemmer may seem too much like a boy, or even a Greek god, to stand in for the Law, he nevertheless seriously enacts its violence and consequently peels Erika away from her mother. Haneke's *The Piano Teacher* suggests that Erika ultimately needs to relinquish the Vienna Conservatory (Schubert and Schumann) altogether, a stately white building/prison pictured for a prolonged time in a stark manner at the very end, a site for Erika of severe discipline or maternal control as well as paternal madness—which she does.

In offering "a sudden sense of open space," the camera coaxes us to recognize that in the end Erika has achieved at least some freedom. As Jean Wyatt observes, "the camera moves to a long shot for the first time in this claustrophobically shot film, together with Erika's swift, flowing stride and her decisive turn away from the Institute and out of the frame," conveying "the free movement out of an entrapping structure" (Wyatt, 2006, 478). We are no longer at the mercy of overhead shots riveted on hands playing the piano, fetishes of the maternal object. Now those hands have been cut off, as Erika "cut off" the hands of Anna, as a necessary sacrifice for the traversal of a deep-seated fundamental fantasy.

Although it is laden with sadness due to the inherently heart-wrenching nature of detaching from one's most precious objects, the outcome of *The Piano Teacher* is ultimately more promising than that of *Secretary*. (*Secretary* itself, as we have seen, offers an inkling of the precariousness of its own ending.) An authentic act is an approach to desiring subjectivity preferable to the *sinthome*, since the *sinthome* is apt merely to be an extension of the trauma that makes it necessary. I also recognize the merits of exceeding a contract rather than entering one. All the potentially transformative excesses of *The Piano Teacher* spring from a necessary contract that is equally necessary to surpass, paradoxically to fulfill. Nonetheless, both films prompt us to acknowledge the value of masochistic acts especially for women negotiating damaged relations with parental passionate attachments. The question might need to be posed, then, of why women can only achieve empowerment through their conventional submissive or even masochistic roles? But perhaps the barrage of films emerging at this cultural moment (circa 2000) that feature female perversion (and we will encounter more of them in the next chapter) suggests an affordable post-feminist exploration of the various benefits of powerlessness.

It does seem wise, in any case, to take into account Kaja Silverman's caveat, in "Masochism and Male Subjectivity," that because masochism tends to be regarded as constitutive of femininity, its capacity to have any potency for women is radically reduced. But it seems that Deleuzean masochism adjusted to suit women has the potential to pull women out of the Imaginary, instead of sucking them back into it, as it does in the case of men, since it leaves the female masochist facing a father figure, structurally positioned to draw her away from the mother, rather than the maternal swamp. And insofar as it drains that swamp, turning it into a hole, Deleuzean masochism is able to draw women into an empty space—the Nothing, which gets carved out through separation from the maternal body—that subsequently can enable desiring subjectivity. At least if Erika Kohut is the model, Deleuzean masochism enacted by a woman with a father figure in the place of the dominatrix has the potential to catapult her into a void, and thereby primes her to emerge into a desiring subjectivity of her own, predicated on a zero-degree point. At least Erika's strategy, as opposed to that of the male masochist, liberates her from the mother through sexual games with a father substitute that drag her down to Nothing and thus produce a vacuum—i.e., a removal of the maternal object. Erika in turn secures this lack by autonomously committing a second authentic act, through which she gives up everything precious, everything entangled with the Vienna Conservatory.

Despite the fact that at various moments the viewer is positioned as a voyeur, which I take to be part of its aim, *The Piano Teacher* also deprives the viewer (not just Erika) of pleasure. In the stark white bathroom scene early on, the spectator cannot help but imagine Erica manually bringing Walter to the point just prior to orgasm and Walter's out-of-frame penis in an erect state of agonizing desire. (Are we being constructed as fetishists here, asked to imagine a phallus that's not there?) At the drive-in movie, where Erika voyeuristically observes a couple making love in a car, the point-of-view shots from Erika's position in the scene make us look at the sex act happening in the back seat. Eventually, the fierce, young man being watched takes a hard look at the viewer, as though to say, you too (like Erika) are perversely observing us. Even during the "rape," the viewer, in effect, sits beside the perverse couple, having been given a front-row seat. For the most part, what we perceive, as we watch the sex scenes of the film, is unpleasurable: unconsummated relations, violence, blood, a scene that borders on necrophilia—all causing our own frustration, tension, and possibly rage. Fomenting disarray, *The Piano Teacher* refuses at least conventional gratification for its spectator, as well. However, at the end, experiencing this thought-specular film, the spectator is drawn in to the point that he/she too might feel penetrated by Walter and even experience vicariously, though in a way that feels real/Real and has actual effects—the slow, laborious act of liberating love. Insofar as the spectator identifies with Erika, *The Piano Teacher* offers the viewer too a chance to escape a cage.

Note

1 In *Contingency, Hegemony, Universality*, Butler suspects that gay marriage would contribute to "assimilationist politics" and that it would extend the power of the institution of marriage by exacerbating "the distinction between those forms of intimate alliance that are legitimated by the state, and those that are not" (Butler, 2000, 175). She also objects to reprivatizing sexuality, "removing it from the public sphere and from the market, domains where its politicization has been very intense." Butler supports, instead, "a delinking of precisely those rights and entitlements from the institution of marriage itself," a "return to non-state-centred forms of alliance that augment the possibility for multiple forms on the level of culture and civil society" (Butler, 2000, 176).

Works cited

Adams, Parveen (2003) "Art as Prosthesis: Cronenberg's *Crash.*" In *Art: Sublimation or Symptom.* New York: Other Press.

Butler, Judith with Ernesto Laclau and Slavoj Zizek (2000) *Contingency, Hegemony, Universality: Contemporary Dialogues on the Left.* New York: Verso.

Coming to Power: Writings and Graphics on Lesbian S/M (1987) Ed. members of Samois. Boston: Alyson Publications, Inc.

Deleuze, Gilles (1971) *Masochism: An Interpretation of Coldness and Cruelty.* Trans. Jean McNeil. New York: George Brazillier.

Fink, Bruce (1997) *A Clinical Introduction to Lacanian Psychoanalysis: Theory and Technique.* Cambridge: Harvard UP.

Foucault, Michel (1994/1997) *Ethics: Subjectivity and Truth.* Trans. Robert Hurley and others. New York: The New Press.

Jelinek, Elfriede (1983/1989) *The Piano Teacher.* Trans. Joachim Neugroschel. London: Serpent's Tail.

Miller, Jacques-Alain (1996) "On Perversion." In *Reading Seminars I and II: Lacan's Return to Freud.* Ed. Richard Feldstein, Bruce Fink, and Maire Jaanus. Albany: SUNY Press.

Reik, Theodor (1941) *Masochism in Modern Man.* Trans. Margaret H. Eigel and Gertrud M. Kruth. New York: Farrar, Straus.

Silverman, Kaja (1988) "Masochism and Male Subjectivity." *Camera Obscura,* 17:31–67.

Wyatt, Jean (2006) "Jouissance and Desire in Michael Haneke's *The Piano Teacher.*" *American Imago,* 62:453–82.

Žižek, Slavoj (1989) *The Sublime Object of Ideology.* New York: Verso.

—(2000) *The Fragile Absolute: Or, Why is the Christian Legacy Worth Fighting for?* New York: Verso.

—(2001) *Enjoy Your Symptom! Jacques Lacan in Hollywood and Out.* New York: Routledge.

—(2002) *Welcome to the Desert of the Real.* New York: Verso.

Žižek, Slavoj with Ernesto Laclau and Judith Butler (2000) *Contingency, Hegemony, Universality: Contemporary Dialogues on the Left.* New York: Verso.

Filmography

La Pianiste (*The Piano Teacher*) (2001) Michael Haneke (writer and director). Kino International. Germany, Poland, France, Austria.

Secretary (2002) Steven Shainberg. Lions Gate Entertainment. U.S.A.

5

Unveiling fetishism in the society of the spectacle: *White, Female Perversions, Mulholland Drive*

[H]ow many Didiers exist in suffering without even considering the possibility of the...representation of the malaise in which they lock themselves and those close to them...?...This is when the freedom and negativity proper to psychoanalytical representation may become mired in fetish. Is this the end of a civilization of questioning and freedom? Or its shift, its mutation?

JULIA KRISTEVA, *INTIMATE REVOLT*

A friend of mine gladly watched two films I recommended: Louis Malle's heavily diegetic *Damage* and David Cronenberg's more self-conscious *Crash*. He became deeply involved in the former; the latter left him cold. Overflowing with glamour and eroticism, *Crash*, I assumed, would appeal to him; but I was being obtuse about his fantasy. In *The Imaginary Signifier*,

Christian Metz discusses the typical, vapid negative response to films—such as "It was depressing"—as interesting insofar as it reflects the disappointment of the spectator's fantasy. In other words, if someone finds a film inadequate for whatever apparently unsophisticated reason, a psychoanalytic explanation, having to do with a disconnect between the spectator's fantasy and the film, is apt to be revealing. Metz, whose work remains rich and enlightening despite feminist attempts to supercede it, reminds us that even intellectuals respond to films according to their particular psychic dispositions.[1]

In Kaja Silverman's *The Acoustic Mirror*, we find the illuminating assumption that a film viewer who responds well to the heavily narrativized film, as opposed to the more self-reflexive experimental film, is apt to be a film fetishist. That is: he tends to be not only the sort of spectator who takes the images on the screen to be real (the kind of film fetishist most of us are inclined to be and a kind that will eventually be explicated in this chapter, in connection with Metz's work) but also one who reaps pleasure from objectifying female figures on the screen, attributing to them his castration at the same time as he paradoxically invests them fetishistically with a plenitude—all in order to alleviate his castration anxiety.

While the topic of the male film fetishist may seem old hat to feminists who have branched out from, problematized, and contested such a by now classic argument, neither the passage of time nor such efforts has done away with the problem of fetishism as a psychic phenomenon that closes off lack and flees from negativity. Silverman proposes that the male spectator's identification of the female figure on the screen "with lack functions to cover over the absent real and the foreclosed site of production—losses which are incompatible with the 'phallic function' in relation to which the male subject is defined" (Silverman, 1988, 2); and sometimes, she adds, "the male subject is even unable to tolerate the image of loss he has projected onto woman, and is obliged to cover it over with a fetish" (Silverman, 1988, 18). Silverman conceptualizes the "'normal' male subject" as in denial of his lack, of his insufficiency, and, she proposes, "the mechanism of that disavowal" is a paranoid "projection" (Silverman, 1988, 18).[2]

Feminist film theory has not vanquished, or caused to vanish, such male neurosis. It is especially naïve to think so now, as the current eruption of especially internet pornography and the popularity of "gentlemen's clubs" go to show. As Kristeva commented in an interview, "male sexuality and the social process of sexualization clearly offer men a greater opportunity to amass fetishes and substitutes capable of replacing the fundamental lack and offering a hope of satisfaction—a satisfaction that may be only temporary but is satisfying both phallically and narcissistically" (Kristeva, 1996, 64). Although some feminist film theorists seem to have graduated beyond thinking about male desire, as well as beyond thinking within heterosexual frameworks, male desire persists (in particular in the world of film) in the apparently archaic forms of objectification and fetishization of women—which can be endlessly fascinating from a psychoanalytic perspective (I am making no moral judgment here). (Possibly nervousness over any sort of kinship with Catherine MacKinnon has led some feminist film theory to blind itself to powerful psychic drives.)

Silverman's male spectator is, in my book, Lacan's obsessional: the type of guy who regards himself as an unbarred subject (S), who derives "more pleasure in fantasy than in direct sexual contact" (Fink, 1997, 112). Because the "obsessive refuses to acknowledge any affinity between the object and the [m]Other" (Fink, 1997, 118), because he refuses to recognize that "the breast is part of or comes from the mOther" (Fink, 1997, 119), he objectifies women in a way that renders each of them fungible, often creating "two classes of women: the Madonna and the whore." His is therefore an "*impossible desire*": the closer he gets to consummating his desire, "the more the Other begins to take precedence over him, eclipsing him as subject" (Fink, 1997, 123). He is therefore apt to fall in love with someone inaccessible or to be Silverman's male film spectator who voyeuristically takes pleasure in seductive women so distant and safe that in fact they don't exist beyond being imaginary signifiers. Obsessionals tend to marry the "madonna" and fail to desire her because of her proximity to the mOther and "desire" the "whore" who is satisfyingly unsatisfying because of her distance from the mOther. They tend to situate a maternal woman at home to coddle them and the kids while maintaining distant objects of desire at strip clubs as well as in magazines and films. This way they can steer clear of *objet a*, the real cause of their desire, as it would lure them too close to the terrifying mOther.[3]

Two forms of fetishism, then, protect Silverman's (obsessional) male film spectator. He objectifies female figures on the screen to disavow his lack, making fetishes of them. He likewise participates in the film fetishist's acceptance of the illusion that there is presence on the screen, where in fact there is nothing but chemical particles, and hence (like my friend) tends to prefer a heavily narrativized film to a more experimental one (the two forms of fetishism often dovetail). In reality, however, as we all know absolutely at some level, and as Metz explains in *The Imaginary Signifier*:

What defines the specifically cinematic *scopic regime* is...the...absence of the object seen. Here the cinema is profoundly different from the theatre as also from more intimate voyeuristic activities with a specifically erotic aim.

(Metz, 1982, 61)

That is: representation in both theater and cinema, as Metz points out, is "by definition imaginary," for "that is what characterises fiction as such." But "the representation is fully real in the theatre, whereas in the cinema it too is imaginary, the material being already a reflection." We experience cinematic fiction as "the quasi-real presence of that unreal itself" (Metz, 1982, 67). Metz draws a parallel between the child who is terrified by his view of the mother's missing penis and who then later in life becomes dependent on a fetishistic prop for a sense of potency and orgasm and the film spectator who, while aware at some level that the screen presents no more than a fiction, respects the diegetic illusion. "Any spectator will tell you that he 'doesn't believe it', but everything happens as if there were nonetheless someone to be deceived, someone who really would 'believe in it'" (Metz, 1982, 72). The fetish, in cinema and elsewhere, is for Metz "the good object" that is "threatened in its 'goodness' . . . by the terrifying discovery of the lack" (Silverman, 1988, 75). We have the fetish to thank for covering the lack—the wound that cinema actually thrives on, as film is predicated on Nothing real/the Real—and thereby for enabling "the object as a whole [to] become desirable again without excessive fear" (Silverman, 1988, 75).

Silverman reviews, still in *The Acoustic Mirror*, Metz's argument in a list of primarily male film theorists (Dayan, Mulvey, Munsterberg, and Oudart) preoccupied with "the specter of a loss or absence at the center of cinematic production." As opposed to Metz who for the most part identifies the film spectator as a genderless fetishist, Silverman reads film theory's concern with lack as a "preoccupation with male subjectivity, and with that in cinema which threatens constantly to undermine its stability." Silverman contends that film theory and film are obsessed with "the coherence of the male subject" (Silverman, 1988, 2). Fetishism, to Silverman, has been marshaled to save, or perhaps we should say "produce," that coherence. Silverman explains Metz as understanding cinema to be "not only invaded by but synonymous with the loss of the profilmic event" (Silverman, 1988, 3). As she so strikingly articulates his position, cinema is structured according to a lack. It is castrated, so that the viewer must protect himself from the trauma of that castration through the defensive mechanism of fetishism, which of course entails disavowal. Silverman gives this compelling emphasis to Metz's work: the spectator shields himself from confronting the lack that cinema is predicated on by accepting a surrogate in the place of the absent reality. Silverman therefore perceives a conflict between the fetishism of "suspended disbelief" and an overt demonstration of artifice, since artifice shatters the illusion of verisimilitude. She believes that the cameramen, directors, critics, and spectators who "fetishize" technique (or style, as in Cronenberg's *Crash*) have "acceded to the loss of reality" and do not experience such a loss as traumatic (Silverman, 1988, 5).[4] Being much more anxiety-ridden than those who acknowledge and even appreciate filmic technique, some spectators, however, dodge technique and films that foreground it, as part of their effort to preserve cinematic illusion, given the psychic danger for them of exposure to castration.

Having synthesized the dominant psychoanalytic theories of fetishism that explain how narrative cinema conventionally functions, this chapter will point out counter-fetishistic moves within three quite distinct films: Kieslowki's *White* (1994), Streitfeld's *Female Perversions* (1996), and Lynch's *Mulholland Drive* (2001). My interest is in thinking—through film—about and beyond fetishism, both in its male (Silverman) and genderless (Metz) forms. Not only is fetishism thriving; film itself engages it as a topic, galvanizing the theoretical debate to work against the globalizing tide of our spectacular, psychically diminished Western world.[5]

And this is where Julia Kristeva's recent commentary on cinema enters, and takes over, the picture. In "Fantasy and Cinema," Kristeva treats film (in a way similar to Metz) as fantasy, which "prompts us to take seriously this other reality—psychical reality." To Kristeva, fantasy "distortedly admits the subject's desire" (Kristeva, 2002, 65) or its lack thereof. And literature and art are "the favored places for [fantasy's] formulation" (Kristeva, 2002, 66). Allies of psychoanalysis, literature, and art "open the verbal path to the construction of fantasies and prepare the terrain for psychoanalytical interpretation" (Kristeva, 2002, 68).

Although most movies reduce the viewer to a "passive consumer," *pulverizing fantasy by substituting their own brash images*, Kristeva makes a special case for "an other cinema"—a cinematic genre she labels "the thought specular" (Kristeva, 2002, 69). Although most contemporary images shrink our psyches—"It is not a time of great works" (Kristeva, 2002, 13)—Kristeva champions cinema that "explores the specular" (Kristeva, 2002, 73), that seizes us at the point of fascination, at the site of the (Lacanian) gaze. The "thought specular" both designates and denounces fantasy: it lures the spectator to locate his/her fantasies and then to empty them out. It puts into play Freud's primary processes, Kristeva's semiotic, and thus is able to seize "drives always in excess in relation to the represented and the signified" (Kristeva, 2002, 74). The thought specular thinks the specular in a way that is itself specular; but even as such ethical cinema, as Kristeva regards it, employs the visual/fantasy, it is protected from it as it demonstrates its fetish-istic logic. Kristeva's ethical cinema displays evil—evil being a non-symbolized death drive—at first taking us for a ride but ultimately "mak[ing] us keep our distance" (Kristeva, 2002, 79). Such cinema is the "privileged place of sadomasochistic fantasy, so that fear and its seduction explode in laughter and distance" (Kristeva, 2002, 80). Kristeva perceives the situation as one of cinema's choice: to indulge in sadomasochism, to authorize perversion, to banalize evil, or to demystify such fixations.

To demystify is precisely what the three contemporary films analyzed in this chapter seek to do, as they loosen and undermine various forms of detrimental fetishisms and thus work against Western social values of performance, success, competition, mindless pleasure, and spectacle. This outbreak of the thought specular especially in non-avant-garde cinema is a striking phenomenon, an intriguing ethical (again, in Kristeva's sense of giving expression to the death drive), theoretical, and psychoanalytic turn. In the form of capitalism (Kieslowski), the objectification of women as Daddy's girls as well as erotic playthings (Streitfeld), and love conceptualized as full, fulfilling, and lasting (Lynch), fetishism is identified as psychic poison.

Here we have, then, more or less mainstream film working against the kind of cinema Kristeva finds pernicious, film that sustains the fetishist's inability to face the negativity that indicates his mortality and that (were it to be encountered) would facilitate desire. Here we observe film that undoes resistance to "the Nothing," without which, in Heideggerian terms, there can be "no selfhood" or "freedom." Kristeva's psychoanalytic work is founded on the Heideggerian assumption that "For human existence, the nothing makes possible the openedness of beings as such. The nothing does not merely serve as the counterconcept of beings; rather, it originally belongs to their essential unfolding as such. In the Being of beings the nihilation of the nothing occurs" (Heidegger, 1929/1977, 103–4). Nothingness constitutes human beings; it is constitutive of Being. In *Hatred and Forgiveness*, Kristeva continues this theme, one she put forward in the spirit of Mallarmé as early as the publication of *Revolution in Poetic Language*, in claiming that the sacred must be rediscovered, "in the very depths of language, to the point of the *nothingness* in which the everyday as well as the absolute are mired" (Kristeva, 2010, 25, my emphasis). Fantasies that "deny the *lack of being* essential to the human condition" (Kristeva, 2010, 33) only preclude our human being as well as our subjectivity, which Kristeva defines as necessarily "open to a search for meaning and sharing" (Kristeva, 2010, 32).

Whiting out fetishism

Krzysztof Kieslowski's *White* (1994), the second or middle film of his exquisite

Three Colours (*Blue*, *White*, and *Red*) trilogy, extends the anti-fetishism protest of the 70s—when feminists, Marxists, and theorists of modernist aesthetics challenged what they took to be an illusory Hollywood cinema—into the early 1990s. Laura Mulvey, in *Fetishism and Curiosity*, lays out the terms of this protest:

> Anti-fetishism, like a portmanteau, linked together different strands of the debates which aimed to exorcise: the cinema's conventional investment in willing suspension of disbelief and denial of its own materiality; the psychic process of defense against a (mis)perception of the female body as castrated; femininity fragmented and then reconstructed in image into a surface of perfect sheen; the erasure of labour processes in the society of the spectacle; the glamour of Hollywood cinema in which fascination with the erotic erases the machinery of cinema and filmic processes....The influence of Brecht met psychoanalysis, modernist semiotics and Althusserian Marxism. In both theory and practice during this period, there was an aspiration towards the defetishisation of the film medium.
>
> (Mulvey, 1996, 9)

White focuses on a Polish hairdresser who works in Paris and is married to a gorgeous woman, Dominique. But she divorces him for his inability to "consummate the marriage." Karol loses all his earthly possessions and is in effect driven out of France by his estranged wife. *White* critiques fetishism both at the level of its personal narrative as well as economically: in terms of post-Communist Poland's new capitalist national identity, that is, in terms of commodity fetishism. Exemplifying Kristeva's thought specular insofar as it plays out Karol's fantasy only to reveal its destructiveness, Kieslowski's *White* weaves psychoanalytic fetishism together with commodity fetishism in an ironic condemnation of them both.

Kieslowski's *White* exposes its protagonist's fetishistic resistance to marital desire leading to consummation—with its threat of an eclipse of his subjectivity—in a way that accords with the film's critique of post-Communism in Poland. *White* implicitly argues for a gap that would enable the co-existence, rather than the conflation, of the Symbolic and the Real—against the threat of capitalist, postmodern instant gratification that collapses the distance between desire and its object. The hero's avoidance of consummation with a woman he finds ravishing chimes with his later obsession with capitalism insofar as both are means of dodging the void, or lack of being, in the system. As part of its effort to liquidate fetishism, *White* exposes such a phobia: fear of an "encounter with the negative, body and soul," a resistance to "symbolic castration" (Kristeva, 2002, 145). Such an encounter depends on negation and is impregnated "with separation and frustration, freighted with oral, anal, and penile losses." At the same time, it serves as an invaluable cut that would "benevolently [generate] the capacity of thinking itself" and open the door to "indefinite questioning" (Kristeva, 2002, 146–7).

Although Karol apparently pleasured his wife prior to their marriage, upon being married, he became impotent and consequently, shocked, finds himself in divorce court. A hairdresser—a possible clue to his fetishistic psychic composition?[6]—Karol steals a delicate bust that resembles, and for a long while displaces, the beautiful wife he fails to keep: upon trans-porting to Poland this figure of a pale young woman in a lacey bonnet, Karol bends to kiss his new fetish object. An obsessional with the obsessional's typical "impossible desire" that precludes satisfaction due to the terror of an accompanying *aphanisis*, Karol seems better suited to capitalism than to marriage. In this economic system, everything is aggressively fungible. Gaps are put into play only immediately to be filled and reopened, only to be refilled and reopened, *ad infinitum*, so that the gap never gains ontological consistency. (Reiterating this fear of openings, in *White*, a hunched-over elderly person pops a bottle into a green recyling bin, where it fails to fall through, plugging a hole.)

Capitalism is fetishistic insofar as the social relation among men is taken to be, as Marx writes in *Capital I*, "the fantastic form of a relation between things" (Marx, 1887/1967, 77). Things stand in for people. Even worse, as Žižek elaborates in *The Sublime Object of Ideology*, "The *value* of a certain commodity, which is effectively an insignia of a network of social relations between producers of diverse commodities, assumes the form of a quasi-'natural' property of another thing-commodity, money: we say that the value of a certain commodity is such-and-such amount of money" (Žižek, 1989, 23). Social relations are obscured—disavowed. An ideological fantasy structures, and gives consistency to, social reality. Capitalists "know that their idea of Freedom is masking a particular form of exploitation," but they persist in following it (Žižek, 1989, 33). Or, as Guy Debord quite clearly puts it in *The Society of the Spectacle*: "The fetishistic appearance of pure objectivity in spectacular relationships conceals their true character as relationships between human beings and between classes" (Debord, 1995, 19).

A flaccid Karol avoids an encounter with an angelic woman to circumvent his constitutive lack, engagement with which has the potential, as he is stuck unconsciously believing, to shatter his Imaginary sense of self—whereas in actuality such an encounter would open up Karol, releasing his drives from their (mere) fixation on Dominique as fetish object (what he wants her to be). Instead, Karol plunges into the pursuit of capitalist profit, where excess is folded into the system, rather than encountered. As Žižek explains: "the labour force is a peculiar commodity, the use of which—labour itself—produces a certain surplus-value, and it is this surplus over the value of the labour force itself which is appropriated by the capitalist" (Žižek, 1989, 22). Like capitalism, Karol is neurotically compelled to retain everything, refusing to conceive of Nothing. He demands from a public phone the release of two unused francs for the call he makes; he not only receives back the two-franc piece, but he hangs onto it for most of the film.

White characterizes Poland as a place where "These days you can buy anything," as Karol's private employee reminds him. "Anything" includes even a corpse, the purchase of which epitomizes the point that excess is re-consumed by the system. Even dead bodies are recycled. Death is deprived of its usual ability to generate a void. Karol buys the nondescript body of a dead Russian man whose head is bashed in, so that he can stage his own death in an effort to bring Dominique to his funeral, allowing him to observe her response to his death and then pin it on her. Driven to profit, Karol cannot bear to lose anything; totally retentive, he cannot face loss: even at the end, when he has arranged things to produce desire between himself and Dominique, and in effect has carved out a lack, Karol has placed an ineradicable distance between himself and his former wife—now that she is incarcerated and he off to Hong Kong—in order to avoid any vulnerability. If he reappears (recall that he had staged his own death, implicating Dominique in his demise), Karol rather than Dominique goes to jail. They can never again coalesce. Future desire leading to shared *jouissance* has been ruled out, since one of them must necessarily be behind bars. Dominique turns out to be such a horrifying threat to Karol's obsessional psychic structure that he must cage her. Perhaps his plot is not so much to seek revenge as to ensure that she can no longer lure him into what he assumes would be psychic disintegration.

On the non-diegetic level as well, *White* exposes fetishism, exposure being an apt way to undermine it given that fetishism operates through disavowal. Kieslowski punctuates *White* with semiotic splashes of color, which often paint the entire frame, so that the film itself undergoes *aphanisis*—but without panic. *White* occasionally loses its diegetic identity and can even be said to flaunt its disbelief in its own reality. Unlike capitalism, Karol, and the obsessional spectator, *White* insists on the leftover, where excess has the power to desubjectify or, in other words, reveal the desubjectification or lack on which all subjectification is founded.

After Karol stumbles verbally in answering the judge's questions early on about his unconsummated marriage, a flashback appears of the moments directly after Karol and Dominique tied the knot at the church. Positioned in the view of Karol, we watch a swirl of whiteness emerge, a veiled and strikingly white Dominique at the eye of this psychic tornado. This flashback at this critical moment in the courtroom would seem to respond to the judge's question: was the marriage consummated? Whiteness traumatizes Karol, as it serves as a blankness in which unconsciously he feels he cannot afford to collapse, a haze, the Lacanian gaze, which the so-called, feminist "male gaze"—actually the male look—avoids like the plague, objet a, the cause of his desire, "something from which the subject," as Lacan defines the objet a, "in order to constitute itself, has separated itself off as organ" (Lacan, 1981/1973, 103).[7] But this dazzling white cloud is celebrated by the film. It is through such a gaze, in fact, that film has the potential to disengage a fantasy from an object, to symbolize drives that, by remaining unsymbolized, cause the fundamental fantasy doggedly to persist. Karol sabotages himself maritally in a desperate attempt, carried out ironically through his impotence, to preserve his fantasy of unbarred subjectivity. And this flashback scene, riveted on Dominique, on whiteness, seems to threaten to elide Karol, representing his obsessional phobia of fading as a subject. But the void avoided by Karol is offered up to the viewer, as though White is intent on spectatorial disruption.

Toward the end when Karol reveals to Dominique in her hotel room that he is, after all, still alive, the film again overwhelms the spectator with whiteness. Mutually impassioned, they make love. Accompanied by Dominique's blissful moaning, the screen fades to pervasive white. Finally, Karol can perform, melt together with her in orgasmic pleasure—now that a huge wall will imminently divide them. (He is "dead" in society's eyes, and soon she will be escorted off to prison.) Karol seems to have met the paradoxical challenge of governing even the very experience whose bliss derives from its breaking down of boundaries. Or, concentrating on Karol's loss here, we might view it as an instance of the obsessional (momentarily) running "aground" on "the Zeitlos" (unbound time), as Kristeva would put it, "hoping to possess the unmeasurable by measuring it" (Kristeva, 2002, 41). In either case, White contrasts Silverman's fetishist who, like Karol, desires only remote objects and the film's ideal viewer who can release him/herself at the moment of Dominique's jouissance as it is represented by the white Nothingness on the screen. The film presents a state of border-lessness at this point, in a way that allows the viewer to revel in a cavernous, amorphous, profound filmic space that exceeds the diegesis. White invites us to watch it in a non-fetishistic way by succumbing to the gaps—the white-outs—themselves, gaps in the narrative, the sites of the Nothing and, in turn, of the gaze.

By building such psychic opportunities, unseized by Karol, technically into his film, Kieslowski subtly punctures the fetishism of the obsessional as well as the related commodity fetishism of capitalism, the very means by which Karol effects his fierce grip on the gaze. In the end Karol in a sense *buys* Dominique's love; but he cannot experience it. He can only conquer it, and so he misses out on the intimacy that might have provided some respite from, and resistance to, the virtual capitalist world he seems instead at the end of the film to re-enter. Separate from Karol, however, *White* itself yields a desubjectifying *jouissance* that plunges its viewer into the void that, as Kristeva describes it, "is not simply the narcissistic or egoistic caprice of man spoiled by consumer society" (where Karol wants to live and in a sense thrives) "or the society of the spectacle. The jouissance at issue here...proves indispensable to keeping the psyche alive, indispensable to the faculty of representation and questioning that specifies the human being" (Kristeva, 2002, 7–8). Associating neurosis with capitalism and promoting negativity or the Nothing as their antidote, *White* provides the space of intimacy that panics Karol.

Feminist fetishism

In contemporary film the tendency to rupture the diegesis by featuring technique, to exhibit rather than cover over or suture the filmic cut, has given way recently to the curious phenomenon of "cutters" popping up as central figures in film narratives. This outburst on the narrative level raises the question of its relation to the fetishistic history of film insofar as the female act of cutting might seem to respond to the male unwillingness to acknowledge a cut. In the latter (male fetishism, based on disavowal), we find an attempt at eliding a lack in being; in the former (women cutting themselves) an attempt, at least as desperate, to effect a split. How does such physical splitting relate to the idea that, as Mary Ann Doane sums it up in "Film and the Masquerade: Theorising the Female Spectator," "[s]pectatorial desire, in contemporary film theory, is generally delineated as either voyeurism or fetishism" (Doane, 1999, 133)?

I propose that the recent outbreak of cinematic representations of women cutting themselves—as this act bears at the very least a paranomastic relation to the cuts in film that disrupt the diegesis and hence, as Silverman believes, break the spell of fetishism, opening up the wound/absence the film is actually predicated on—might be read, within the genre of Kristeva's "thought specular," as a response to the predominance of fetishism in the operations of filmmaking and viewing. Simply put: whereas a fetishist disavows a lack, a cutter carves out a lack that she seems to be insisting must be avowed. Such cinematic cutting of the body might signal a mutation, in relation to the dominant fetishistic mode. It would seem to question the way that "the freedom and negativity proper to psychical representation [has] become mired in fetish," again to translate into Kristeva's psychoanalytic and philosophical terms (Kristeva, 2002, 129), by opening up a gap to disturb fetishistic fixation.

Such an act, for one thing, tends to disarticulate male systems of viewing by rendering the film tough to watch, to inject a disorienting dissonance, perhaps pressuring the viewer defensively to think, "Oh well, this is just a film, not a woman actually slicing up her genitals," thus bursting the filmic fetish standing in for the filmic void. Cutting isn't sexy. The reasons typically proferred for why women cut themselves—to feel *something* rather than numbness, the urge to be a subject, the desire to desire—are not disconnected from this reading of women's self-cutting as a challenge to fetishism. If fetishism objectifies women, then it very well might compel women to subjectify themselves, a process requiring the opening of a space, a lack, a site of desire, even through behavior that might itself be characterized as perversion. If my hypothesis is valid, then, voyeurism, fetishism, and sadism will have produced a beneficial masochistic reaction.

If the reason women cut themselves were based on three contemporary films that feature cutters—*The Piano Teacher* (2001), *Secretary* (2002), and *Thirteen* (2003)—it would appear that women resort to self-mutilation due to an overly intense, suffocating maternal bond, unobstructed by a paternal metaphor. Cloying or controlling maternal love coupled with paternal absence or neglect that coexists with a lack of maternal desire, which in turn enjoins the mother unconsciously to take her daughter for the phallus that fulfills her, these films suggest, produces a daughter who engages in self-laceration. A daughter with roughly such a parental background (like Erika in *The Piano Teacher*) might deploy a razor or knife as *her* phallus, to secure release from the Imaginary mOther prison. Such melancholic daughters, prisoners of "the affect, of the archaic Thing, of primary inscriptions of affects and emotions" have in effect swallowed "but not digested," as Kristeva explains, "the mother-Thing" (Kristeva, 2002, 24). They need to release the invading maternal object. They may use various methods to expel her, such as vomiting, giving birth, and, I am suggesting, cutting. Such young women vulnerable to becoming the object of their mother's desire, or *jouissance*, might even (ironically) be enthralled by male fetishizing, that is, by being objects of the "male gaze," but only in an effort ultimately to slide out of the jaws of the all-consuming mOther, a psychic metonymy that also can be observed in *Secretary* and *The Piano Teacher* (as we have seen) as well as in *Thirteen*. The heroines of these three films seem driven, to varying degrees, to objectify themselves in relation to someone else besides the mOther, in an attempt to achieve finally, subsequent to two phases of objectification, subjectification.[8] Male fetishism in this scenario, in other words, is *used* by such heroines to escape the clutches of the suffocating mOther.

Cutting in film, at the level of the diegesis, I am suggesting, has the potential (like the non-diegetic filmic cut) to awaken the male spectator from his fetishistic stupor and to preclude objectification of women. It might also be read as the woman's attempt to achieve Symbolic castration in the psychoanalytic sense of becoming a desiring subject. It can work specifically by distancing the daughter from an overbearing mother as that suffocated daughter strategically deploys a lover, providing a guarantee against future maternal objectification. And insofar as cutting, however it is done, achieves such goals, it demonstrates Kristeva's practice of employing perversion for therapeutic purposes.

Kristeva holds a special place for perversion in psychoanalysis. She reads perversion in Proust, for example, as a way of seizing an "enclosure of incommunicable pleasure" and of narrativizing "the (inevitably sadomasochistic) intrigues inherent in eroticism" (Kristeva, 2002, 57). Perversion has the capacity to access the drives, the death drive, *jouissance*, and the (Lacanian) Real. Traversing autistic enclosures is facilitated by perverse objects that serve as pseudo-objects. Deploying perversion for such purposes, a film enters the category of the "thought specular." Rather than participating in sadomasochistic drives for their own sake, it exhibits them to think them through, by giving them, through the specular, self-conscious representation. By inscribing the drive, the specular enables it to morph into desire, transforming aggression into seduction. It is the specular—film, in particular—that has the capacity to do this, being at the point of "departure of . . . signs, narcissistic identifications, and phantasmatic trances" (Kristeva, 2002, 72).

Susan Streitfeld's *Female Perversions* (1997) traces the self-destructive daughter's over-identification with the mother to the father's brutalizing of the mother. The film presents a heroine whose ritual cutting seems at least in part the consequence of a childhood in which she meant, at a key moment of her father's violence toward her mother, to offer solace to her mother, although, instead, somehow she ended up succoring her father, the implication seems to be, in an incestuous relation of some stripe. In one scene late in the film, Eve slowly cuts her breast, methodically encircling her nipple in imitation of her mother's writing (in the distant past but now in Eve's present nightmarish daydream) similarly on her breast with a pen as part of the mother's effort to seduce Eve's father, who responds by pushing Eve's mother down.

To outshine her mother vis-à-vis her father, Eve evolves thereafter into a "phallic woman" insofar as she dresses the part (short skirts, high heels, elegant lingerie, long hair, impeccable make-up, etc.) and is professionally a high-powered lawyer on the elevated social road to a judgeship. It seems plausible that Eve turns into a phallic feminine object to succeed with her father (and father substitutes) where her mother failed. I find Eve's sister's, Madelyn's, charge that Eve strives for the "big Daddy dick" counter-intuitively compelling if it is translated into the notion that Eve wants to be the phallus for her father, so that he can avoid anxiety over losing his. Eve (like Madelyn herself, in fact) wants to be the fetishistic object of her father's desire. In a clear rivalry, both sisters make repeated attempts to attract their father's attention by becoming the phallus, a fantasy that *Female Perversions*, as itself fantasy, engages in—only in the end to deflate.

One might even read Eve as flaunting a certain excess of femininity, as wearing a compensatory mask of femininity, and therefore as reflecting Joan Riviere's idea of masquerade in "Womanliness as a Masquerade." It seems arguable that Eve exemplifies Riviere's thesis about the professional or intellectual woman having to "make up" for seeming to pilfer the phallus by exaggerating her femininity, by flirting as a way of insisting that she "is" the phallus (for them) rather than "has" it (for herself). In fact, an uncanny continuum appears to emerge within *Female Perversions* starting from Eve's psychic trouble with her father, reflected specifically in her compulsion to fill his lack, to her phallic feminine image in her professional life. Just as the phallic feminine daughter, the Daddy's girl, comforts her father, the professional/intellectual phallic feminine woman serves as an anxiety-relieving fetish for surrounding anxiety-ridden male colleagues. Cooperating with the man's tendency to fetishize women, such a woman is pleasing, rather than a threat. This, I submit, is the most apparent feminist reading of the film, yet only a first phase in the many permutations in *Female Perversions* on the topic of femininity.

The film may be read, then, as an exposé of "normal female perversion" as this concept is laid out in Louise Kaplan's voluminous book *Female Perversions*. As Kaplan's "pervert," Eve adheres to patriarchal ideals of femininity, the very ideals that draw Silverman's male spectators to movies. Even the masquerade of femininity—which Mary Ann Doane reads as a sophisticated distancing of the woman from herself, as a disorienting way of keeping herself from being imaged as incapable of lack, from being objectified—may be seen à la Riviere and Kaplan as falling, after all, into the patriarchal trap of objectification. The woman in feminine masquerade—who to Doane challenges the concept of essential womanhood, where womanhood is defined as all body with no capacity for performance or rather performativity—might be perceived as the pusillanimous white doll of patriarchy, who possesses no power, lacks lack, and is constituted by perverse cultural behavioral norms. In a way Eve lends herself to this description. She expresses major doubts to her male superior about receiving the judgeship and is haunted throughout the film by hallucinatory voices that question and ridicule her professional ambitions. Such behavior seems part pretense but also insinuates that Eve has internalized and wrestles with the uneasiness that male-dominated society bestows on women who excel in traditionally male arenas. "Eve," as Jean Walton put it in a "Women Filmmakers: Refocussing" Conference paper in Vancouver, "is an unconscious collaborator with the patriarchal system, apparently unaware of how her adherence to feminine phallicism has constrained her sexual and emotional life" (Walton, 1999, 6).

Although Walton senses a link between what she calls an Oedipal, traumatic primal scene with Eve's father and Eve's "bondage scenario she constructs for herself to reach orgasm during sex," and consequently interprets Streitfeld's film as complicating the social issue of femininity with what I would call a personal dimension, Walton for the most part stresses that Eve is "hopelessly implicated in the social system that produces [her] as 'feminine'" (Walton, 1999, 6). The film could in turn be read as italicizing in particular the "whiteness" of female perversions, by taking into account the Latina women who stare impassively at an Eve who initially is oblivious to them and eventually disturbed by these women of color who seem to "see through her," to gaze at her—from the site of the Lacanian (not of course the male) gaze. One could interpret *Female Perversions* as admiring these Latina women over the pale, brittle, phallic, feminine collaborator, Eve. In fact, Walton reads the racial others in *Female Perversions* as being transformed, through the mediation of Madelyn's thesis, into the "terrifying matriarchal Earth Woman of [Eve's] dreams" who equips Eve "to acknowledge the unconscious Oedipal determinants of her erotic fantasy life" (Walton, 1999, 10). The climactic result is that Eve can cut the "rope," imaged over and over in her nightmares, that knots together her psycho-sexual world. Read along these compelling lines, *Female Perversions* enacts Kristeva's thought specular in setting up Eve's fundamental fantasy of being a (her father's) fetish and lets the spectator ride with it, lays it bare, and subsequently represents its demise, through the heroine's encounter with her unconscious, with what she is not. The scrutinizing eyes of the Latina women grant Eve the tools that allow her to cut herself free.[9]

Female Perversions reinforces its critique of conventional femininity by including Ed, a 13-year-old girl who also mutilates herself literally in ways that can be analyzed from both cultural and psychoanalytic perspectives.

Ed tends to cut herself in response to her mother's traditional romantic attachment to Rick, so that one might argue that Ed abuses herself because she feels slighted emotionally by her mother. Given her mother's hopelessly sentimental aspirations, Ed's self-mutilation can also be regarded as a radical act of protest against Kaplanesque "female perversions." In this reading, Ed's cutting rebels against such romanticism, which causes Emma (Ed's mother) to metamorphose into a foolish feminine bauble, and serves as explicit testimony to my thesis that women's cutting is meant to undercut men's fetishism. Insofar as *Female Perversions* features such a character (who also hacks away at her short hair as part of her campaign to avoid becoming the object of the "male gaze"), the film might be said to deploy *feminist* perversion that slices away at conventional feminine, actually masculine, fantasy. Emma aspires to be like the mannequins of her frilly dress shop; Ed's cutting speaks to that dehumanization by implying the necessity of women having a lack rather than being the object that fills his lack. Ed's final act of carving the word "LOVE" into her leg in a way epitomizes this point of her resistance to the sick fetishistic relations between men and women. Innocent 13-year-old Ed believes in "LOVE." She fails to realize, however, as Lacan does, that, being "the desire to be One," love "leads us to the impossibility of establishing the relationship between 'them-two'...sexes" (Lacan, 1998/1975, 6), that love cannot be inscribed, and that "love is impossible" (Lacan, 1998/1975, 87).

This impasse—Love as aporia—is where I think *Female Perversions* gets especially shrewd, in particular through Ed's aunt as she overlaps with Lacan who teaches that love is giving what you don't possess: the true cause of the other's desire, *objet a*. I take Ed's aunt's didactic erotic dance to be the centerpiece of the film. Ironically in a way like Simone de Beauvoir, or Cindy Sherman, she makes the critical point that femininity is supplementary to women: "you can learn to be feminine too," she instructs Ed. "It's not something that comes to you naturally. You gotta work at it." The aunt trained herself to be feminine; she advises Ed to practice every day, and she'll catch on. More specifically, a woman has to learn how to convince a man that she has what he desires. She then proceeds, in fetishistic garb (lots of black, high heels, lingerie, even a veil she waves around), to show Ed how to dance to seduce a man: "You do this well, and any man will want you." "It's all about power," Ed's aunt concludes.

But Ed's vulgar aunt does not really mean "you" in her statement that "any man will want you," since she tells Ed that "you gotta erase yourself"; "you gotta become, like, generic." *Female Perversions*, I think, may "fail" in this way—fail, that is, to be straightforwardly feminist. The aunt tries to teach

Ed how to conform to a Kaplanesque perverse norm, about which the film is clearly self-conscious; nevertheless, *Female Perversions* nowhere offers an attractive alternative. Can Emma's outburst that the problem with the women of Madelyn's dissertation is that they are fat and unattractive simply be dismissed? The grotesque, curvaceous Earth woman of Eve's dreams and daydreams who effects Eve's ability to cut her rope is certainly no role model, nor is she (I think) meant to be. Eve albeit carts off at the end her sister's picture of a Mexican woman with iguanas curled on top of her head—a Mexican Medusa-figure, perhaps reminiscent of Cixous's famous essay, "The Laugh of the Medusa." But *Female Perversions* offers no glimpse of Eve (as judge) incorporating such an image or a sense that she might or should relinquish "femininity."

Let's consider further, then, that the film's take on "femininity" resembles Doane's understanding of the feminine masquerade rather than Riviere's. To Doane, the mask holds femininity at a distance. Hence it can work against "patriarchal positioning," or male fetishizing, by undermining the notion of woman or femininity as "closeness, as presence-to-itself, as, precisely, imagistic" (Doane, 1999, 138). Masquerade, in Doane's conception, produces a gap between a biological woman and her image, splitting or cutting the female subject in this way. Doane's feminist logic is that because of its instability, its destabilizing of the image, the feminine masquerade confounds the "masculine structure of the look" (Doane, 1999, 139), shattering what feminists call "the male gaze." This, then, is the more complex and smart "advice" the film, operating paradigmatically as Kristeva's "thought specular," offers women on how to cut across the fundamental fantasy of serving as a phallic object.

It is not that I think Eve will set out as a judge to frighten rather than comfort men but that the film positions her at the end as a multi-dimensional subject whose "femininity" has become conceptually sophisticated in part by the film's own unwillingness to make up its mind, so to speak, about whether or not to value this concept. In the course of *Female Perversions*'s equivocations—between presenting femininity as something to be avoided at all costs, the product of a girl's sick relations with her parents as well as of patriarchal manipulation, and as attractive (who isn't "enchanted by Tilda Swinton's brilliant and nuanced acting"? to quote Walton [Walton, 1999, 2]), or even as an empowering performance—femininity itself emerges as complicated.

Finally, because *Female Perversions* does not quite resolve the issue of femininity but offers at least two positions—that femininity is a white perverse norm of patriarchy, and even that idea is made more intricate, as we have seen, by the personal dimension of the film, *and* that femininity is a clever mask, a role that women can learn in order to manipulate men's desire—the film ends up being a kind of (conceptual) fetish itself. I almost wrote "ironically." However, if we consider Doane's point that "The female...must find it extremely difficult, if not impossible to assume the position of fetishist" as well as her reference to the "abolition of a distance" in women, their "inability to fetishise" (Doane, 1999, 137), we might be inclined to congratulate Streitfeld for producing a film whose double take on femininity does just that. *Female Perversions* counters fetishism with (thought?) fetishism, insofar as it "disavows" the femininity that is a strategic construction of patriarchy (in and beyond the family) and simultaneously "avows" "femininity" by preserving its appeal (refusing to offer an alternative), even seeming practically to suggest that women learn how to put it on as a mask or advocating femininity as a kind of costume. *This* "fetishistic" position on "femininity" is sufficiently cracked open, however, so that nothingness holds a place in it. That is: *this* "fetish" opens gaps, providing for negativity and freedom.

For one thing, femininity is not discarded, although (as mask) it is de-essentialized, excavated, emptied out. Given that Ed's aunt's lesson teaches the value of femininity as costume, as though a woman ought to assume it so long as men are built psychically the way they are, the film can be read as giving license to women to play the role of the fetish/ phallus. This idea of masquerade of course connects with Doane's sense of it as effecting a "defamiliarisation of female iconography" (Doane, 1999, 139).[10] Second, thematically "disavowing" femininity, insofar as it is female (Kaplanesque) perversion that (patriarchy tricks women into thinking) is natural and necessary, even as the film "avows" "femininity" as a politically useful mask, *Female Perversions* cuts through the Daddy's girl's fundamental fantasy that she is bound to be his feminine object of desire, for real, all the while giving a glimpse of the split between these two positions.[11] And then by presenting femininity as even possibly an attractive and enjoyable inhabitation, an actual experience of desire, on its own, founded on the absence carved out by all the cuts, the film adds a third "cutting through." Femininity has been set in motion on its own, to live an autonomous life cut off from the demands of the father. To cede it entirely would only be another way of remaining tied—oppositionally—to the fantasy of pleasing Daddy. And this is the brilliance of such a position.

Operating as part of Kristeva's notion of the thought specular, perversion in Streitfeld's *Female Perversions* ultimately functions on behalf of psychic expansion. Eve's self-mutilation, her eventual cutting of the rope, Ed's cutting, and the aunt's figurative slicing of herself into, on the one hand, who she thinks she is and, on the other, the erotic object she deliberately becomes when she dances—all culminate in fetishistic splits that save women from being mere objects of the "male gaze" or, perhaps worse, the non-entity Emma would have collapsed into had Rick been slightly compassionate or more conventional and less obsessional. By unveiling the nothingness at the base of femininity and thereby cutting through the Daddy's girl's fundamental fantasy, *Female Perversions* as fetish object ironically underscores the void at the heart of all fetishism and becomes in turn an anti-fetish fetish.

What do film and love have in common?

In *Intimate Revolt*, Kristeva distinguishes between "noble" fantasy that serves desire and the ignoble "spectacular imaginary" that currently "assaults us and that we all consume more or less complacently" (Kristeva, 2002, 180). One trouble is that the spectacular imaginary keeps us "mired in fantasy." It offers an opaque reality without "arranging the escape hatch of clarity." Instead, Kristeva favors "critical" representations of fantasy that are self-conscious rather than stereotypically protective and numbing. Self-conscious fantasy, to which Kristeva ascribes a "thetic value[,] stabilizes the subject and permits him/her to continue to symbolize, be free." It can serve as a "source of survival and rebirth," diverting the death drive "from hand-to-hand combat" (in particular with "the primordial idol, the mother"), by bringing "to life this metabolized-negativized drive in indefinite, infinite psychical life" (Kristeva, 2002, 180). David Lynch's *Mulholland Drive* (2001) is not only such a self-conscious fantasy, but it also is explicitly *about* the value of fantasy in slicing through a debilitating love fantasy. *Mulholland Drive* demonstrates how fantasy can offer an "escape hatch."

Fantasy, then, can escort one to the negativity that complements desire and is necessary to ignite it, or it can plug lack, thus serving as a fetish. Lynch's *Mulholland Drive* contests such fetishism. Leaving behind a Freudian notion of castration in favor of rendering a universal abyss at the heart of things, *Mulholland Drive* is a thought-specular, anti-fetishism film that operates at a non-gendered, Lacanian level. Here it is not a question of a particular voyeuristic male spectator experiencing, and then defending against, castration anxiety because the film exposes his lack or powerlessness but that *all* spectators are given the opportunity to encounter a certain inarticulable absence, to which site they are brought through a story about the effectiveness of fantasy in dissolving fantasy.

More specifically: *Mulholland Drive* unveils the gap between a supposed object of desire and the *objet a*, or cause of desire, that renders that object alluring. The film in this way seems cognizant of the Nothing on which love is founded. At the same time, as a meta-film, a film preoccupied with matters of film and the film industry, *Mulholland Drive* reveals the illusory nature of film itself. Hence an analogy takes shape, one Godard already insinuated in *Contempt*—between cinema and love—perhaps implying the reason why cinema is enthralled with this topic. In revealing the void on which love and film are predicated, *Mulholland Drive* attempts to explode the fetishistic ideas of the fulfillment or satisfaction of Love and the verisimilitude of film. Lynch's film offers a full disclosure about cinema (that it is not full!), puncturing the fetishism of film in the Metzian sense. And it does so through a complex narrative about a love affair, offering the revelation that absence founds them both. Lynch demonstrates Lacan's conception of "the only conceivable idea of the object, that of the object as cause of desire, of that which is lacking," a lack situated in the Real. "[A]nd the little we know about the real," Lacan elaborates, "shows its antinomy to all verisimilitude" (Lacan, 1981/1973, ix). Lynch, I am suggesting, is faithful to this Real antinomy.

Mulholland Drive's exposure of love's underlying absence depends on the film's two-part structure. While some debate may linger over whether roughly the first two-thirds of *Mulholland Drive* can be considered fantasy and the last one-third reality, I would venture to assert that most viewers regard the former as Diane's fantasy of a successful relationship with Camilla and the latter as the preceding actual story of a failed sexual relation that explains the rationale of the fantasy. As Todd McGowan writes in "Lost on Mulholland Drive: Navigating David Lynch's Panegyric to Hollywood," "The first part of *Mulholland Drive* portrays the experience of fantasy, while the second part depicts the experience of desire." That is:

> The second part of *Mulholland Drive* is structured around the incessant dissatisfaction of desire as Diane (Naomi Watts)—and the spectator—are denied any experience of Camilla (Laura Elena Harring), Diane's love object. By contrast, in the first part Diane, appearing as Betty, can enjoy the object.
>
> (McGowan, 2004, 67)

Diane's desire is not only dissatisfied the way all desire is by definition dissatisfied—since to desire is precisely to seek or lack satisfaction—but Diane's already intense desire is abruptly terminated at its apex. Lynch is astute in capturing a lover's urge to kill a beloved who tortures her with desire that gets expressed simultaneously along with an edict against it. In the last third of the film, Diane has a hallucinatory memory of herself in an erotic pose with Camilla, as Camilla gushes to her, "You drive me wild," yet immediately follows that incitement to Diane's desire with her decision that they "should not do this anymore." Devastated, Diane feels compelled to expunge Camilla from the face of the earth. She hires a hit man to do so. Diane knows that she must expel Camilla: as Betty, she reiterates passionately this murderous impulse in the Hollywood audition (enacted after the hit man has done the job) as well as in the practice audition, which Betty performs with Rita. In both, Betty asserts to her partner, "I'll kill you. I'll kill us both," again reiterating insistently that the elusive love object must be removed. Laid out in the first two-thirds of the film, however, Diane's fantasy offers, more profoundly, a psychoanalytic approach to canceling the love object. It is a fantasy that works to extinguish Diane's cathexis of Camilla, which requires that it engage the Real of Diane's desire, that it bring down Diane's desire to its root in the Real to enable her to face unconsciously that its object is "merely" an absence, a missing piece cast off during the early separation from the mOther, a remainder, so that to chase after Camilla is to pursue an illusion.

Mulholland Drive is comprised of three ontological levels: fantasy and reality, as I have said, and the Real. Something horrific suffuses this film. The Real is represented as monstrous: through the monster behind Winkie's café; the creepy, ominous figure of Louise who arrives at Betty's aunt's door and proclaims forebodingly that someone is in trouble; the corpse that Betty and Rita traumatically encounter in Diane's apartment; and perhaps the ghastly, tiny, elderly couple (aged parents? emblems of a gross heterosexual satisfaction?). Diane's fantasy includes a terrified man who returns to Winkie's with someone who appears to be in the position of his therapist since the shaken young man explains to him that they are there because he has had two dreams that took place at this coffee shop. The young man at Winkie's, whom I will call the analysand, was scared in his dreams as was his analyst, scaring the young man even more so. Why? Because there is a man in back who is "doing it." The analysand can perceive, in the dream, that man through the wall; in the dream he can perceive his face. The therapist suggests that the analysand has come to Winkie's, to observe if the man "doing it" is actually out there. They take a peek. The monster emerges, frightening the analysand, it seems, to literal death.

Later, Betty and Rita sit in what appears to be the same Winkie's for coffee, loosely establishing a parallel between Betty and the analysand and Rita and the monster. In yet a third Winkie's scene, we have Diane sitting with the hit man, ordering the extinction of her "object of desire," so that the following chain of associations forms on the side of the monster: the monster, Rita, and then death or an extinguished Camilla. If we accept that the monster is in the register of the Real, this chain enables us to read Diane's fantasy as an encounter with the Real of Diane's desire as that monster is identified with Rita, the fantasy's stand-in for Camilla. In addition, the corpse that Betty and Rita discover in Diane's apartment is taken by the two young women in the first place to be Rita (since their hunch is that Rita is Diane Selwyn, and they are now in her apartment), and then later as someone mistaken by the murderer as Rita. The body is laid out on the bed in a way reminiscent of how Rita lay on the aunt's bed in an early scene, on her side with her legs stacked up. Upon giving us a close-up of the face of the dead person, the camera reveals a monstrous face, so that again Rita is linked to the monster. Rita is the monster in that she—as the stand-in for Camilla—has captured Betty's/Diane's desire or appears to be the *objet a*: refusing to fulfill Diane's desire in real life, Camilla fixes her in an utterly miserable position. Diane needs to rectify this situation, by confronting its monstrosity, so to speak, meaning its rootedness in the Real. As Coco warns in the fantasy, "If there is trouble, get rid of it!" Camilla is Diane's "trouble," and in real life (in the film) she gets rid of it literally. Her fantasy, though, offers another, more effica-cious psychoanalytic way to detach from a painful love object, to "kill," or uproot, such a monster.

Prior to such an extrication, though, Betty and Rita (in the fantasy) begin to merge. In order to avoid being killed, Rita needs to disguise herself. Betty tells Rita that she knows what Rita has to do, which turns out to mean—melt together with Betty (Diane's ultimate fantasy). In her dream, then, Diane transforms Camilla into a woman (Rita) who does not know who she is and who therefore is empty enough to fuse with Betty/Diane. When they try by phone to reach Diane Selwyn, Betty comments that it is strange calling yourself. But at this moment it is not clear who is calling Diane or "herself" because it is not obvious which one of them is Diane. Rita dons the white wig, causing her to resemble Betty physically. And the fantasy is in general about their merging in love, so that the idea of love here would seem to be of a subject uniting with her missing piece. "I'm in love with you," Betty repeats emphatically and erotically. The bed scene of them making love is what we might call a Lacanian Love encounter, where the subject in love (Betty) coalesces with her beloved. Lacan asks:

Is love—as psychoanalysis claims with an audacity that is all the more incredible as all of its experience runs counter to that very notion, and as it demonstrates the contrary—is love about making one (*faire un*)? Is Eros a tension toward the One?

(Lacan, 1998/1975, 5)

simultaneously positing Oneness as the lover's goal *and* casting a cynical psychoanalytic eye on its possibility.

But especially given that this attempted union occurs in the fantasy segment of the film, *Mulholland Drive* (too) seems to know that the missing piece can never be annexed. Being a constitutive lack of the subject, such a piece, upon being embraced, would threaten subjectivity. "[D]esire merely leads us to aim at the gap" (Lacan, 1998/1975, 5). The subject lacks, but it lacks nothing. To fuse with what it lacks consequently would be threatening, if not shattering (which is not to imply that the pursuit of love should be avoided). *Mulholland Drive* also seems keenly aware that those subjects who believe they come close to consummating their desire, upon being cut off in the midst, would wish to "kill" what they take to be the missing piece with which they almost coalesced, for it would be agony to have that "missing piece" of oneself walk away—with or as a piece of oneself. Instead, however, the missing piece, or missing emptiness—since the *objet a* or cause of one's desire is only a structural absence, the residue of one's splitting off from the original Other—needs to be pried loose *in the suffering lover's psyche* from the contingent object that only appears to house the *objet a*. That one's cause of desire actually inheres in one's ostensible object of desire is a psychic illusion. It is this illusion, not the object, that must be destroyed. This is Lacanian logic as well as, I am proposing, the logic of Lynch's film.

Mulholland Drive advances the idea that Diane needs to relinquish her psychic grip on Camilla, to realize, at the level of the unconscious, that Camilla is merely a contingent object. At Club Silencio, Rita and Betty sit and watch all sorts of paradigmatic separations. One would assume that here, at the Club, there would be a band, but "No hay banda." There is music, but it is recorded. The emcee proclaims the theme: "It is an illusion." The singer belting out Roy Orbison's "Crying" herself bewails a lost love, helping us to link the splitting the scene effects—between what appears to be true and the reality ("No hay banda")—with a certain psychic/emotional detachment that Diane needs to undergo. The singer collapses onto the stage, but her singing eerily continues.

The voice, one of the four forms of the *objet a* in Lacan's *The Four Fundamental Concepts*, persists without embodiment.[12] In this scene of the singer with the blue hair, it is emphatically disembodied. The collapsed voiceless singer suggests that the voice, or *objet a* (the cause of Diane's desire), is located someplace else besides the body of the singer, or the body of Camilla—that Diane loves Camilla for "something more." And at this moment, the fantasy that Camilla is that excess is crumbling, as McGowan suggests:

> The structure of fantasy breaks down when the subject confronts the total emptiness of the *objet petit a*, which is what occurs as Rebekah Del Rio's song continues after she has fainted.... Betty looks down in her purse and sees a blue box, which represents the point of exit from the fantasy world.
> (McGowan, 2004, 83)

Betty, then, shakes as she observes all the stage effects that indicate illusion, especially the singer as she physically detaches from her song, because Betty senses—and is experiencing—the deterioration of her fantasy. Like McGowan, I too think that Betty shakes upon confronting the Nothingness of the cause of her desire. But we might arrive at yet another reading, first by disagreeing with McGowan's proposition that Betty cedes her desire and hence commits an unethical act.[13] For Betty/Diane does everything she can to act on her desire, whereas what she actually needs to do is quite the opposite: to distance herself from it, to *recede* from her object of desire (Camilla) by examining the relation between it and the cause of her desire (something other or more than Camilla) or, in other words, by learning the lesson of Club Silencio—"It is an illusion." Yet the horror that Betty's brittle shaking indicates is not merely due to Diane's unconscious confrontation with the ineluctable lostness of the lost object, but also to the fact that it is, practically speaking, too late for Diane.

In sum: Diane's fantasy, produced unfortunately after the hit man has enacted the murder commissioned by Diane, reveals to her the logic of love as fantasy—the lover pursues an *objet a*, a cause of desire, a missing piece, rather than a bona fide object—as well as therefore (this is the "up" side) the possibility of squashing a fantasy that makes one miserable. (We can assume that this is the chronology, i.e., that the dream-fantasy occurs after the actual murder, for one thing because Rita shows up in the fantasy with a pile of money that Diane presumably paid to the hit man to have Camilla killed and also because Diane's fantasy is preoccupied with myriad perceived threats to, and the possible imminent death of, Rita.) The anguished subject in love needs unconsciously to recognize the skewed relation of the object of desire and the *objet a*—that they are by no means synonymous. Diane's fantasy (the first two-thirds of the film) functions—by foregrounding various splittings between things usually taken to be fused and engaging an abyss with the potential to erase and reconfigure psychic structures—to aid her in breaking apart her psychic fantasy predicated on a certain false object. Noble fantasy here, then, effectively destroys fantasy. But Diane has acted too rashly in reality, not taking into account that literally to kill an object of desire only makes things drastically worse, that the "killing" needs to be psychic. This twofold realization—unconsciously Diane is belatedly coming to grips with the Real absence of her obsessive attraction to Camilla and simultaneously facing her fatal mistake of murder—as it emerges in Diane's fantasy at Club Silencio is surely what makes Betty/Diane quake.

Lynch redoubles this theme of illusion by deliberately setting it within the context of Hollywood, fulfilling Kristeva's desideratum that the thought specular be self-aware, as a way of distancing the spectator from the film itself as fantasy. Rita, Camilla's substitute in Diane's fantasy, whimsically names herself after Rita Hayworth depicted on a poster for *Gilda*. All the flamboyant camera shots that lead the way to horror—creepily down the hall to Rita in the shower, down the steps to the monster behind Winkie's, and perhaps most suspensefully to the grotesque corpse in bed—scream out that we are watching a psycho-horror film. Betty (Davis?) in the fantasy sequence remarks to Rita that, in checking out with the police if an accident indeed happened on Mulholland Drive, they can pretend they are someone else, just "like" in the movies. Within the context of Diane's dream-fantasy (about a sexual relation with Camilla, in the guise of Rita), Betty designates Hollywood and specifically her aunt's Los Angeles apartment as a "dreamplace," referring to her dream of making her debut in Hollywood. And, again in imitation of Godard's *Contempt*, the last word of *Mulholland Drive* ironically is "Silencio," which points not simply to the absence at the core of the love fantasy the film encloses but also, à la Metz, to an absence imbricated with the film, or film as a whole, and on which the film, or film in general, is founded.

By ending this film with this word "Silencio" as well as with the voiceless singer with the blue hair from Club Silencio, by featuring finally this scene of disembodiment, Lynch points to *Mulholland Drive* itself as the illusion. Just as *Camilla* (not Rita!) is the illusion of Diane's love—"I'm in love with you," Diane breathlessly but erroneously asserts to Camilla—*Mulholland Drive*, while signifying "unaccustomed perceptual wealth," is (to quote Metz in general) "stamped with unreality to an unusual degree." Like all cinema, *Mulholland Drive*, as *Mulholland Drive* itself discloses, "drums up all perception, but to switch it immediately over into its own absence, which is nonetheless the only signifier present" (Metz, 1982, 45). Such a defetishizing exposure of the film enhances *Mulholland Drive*'s status as thought specular, insofar as it precludes any pretense of its subject matter actually being there, thus removing the spectator from its fascination. It is insofar as *Mulholland Drive* is a Metzian imaginary signifier that it can serve as Kristeva's Imaginary register, where (to Kristeva) the Real is inscribed within consciousness, engagement with which can release the grip of a misery-producing love "object."

By exposing the chasm at the heart of love and film, Lynch's film doubly undermines fetishism: the phantasmatic form that plugs the lack of love with an object as well as the fetishism of filmic verisimilitude. *Mulholland Drive* drags the fetishism of *White*'s capitalism (especially as it is manifested in Hollywood), of the obsessional (on the screen and in the audience), of love as well as film itself—insofar as it projects itself as present—down to its vacuous base, a blue box, unmistakably an escape hatch, containing Nothing. Targeting a primary generator of the glittery images of the society of the spectacle—Hollywood itself (the famous sign of which is put on display in the film, along with one shot after another of Los Angeles, illusorily radiant by day and sparkling by night)—Lynch's film grants the spectator an opportunity of intimate revolt or return, through an especially sensuous cinematographical encounter with images of interiority that collapse ultimately in a way that can catalyze a new start. Facing the oblique relation of the object of desire and the *objet a*, at the level of the unconscious, within this savvy and sophisti-cated example of Kristeva's thought specular, the spectator is prompted to exit through the blue box, to extricate him/herself from psychic fixations, by working through them, to enter eventually into fresh psychic space.

Like *White* and *Female Perversions*, *Mulholland Drive* as the thought specular has the potential to absorb, and in doing so connect with, the specta-tor's own suffering in love. Through such attachment to the screen—a way of drawing the spectator's emotional plight into semiotic *representation*—all three films offer "forgiveness," that is, as Kristeva defines it, the transfigu-ration of the spectator's pain into meaning. Perhaps directors as distinct from one another—and as ostensibly removed from Eisenstein, Godard, Bresson, Hitchcock, and Pasolini—as Kieslowski, Streitfeld, and Lynch can succeed where the fetishist fails. By bringing the spectator into relation with his/her unconscious, by luring the spectator through the wealth and potency of their semiotic qualities into the abyss, into "hazardous regions" wherein "unity is annihilated" (Kristeva, 2002, 10)—which in the case of *Mulholland Drive* is shown to found love and film—thought-specular films can restore psychic depth and activate desire. *White*, *Female Perversions*, and *Mulholland Drive* all thereby do their part in arming the spectator against the contemporary robotization process.

Notes

1 Metz identifies two sources of filmic unpleasure, for all. "It can arise on the side of the id when the id is insufficiently nourished by the diegesis of the film; instinctual satisfaction is stingily dealt out, and we have then a case of frustration" (Metz, 1982, 111). Or the id, on the contrary, might be overly satisfied, producing aggressivity against the film. In the latter case, the super-ego and defenses of the ego may intervene or counter-attack.

2 Silverman's sense that lack and the phallic function are incompatible seems invalid from a Lacanian standpoint, since Lacan defines the phallus as the signifier of desire/lack. This difference perhaps explains why I (as opposed to Silverman) do not assume that men are universally anxious. In "Fetishism," Freud sets up three categories in relation to fetishism: men who inexplicably manage to surmount their anxiety, men who need a prop to protect them from the lacking female genitals, and homosexuals who, without such a prop, flee in the direction of other men.

3 In *Encore*, Lacan proposes that the Other qua locus does not hold up and that therefore "there is a fault, hole or loss." *Objet a* functions "with respect to that loss" (Lacan, 1998/1975, 28). He addresses this concept again later in this same seminar: "Object *a* is the void presupposed by a demand." That is: "in the desire of every demand, there is but the request for *objet a*, for the object that could satisfy jouissance." Objects are laid claim to and made into the cause of desire or *objet a* "as substitutes for the Other" (Lacan, 1998/1975, 126). Yet we delude ourselves into thinking that our object of desire embodies this substitute. Instead, *objet a* only haunts that object. In his extremely useful (first) book, *The Lacanian Subject: Between Language and Jouissance*, Fink offers a neat explanation of this concept: it is a rift in the hypothetical mother-child unity that leads to the advent of *objet a*. It is the "*remainder* produced when the hypothetical unity breaks down, as a last trace of that unity, a last *reminder* thereof. By cleaving to that rem(a)inder, the split subject, though expulsed from the Other, can sustain the illusion of wholeness; by clinging to *objet a*, the subject is able to ignore his or her division" (Fink, 1995, 59).

4 Consequently, Silverman is puzzled by Metz's inclusion of technical virtuosity as part of the cinematic fetish. As opposed to Silverman, Metz has no trouble thinking about cinematic technique as part of the film as fetish. He writes that the "fetishism of technique" that cameramen, some directors, some critics, and even some spectators engage in is an instance of fetishism taken "in its ordinary sense." He describes the "apparatus of the cinema" as "a *prop*, the prop that disavows a lack," "a prop which is the penis, since it negates its absence." Cinema as a technical feat, to Metz, facilitates the spectator's ability to denounce "the lack on which the whole arrangement is based (the absence of the object, replaced by its reflection)" (Metz, 1982, 74). Not just the connoisseur, the cinephile, proposes Metz, but also the ordinary cinema-goer appreciates the machinery that carries him/her away, that helps him/her to regard the film as a "good object."

5 A full account of feminist work on fetishism is beyond the scope of this chapter. But it is important to mention Teresa de Lauretis's *The Practice of Love*, in which (following in the footsteps of Bersani and Dutoit) she regards the very structure of desire as fetishistic and posits that the lesbian mourns the loss of the female body and so is attracted to fetish substitutes of it. Also see *Space, Time, and Perversion* by Elizabeth Grosz, who rehearses the history of fetishism in psychoanalysis, explaining why it is considered a "uniquely male perversion" (Grosz, 1995, 9). Grosz seems to take a fetishistic position on the question of the relevance and validity of psychoanalysis in relation to feminism (one similar to the case I make in my analysis of *Female Perversions* upcoming). She recommends a "cultivated ambivalence" that "may provide the distance necessary to extract what may be of use in psychoanalysis while using psychoanalytic concepts, such as fetishism, to problematize psychoanalytic assumptions and to move beyond them" (Grosz, 1995, 154).

6 In "Fetishism," Freud discusses the pervert who reaps pleasure from cutting off women's hair, to illustrate the fetishist's divided attitude toward women's castration: he is compelled to carry out the very castration he disavows.

7 These two concepts of the gaze are distinct, if not antithetical. Lacan defines the gaze as the subject's constitutive lack. Feminist film theory has in mind the man's visual objectification of the woman. While Lacan's "gaze" is not gendered, the "gaze" in feminist theory is almost always projected by a man. Feminist film theory at times mistakenly appropriates Lacan's gaze as the male look. But one looks or tries to look, in Lacan, at the gaze, which looks back only to shatter the subject. To encounter the Lacanian gaze is to coalesce with what one is *not*, and therefore to desubjectify.

8 Other relevant films are *In My Skin* and, less directly, Jane Campion's *In the Cut*.

9 Lest I distort Jean Walton's position, with my earlier speculative spinning off from her various observations, I want to clarify that Walton is especially critical of *Female Perversions* for "its participation in the quite routine practice in mainstream (and apparently independent) films of using marginalized, two-dimensional characters of color as a foil to set off the white characters' problems, or as catalysts to guide them to a psychological resolution of their problems, or even as un-complex wise figures who know 'instinctively' what the white people must learn through a process of development," to quote correspondence I have had with her.

10 In *What Lacan Said About Women*, Colette Soler allows us to observe that such a position is close to Lacan's. She explains why women are not masochists even as they may engage in feminine masquerade. She suggests that women's charms owe a great deal to semblance, which is not at all tantamount to lying. Feminine masquerade is instead "an accommodation with the semblances; there is no limit, as Lacan says, to the concessions that a woman is ready to make for a man: of her body, her goods, her soul, everything that is good for her." Soler acknowledges a certain "note of derision" that the woman may bring to her masquerade, but she locates this too on the surface, "although it marks with a touch of protest the alienation of her being to which the structure of sexuation condemns her." On the whole, however, Soler stresses the benefits to women of their concessions as part of masquerade. She explains that "a woman sometimes takes on a masochistic appearance, but only to give herself the appearance of a woman, by being a woman for a man, for want of being Woman. The love that she calls upon as a complement of castration in order to locate her being defines her subjection to the Other and her alienation; this alienation intensifies the alienation that is characteristic of the subject. Yet this is also the field, which feminists would almost make us forget, of her power as object-cause of desire" (Soler, 2006, 80–1).

11 Such a notion of the fetish that exposes its split structure is akin to Homi Bhabha's idea in *The Location of Culture*. To Bhabha, racist stereotypes are fetishistic, involving a mask inscribed on a lack, which "gives the stereotype both its fixity and its phantasmatic quality" (Bhabha, 1994, 77). "[F]etishistic identification . . . provide[s] a process of splitting and multiple/contradictory belief" (Bhabha, 1994, 80). It allows "substitution and fixation" always with "the trace of loss, absence" (Bhabha 1994, 81). Bhabha grants power to the fetish, since it, like mimicry, "radically revalues the normative knowledge of the priority of race, writing, history." It mimes "forms of authority at the point at which it deauthorizes them" (Bhabha, 1994, 91).

12 In *The Four Fundamental Concepts*, Lacan establishes that the drive is recognized in "a certain type of objects which, in the final resort, can serve no function. These are the *objets a*—the breasts, the faeces, the gaze, the voice. It is in this new term that resides the point that introduces the dialectic of the subject *qua* subject of the unconscious" (Lacan, 1981/1973, 242).

13 A word about Lacanian ethics: in his seventh seminar, *The Ethics of Psychoanalysis*, Lacan urges the subject to act in conformity with his desire. "Traditional morality concerned itself with what one was supposed to do 'insofar as it is possible,' as we say, and as we are forced to say. What needs to be unmasked here is the point on which that morality turns. And that is nothing less than the impossibility in which we recognize the topology of our desire" (Lacan, 1992/1986, 315). To Lacan, it is ethical not to cede one's desire, *as desire is defined in relation to "impossibility," death, the Real*. "[T]he only thing one can be guilty of," Lacan in a sense admonishes, "is giving ground relative to one's desire" (Lacan, 1992/1986, 321).

Works cited

Bhabha, Homi K (1994) *The Location of Culture*. New York: Routledge.

Debord, Guy (1995) *The Society of the Spectacle*. Trans. Donald Nicholson-Smith. New York: Zone Books.

De Lauretis, Teresa (1994) *The Practice of Love: Lesbian Sexuality and Perverse Desire*. Bloomington: Indiana UP.

Doane, Mary Ann (1999) "Film and the Masquerade: Theorising the Female Spectator." In *Feminist Film Theory: A Reader*. Ed. Sue Thornham. Washington Square, New York: New York UP.

Fink, Bruce (1995) *The Lacanian Subject: Between Language and Jouissance*. Princeton, NJ : Princeton UP.

—(1997) *A Clinical Introduction to Lacanian Psychoanalysis: Theory and Technique*. Cambridge: Harvard UP.

Freud, Sigmund (1927) "Fetishism." *Standard Edition of the Complete Psychological Works of Sigmund Freud*. Oxford: The Hogarth Press, Vol. I, 295–343.

Grosz, Elizabeth (1995) *Space, Time, and Perversion: Essays on the Politics of Bodies*. New York and London: Routledge.

Heidegger, Martin (1929) "What is Metaphysics?" In *Martin Heidegger: Basic Writings*. Ed. David Farrell Krell. New York: HarperCollins Publishers.

Kaplan, Louise (1991) *Female Perversions: The Temptations of Madame Bovary*. New York: Doubleday.

Kristeva, Julia (1996) *Julia Kristeva: Interviews*. Ed. Ross Mitchell Guberman. New York: Columbia UP.

—(2002) *Intimate Revolt: The Powers and the Limits of Psychoanalysis*. Trans. Jeanine Herman. New York: Columbia UP.

—(2010) *Hatred and Forgiveness*. Trans. Jeanine Herman. New York: Columbia UP.

Lacan, Jacques (1981/1973) *The Four Fundamental Concepts of Psycho-Analysis: Book XI*. Ed. Jacques Alain-Miller. Trans. Alan Sheridan. New York: W.W. Norton & Co.

—(1992/1986) *The Ethics of Psychoanalysis 1959–1960: Book VII*. Ed. Jacques-Alain Miller. Trans. Dennis Porter. New York: W. W. Norton & Co.

—(1998/1975) *Encore: 1972–1973: On Feminine Sexuality/The Limits of Love and Knowledge: Book XX*. Ed. Jacques-Alain Miller. Trans. Bruce Fink. New York: W. W. Norton & Co.

McGowan, Todd (2004) "Lost on Mulholland Drive: Navigating David Lynch's Panegyric to Hollywood." *Cinema Journal*, 43 (2): 67–89.

Marx, Karl (1887/1967) *Capital: A Critique of Political Economy. Volume I: The Process of Capitalist Production*. Trans. Samuel Moore. New York: International Publishers.

Metz, Christian (1982) *The Imaginary Signifier: Psychoanalysis and the Cinema*. Trans. Celia Britton, Annwyl Williams, Ben Brewster, and Alfred Guzzetti. Bloomington: Indiana UP.

Mulvey, Laura (1996) *Fetishism and Curiosity*. Bloomington: Indiana UP and the British Film Institute.

Riviere, Joan (1929) "Womanliness as a Masquerade." *International Journal of Psychoanalysis*. 10: 303–13.

Silverman, Kaja (1988) *The Acoustic Mirror: The Female Voice in Psychoanalysis and Cinema*. Bloomington: Indiana UP.

Soler, Colette (2006) *What Lacan Said about Women*. New York: Other Press.

Walton, Jean (1999) "(White) Female Perversions." Paper at "Women Filmmakers: Refocussing" Conference, Vancouver, British Columbia.

Žižek, Slavoj (1989) *The Sublime Object of Ideology*. New York: Verso.

Filmography

Female Perversions (1997) Susan Streitfeld. Trimark. U.S.A.
Mulholland Drive (2001) David Lynch. Universal Pictures. U.S.A.
White (1994) Krzysztof Kieslowsk. Miramax Films. France.

6

Psycho: the ultimate seduction

In *Intimate Revolt*, Kristeva laments the loss of what she considers to be essential components of European culture—"a culture fashioned by doubt and critique." The "moral and aesthetic impact" of Europe, she contends, has become marginalized, as it now is, at best, "tolerated by the society of the spectacle, when it is not simply submerged, made impossible by entertainment culture, performance culture, and show culture" (Kristeva, 2002, 4). Kristeva's concept of intimate revolt involves reviving the profound and acute logic of this rich, multi-faceted, analytical culture, to restore its aesthetic and ethical dimensions now under the threat of extinction. In *Hatred and Forgiveness,* Kristeva celebrates, and urges us to hang on to, "the art of living, taste, leisure, the so-called 'idle' pleasures, grace, pure chance, playfulness, wastefulness, our 'darker side' even, or, to put it in a nutshell, freedom as the essence of 'Being-in-the-World' prior to any 'Cause'"—as an alternative to, or even a mode of revolting against, our performance-oriented globalized world (Kristeva, 2010, 17).

Also in *Hatred and Forgiveness*, Kristeva shares her experience of frequenting museums when the rat race of contemporary life starts to feel unbearable—to get her psychic blood to flow. Kristeva proposes:

> When the speed or brusqueness on the streets of New York, Paris, or Florence have gotten to you, and you have nothing else to do, or no longer know what to do, do what I do: go into a museum or a gallery and refashion your psychical life.

(Kristeva, 2010, 78)

We can without a doubt deduce from Kristeva's work that interacting with a film at the level of the unconscious can be even more effective in recharging one's psychic battery. In a similar vein, as early as the beginning of his thriller cycle in the 1930s, Alfred Hitchcock himself conceived of film as a way of thawing numbness and renewing moral acuity. His stated aim at that time was

> to provide the public with beneficial shocks. Civilization has become so protective that we are no longer able to get our goose bumps instinctively. The only way to remove the numbness and revive our moral equilibrium is to use artificial means to bring about the shock. The best way to do this, it seems to me, is through a movie.
>
> (Barr, 1999, 147)

On an individual scale, Kristeva's intimate revolt entails questioning and displacing the past—a search for oneself at the level of one's Being—resulting ideally in the opening up of "psychical life to infinite re-creation" (Kristeva, 2002, 6). In between these two phases of the process—questioning and searching and then achieving the *jouissance* necessary for the expansion of psychic life to infinite re-creation—is an arduous journey that exceeds the limits of the representable, thinkable, and tenable, a period of "untenable conflict." Such an adventure of the psyche is analogous to the dark night of the soul undergone by St. John of the Cross, within the borderline region of psychosis.

Turning especially to modern art—literature, painting, and film—including the most hellish and heartrending creations, for a resuscitation of our intimacy, Kristeva locates a refuge from, as well as resistance to, the "so-called virtual world" (Kristeva, 2002, 12). In the fifth chapter of *Intimate Revolt*, "Fantasy and Cinema," Kristeva lays out a fascinating piece of psychoanalytic film theory, in which she explains the special power of *cinema* to access the intimate. Given that Kristeva's designated path to intimacy is the Imaginary, the privileged place of the manifestation of the logic of the Imaginary is fantasy, and fantasy (needless to say) flourishes in cinema, film is a charged psychoanalytic space. The Greek root of fantasy—"*fae, faos, fos*"—signifies "light," and thus Kristeva associates fantasy with a "coming to light, shining, appearing, presenting, presenting oneself, representing oneself" (Kristeva, 2002, 63). Through fantasy, the subject exposes his/her desire or (and perhaps more often) reveals the reason it is blocked. Fantasy is, as Kristeva formulates it, "the reality of...desire," and hence it encourages us to take seriously the reality of the psychical (Kristeva, 2002, 65).

It might therefore be assumed that, given the barrage of images we experience in contemporary Western society, we are all set to explore our intimate depths. But, as Kristeva points out, our spectacular society obstructs the formation and analysis of individualized fantasies. We are deluged with controlling images that are unfavorable to psychic liberation. The society of the spectacle's stereotypical, soap-opera images, in Kristeva's estimation, reduce the spectator to a passive consumer, making him/her the recipient of *its* mass-produced fantasies and thus destroying the possibility of, rather than enabling, the formulation of a particular spectator's singular fantasy—whose singularity is essential for it to do any psychoanalytic good. Fantasy with the power to cut across a spectator's fundamental fantasy causing a blockage or a condition of being stuck would need to be tailored to that psychic story and its protagonist's special psychic needs.

However, inasmuch as "the visible is the port of registry of drives, their synthesis beneath language," it is hard not to persist in thinking of cinema as "an apotheosis of the visible" that "offers itself to the plethoric deployment of [drive-based] fantasies" (Kristeva, 2002, 69). It is thus fortunate that there is another type of cinema, other than the non- or even anti-meditative kind that flourishes in the society of the spectacle—what Kristeva in fact labels "an other cinema"—that serves as a "condensed and meditative mode of writing" with the potential to seize us from the place of the gaze (Kristeva, 2002, 69). The thought specular possesses the power to represent specific instinctual dramas, insofar as it can bring about "the initial specular synthesis at the borders of the sadomasochistic drive" (Kristeva, 2002, 70), through a staging of an encounter with the spectator's constitutive lack, i.e., the gaze.

In the divided world in which we now live, the image thus has

two valences: the stereotyped, lulling image…the new opium of the passions of the people and the cathartic image, a sublimatory activity, whose complex panoply goes from brilliant performances to auxiliary activities in art studios or art therapy.

(Kristeva, 2010, 93)

Accessing the Imaginary, the latter image defuses passion without denying it, by keeping in contact with the drives as well as calling "on the secret drives of the other, the art lover, the recipient, the public" (Kristeva, 2010, 93). Kristeva regards films that she labels the thought specular as the "most advanced medium for the inscription of the drive"—which she sees especially "in relation to sound [and] tactile material."[1] Moreover, it is because cinema offers a "collision with our impossible identities to the point of psychosis" that Kristeva posits the power of the thought specular to transform the drive into desire. The thought specular brings the specular usefully to the limit of its "untenable logic" (Kristeva, 2002, 72–3), a threshold it is necessary to cross, to reconfigure and renew desiring subjectivity.

In her chapter "Fantasy and Cinema," Kristeva defines the specular as "the final and very efficient depository of aggressions and anxieties and as brilliant purveyor-seducer" (Kristeva, 2002, 72). She then proceeds to announce—very strikingly: this is not what one expects—that the

> ultimate seduction, if it existed, would be the ideal mother, the one who holds up the ideal mirror in which 'I' see myself, sure and autonomous, finally rid of the narcissistic throes of the 'mirror stage' and the paradises, both perfumed and abject, where 'I' depended on the mother, more or less indistinct from her.
>
> (Kristeva, 2002, 72)

Here Kristeva suggests that film in the category of the "seductive and terrifying" thought specular, which plays with the uncertainties of who we are, can dissolve the osmosis with the mother of the mirror stage through an ideal mother, holding up the ideal mirror, with the capacity to grant autonomy (Kristeva, 2002, 72). In "The Passion According to Motherhood," in *Hatred and Forgiveness*, Kristeva elaborates her notion of the supportive mother as one who also engages in "dispassion," a "defusing of the amorous link that is nevertheless maintained" (Kristeva, 2010, 92, 91). We can locate versions of both of these mothers in Hitchcock's *Psycho* (1960): the one who consumes Norman and whom Norman consumes but also the cinematic one who sets him free.

Hitchcock's perfumed paradise

Isn't it on the *Zeitlos* that the melancholic runs aground, suffering from a past that will not pass?

JULIA KRISTEVA, *INTIMATE REVOLT*

Using "shock techniques" to thaw numbness, *Psycho* stages the very perfumed and abject paradise *from which* Kristeva's "ultimate seduction"—that of the "ideal mother" who can bestow an "I" on the subject—has the potential to liberate the subject suffering from a fragile, perforated border. By recreating such a steamy paradise, *Psycho* offers the spectator the opportunity to confront and experience its cinematic semiotic fusion with the mother as a way of demystifying "the steam." *Psycho*, in simple terms, can be experienced as an antidote to melancholia. To apprehend how such a cinematic psychoanalytic process might operate, we need to establish how

Psycho presents melancholia, or serves as a case study of a melancholic psyche, and then assess the film's attitude toward that case study.

As I see it, Hitchcock's film features melancholia in order to distance the spectator from its sadomasochistic drives. It lays out on the screen the epitome of this sickness of the soul so that the spectator can formulate such fantasies through *Psycho*'s lektonic traces—its semiotic "expressibles" that absorb and put into play the spectator's unconscious fixation—in an effort to relieve such misery. *Psycho* invites the spectator to throw his/her traumatic material up onto the screen to work through it. As Kristeva explains the process:

> It is essentially a matter of introducing supplementary displacements and condensations to the raw image, associating tones, rhythms, colors, figures—in short, putting into play what Freud called 'the primary processes' (the 'semiotic' in my terminology) underlying the symbolic, this primary seizure of drives always in excess in relation to the represented and the signified.
>
> (Kristeva, 2002, 74)

I am proposing that the melancholic spectator, by opening him/herself up to the lektonic traces of *Psycho,* might face the dark night of Norman's soul, his burdensome melancholic incorporation of the mother, as a way of unlocking his/her own maternal encryptment.

As Kristeva elaborates in *Black Sun: Depression and Melancholia*, melancholia is the product of the withdrawal of an "essential being" who deprives one of what is most valuable in him/herself. Such an agonizing deprivation is lived "as a wound," and the ensuing sadness indicates a deferral of hatred or the desire to ascend that the melancholic nurtures toward the one who inflicted the betrayal or abandonment. Depression covers over aggression and exposes the melancholic's ambivalence. He/She loves the object, but since the melancholic lost the object, he/she consumes it. But since the melancholic also despises the object, the consumed object is rotten. And therefore the melancholic is rotten or non-existent. In other words the attack on oneself is a disguised massacre of another. All of this psychic turmoil is founded on a solid identification of the melancholic with the loved-hated Other that results in a debilitating psychic incorporation. The incorporated Other can even become a "tyrannical judge" who demeans the melancholic, triggering the melancholic's impulse to rid him/herself of the tyrant. But the melancholic's counterattack turns out to be primarily a means of punishing him/herself in the role of the hated Other.

The melancholic's depression signals an inability to lose. The cannibalistic melancholic imagination repudiates the reality of loss. The melancholic has trouble finding a worthy compensation for the loss of his/her being or Being itself and so clings desperately to the lost object. Desire is thwarted. The melancholy Thing blocks the movement of desire that would ensure "continuity in a metonymy of pleasure" and precludes a coming to terms with psychic loss. Rather than fearing death, depressives unconsciously seek protection from a captivating erotic object that challenges the desperately clung-to, deadly bond with the maternal Thing. A debilitating anality is preferred over a fortifying one. The melancholic "fails to summon the anality that could establish separations and frontiers as it does normally.... On the contrary, the entire ego of those who are depressed sinks into a dieroticized and yet jubilatory anality." Such a self-shattering anality "becomes the bearer of a jouissance fused with the archaic Thing, perceived not as a significant object but as the self's borderline element" (Kristeva, 1989, 15).

One of Norman Bates's early, and rather amusing, comments in *Psycho* is that there's "No sense dwelling on our losses." This line immediately strikes one as ironic, if not hilarious, given that Norman does nothing but dwell monstrously on the loss of his mother. But his assertion might be read in a Kristevan vein as commenting on his unwillingness to encounter loss insofar as he has retained his mother psychically and therefore has no loss to dwell on: i.e., there's no sense in obsessing over loss, when you can cleverly circumvent loss (as I have). Norman's line could also be taken to italicize "sense," in which case it might imply some shrewd, momentary (and again Kristevan) self-analysis: there is no "sense" in doing such a thing. It is "non-sense," or crazy, to dwell on the lost object, that is, psychically to encrypt one's mother.

Norman's taxidermy hobby is another blatant clue that he has psychically ingested the maternal object. (My aim here is not to list all such obvious clues but to use them to illustrate dominant features of *Kristeva's* theory of melancholia.) Norman remarks to Marion that actually taxidermy is for him "more than a hobby—a hobby's supposed to pass the time, not fill the time." Norman's taxidermy hobby stops time, expanding the timeless realm he inhabits with his mother—the timelessness that, according to Kristeva's theory of intimate revolt, needs eventually to be channeled into linear time, through a coming into consciousness of timeless psychic matter.

For Kristeva, psychic renewal initially requires an encounter with a "time outside of time," a temporality that Freud called the *Zeitlos*, "an unconscious time that is not only not conscious time but encroaches on a prepsychical time and approaches the somatic." "Unconscious time" or "the time of death" and of the drive (however) is "not a dead time" or a "time [to be kept in a frozen] beyond" (Kristeva, 2002, 31)—and so ought not to be abjected. In Kristeva's view, a folding of this prepsychical, somatic time or timelessness into time— the intersection where working through takes place—is necessary insofar as pathological symptoms and structures thrive on an *inability* to "integrate the atemporal," a psychic talent Norman Bates clearly lacks. The atemporality of death must be inscribed in the linear time of consciousness. Once woven into linear time, immanent within that trajectory, the *Zeitlos* subsequently enables every human manifestation to connect with the unconscious, prepsychical, somatic, and physical, so that the subject can thrive. It is the subtraction of such a thanatology, practiced by the society of the spectacle, that results in psychic trouble, cutting off the subject from unknown reservoirs that establish his/her Being.

It is not as if Hitchcock makes even the first-time viewer struggle to locate evidence of Norman's incorporation of the atemporal maternal object. "A boy's best friend is his mother," Norman asserts to Marion, as well as: "We're all in our private traps, clamped in them, and none of us can get out. We never budge an inch." Norman's "I was born in my trap"—the literalness of it—makes his melancholic incarceration explicit. Norman even harbors the melancholic's usual ambivalence toward the encrypted maternal object. In response to Marion's question of why Norman cannot go away, he explains:

I couldn't do that. Who'd look after her? She's be alone up there. The fire would go out. It'd be cold and damp like a grave. If you love someone, you don't do that to them even if you hate them.

There is hardly any content in *Psycho* that is not soaked in the meaning of Norman's melancholia—the obviousness of which I take as a sign directing us to look elsewhere, beyond the diegesis, as I will discuss. Norman clearly disavows the loss of his mother by seizing and retaining her corpse, which becomes his fetish object in the place of the literally lost (actually, killed, by Norman) maternal figure. A Kristevan reading of Norman's melancholic plight would put it this way: "Depressive persons cannot endure Eros, they prefer to be with the Thing up to the limit of negative narcissism leading them to Thanatos" (Kristeva, 1989, 20). Death is befriended, whereas the erotic object instills anguish. That Marion is, nevertheless, an erotic object for Norman seems confirmed by his generous, attentive, scopically driven treatment of her. That she also causes him anguish is supported by his "mother's"—really his own—attack on his relations with Marion: "No, I tell you, no," she—his tyrannical judge positioned by the melancholic to demean the melancholic— yells at Norman about Marion, accusing him of having a cheap, erotic mind. The "mother" refuses to speak of disgusting things because they disgust her.

"Shut up, shut up," she screams at Norman, shutting down Norman's desire. "They" (Norman and his mother or Norman-as-his-mother) have already murdered two other girls and buried them in the swamp. It is not quite that Norman assumes the mother is jealous (as the pompous psychiatrist in the film believes) but that Norman and "his mother" collude in protecting him from objects of desire that would break their melancholic bond. In profound conflict with himself, an erotically minded Norman voyeuristically peeks through his peephole at a naked Marion enjoying her shower (at some level Norman would like to rid himself of his tyrant), even as he as "his mother" is preparing Marion's vicious murder.

What is even more pertinent from the perspective of Kristeva's theory of the thought specular is that, from the beginning, the spectator is drawn directly into that voyeuristic position, lured to identify with Norman. As Raymond Bellour establishes in "Psychosis, Neurosis, Perversion (on *Psycho*)," "from the start, emphasis is placed on the voyeuristic position, which deliberately constitutes the position of enunciation" (Bellour, 2000, 248). "Never before," comments Linda Williams, "had a film so blatantly enlisted voyeuristic pleasures" (Williams, 1998, 92). *Psycho* begins, after the camera pans to the right, by penetrating an open window. We observe partially raised Venetian blinds that leave a black strip, and we thereby encounter the first site of the film's "jubilatory anality." It is into that dark, rectangular strip that we, glued to the camera, descend. We discover Marion enjoying an afternoon rendezvous with her lover and watch her, dressed in a strikingly pointed white bra, frolic with Sam in the bed. Later we spy on Marion, now in black lingerie (having stolen the $40,000 and turned criminal), preparing for her flight. Like Norman, we voyeuristically view her prolonged, blissful shower, in which Marion seems to succumb, in a state of *jouissance*, to the water spraying forth. (Her sexual pleasure in the shower is no doubt the irrevocable spur to Norman's "mother's" attack, given that depressives cannot tolerate Eros.) We are in turn riveted to the stabbing and imagine her nude body as Norman drags the now-dead Marion out of the bathroom. Wrapped in an incandescent shower curtain, Marion is carried over the threshold of the Bates Motel room backwards, from an interior space to her outdoor death—like a bride in reverse, a bride ravished by death. We are privy to this macabre wedding scene as well, pulled down into its horror, or bliss, as the case may be, as Thanatos conquers Eros.

At the level of the lektonic trace—again, semiotic elements of the film capable of embedding the spectator's fundamental fantasy—we are also guided by the camera (beyond the bounds of the narrative) into the black hole of the bathtub drain, into which the blood-stained water swirls. Our attention is in addition called to the black bathroom sink hole, down which blood also descends; to the tiny black eye of the shower spout; to the flushing toilet bowl at the Bates Motel; and to Marion's navel, which is flashed at us during the stabbings. We are likewise made to witness Norman's cemetery swamp—an enormous black hole. And our eyes are drawn to license plates at the rear of cars, one of which features the famous insinuating letters ANL, as well as to Norman's silhouetted backside, which becomes our unavoidable focus as he drags Marion's body out of the Bates Motel room. In an initial celebration of a jubilatory anality, Hitchcock's camera sucks us into multiple opaque holes that emblematize the gaze—thereby giving us a space on which to project our own fantasy of fusion with the maternal object as well as our anxieties over that psychic melding.[2]

Psycho clinches our sense of the relation of these black holes to the destabilizing Lacanian gaze in switching directly from the vortex of water heading into the black hole of the bathtub drain to a stark close-up of Marion's *dead eye* with its prominent black iris. Linda Williams has her own (albeit less psychoanalytic) helpful way of noting the disorienting spectatorial power and pleasure—I would say *jouissance*, which fits better with Williams's sense of the terror involved—of such "eyes":

> When the forward-moving, purposeful, voyeuristic camera eye 'washes' down the drain after the murder of Marion and emerges in reverse twisting out of her dead eye, audiences could, for the first time in mainstream motion-picture history, take pleasure in losing the kind of control, mastery, and forward momentum of 'classical' narrative.
>
> (Williams, 1998, 96)

As Lacanians know, the eye is not the unapprehensible Lacanian gaze; and to *look* is not to enact the gaze, the gaze being the void on which one's subjectivity depends. In *The Four Fundamental Concepts of Psycho-Analysis*, Lacan explains that there is a split between the eye and the gaze insofar as their functions are distinct. Being on the side of the object (rather than on the side of the subject who looks), the gaze "contain[s] in itself the *objet a* of the Lacanian algebra where the subject falls." Qua *objet a*, it symbolizes the "central lack expressed in the phenomenon of castration" (Lacan, 1981/1973, 77): in other words "It reflects our own nothingness" (Lacan, 1981/1973, 92).[3] In the field of the visible, the gaze "stands for the blind spot...from which the picture itself photo-graphs the spectator" (Žižek, 2004, 263). Yet, despite the lack of coincidence between the eye and the gaze, their dialectic constitutes "a lure" (Lacan, 1981/1973, 102). Enacting this interplay, "Hitchcock's pupil"—a dead, unapprehensible eye—duplicates Lacan's own theoretical "pupil behind which is situated the gaze" (Lacan, 1981/1973, 108), with its power to signify our own nothingness and thereby to elide the subject. Marion's dead pupil (like Lacan's sardine can) does not envision us, but it is gazing at us nonetheless.

Through the subtle black, gray, and white shades of the film as well as the screeching of the *Psycho* theme-song, which draws out the non-sense within the spectator that keeps him/her plastered to the maternal body, and the high-pitched, penetrating screams of both Marion and Lila, as this noise is accompanied by the high-pitched theme-song, in addition to all the black holes that provide the space of the Real, through all such lektonic traces—semiotic colors, sounds, and shapes that have the capacity to absorb the spectator's psychic trouble—we can encode our own maternal fantasy within *Psycho*. The mother's ghastly skeletal head, itself made of black eye sockets and an open black mouth, offers the spectator a final terrifying confrontation with the abject. It is in particular Lila's (Marion sister's) trajectory toward the core of Norman's uncanny world and her point of view that finally carry along the viewer to the mother's gaze. "Lila's look becomes a surrogate for the spectator's [urge] to see inside this forbidden and frightening space" (Mulvey, 2004, 240).

Norman's total collapse with his mother at the end of the film is the icing on the decaying cake. Witnessing this catastrophe of Norman's having become his own fetish object, the melancholic spectator can take a step toward deposing his/her melancholic fundamental fantasy. *Psycho* pulls one into the unconscious space of psychosis through lektonic traces necessarily situated outside the diegesis. Most powerfully, the film deploys its myriad black holes that, in sucking the spectator into the terrifying abyss of his/her maternal attachment, enable the spectator to convert jubilatory anality into a basis on which to establish a frontier separating him/her from that abyss, to transform the gaze from being a threat to being a support of desiring subjectivity. The gaze is, after all, what the subject separates from in order to become a subject. "The subject," asserts Lacan, "is strictly speaking determined by the very separation that determines the break of the [*objet*] *a*, that is to say, the fascinatory element introduced by the gaze" (Lacan, 1981/1973, 118). If *Psycho* is operating as a thought-specular film, the spectator, experiencing Norman's collapse, unconsciously slides from—or is jolted out of—a terrifying psychotic quagmire into a clear space of absence opened up by the various sites of the gaze in the film.

The splendor of abjection

Or, on the contrary—and here we make an aboutface—might *Psycho* be read as a celebration of the abjection of melancholia?[4] Granted, it is difficult to discern much joy in the film's final image of Norman completely vanquished by his mother. However, if we set our sights less on the narrative of Norman's fixation on his mother and his consequent descent into psychosis and read *Psycho* more as we might respond to a Francis Bacon painting, with Norman as the key Figure set within a wide structure that subsumes him, we can perhaps apprehend the film as a field of forces that follow the "logic of sensation," as Gilles Deleuze describes such a logic in his study *Francis Bacon: The Logic of Sensation* (2003). Moving away from figuration (that is, the illustrative and figurative), we might attend instead to the violence of sensation itself. I sense a kinship between Hitchcock's aims in *Psycho* and Francis Bacon's fascination with (in Deleuze's conception) "invisible forces that model flesh or shake it," with Bacon's urge to make such forces visible, as well as with his "intense pity . . . for flesh"—which can, I think, be translated into pity for people miserably encased in their flesh, people for whom abjection might provide relief. It is *Psycho*'s status as postmodernism that allows for this comparison with Bacon's paintings. As Linda Williams points out in "Discipline and Distraction,"

> *Psycho* (1960) marks a moment in popular film reception when the more stable qualities of the 'classical Hollywood cinema'—defined as a cinema of strong narrative logic and causality, psychological motivation, character-driven events, spectatorial absorption into a diegesis, and identification with characters (Bordwell et al. 1985)—began to be replaced by postmodern styles and themes.
>
> (Williams, 1998, 89)

Using Deleuze on Bacon to read *Psycho* also puts us in sync with Deleuze's own non-narrative conception of cinema, in *Cinema I*, as "a composition of images and of signs, that is, a pre-verbal intelligible content (pure semiotics)" (Deleuze, 1986, ix). Such an overlap makes perfect sense in that the various trajectories featured in Deleuze's Bacon book link up with those in other arts "such as music, cinema, and literature," as Daniel W. Smith notes at the end of his Translator's Introduction to *Francis Bacon: The Logic of Sensation*. Smith regards this text as "an entry point into the conceptual proliferation of Deleuze's philosophy as a whole, and his other writings on the arts" (Smith, 2003, xxvii). In his work on film, Deleuze concentrates on "cinematographic concepts" defined as "types of images and the signs which correspond to each type" (Deleuze, 1986, ix). Great film directors, to Deleuze, are thinkers who "think" not with concepts but with images: movement-images (up to Hitchcock) and time-images (after Hitchcock). In fact, Deleuze points to Hitchcock as the director who invented "an extraordinary type of image: the image of mental relations" (Deleuze, 1986, x). Hitchcock's frames turn an image into a mental image that is open "on to a play of relations" that always produce an "out-of-field" that reaches "on to infinity" (Deleuze, 1986, 18).[5]

Still, it is by way of Deleuze's analysis of Francis Bacon that I think we can best access what is operating imagistically in Hitchcock's *Psycho*. To Deleuze, a painting avoids the figurative through abstraction and isolation, both of which disrupt narration. When a Figure is put into relation with an isolating area, it becomes an image, an icon, breaking representation and liberating the Figure. This is a positive substitution—fact and event for representation and narration—given that a story cancels out possibilities of what can be done *with paint on its own*. (Deleuze's film theory is similarly focused on what can be done *with film on its own*.) As Deleuze observes, Bacon isolates a Figure within "a round area or parellelepiped...to avoid the *figurative, illustrative,* and *narrative* character the Figure would neces-sarily have if it were not isolated" (Deleuze, 2003, 6). In Bacon, according to Deleuze, flat fields of color curl around the Figure, and the Figure in turn presses outward to dissolve into the field: hence the role of the spasm or the scream. The entire body attempts to flee, to disgorge itself through a hole or tip, and in some paintings the Figure has disappeared, entering completely the realm of abjection.

Analogously, in *Psycho*, the Figure of Norman is surrounded, closed in upon, by several assailants. In turn, he finally becomes assimilated in the field itself—a vanishing that commences at the point where he peeps through the hole at Marion showering. Norman metamorphoses through that peephole, becoming immediately afterward his mother, murderer of Marion, whose murder results in a Baconian scream. It is obviously Marion's, rather than Norman's, scream, but this matters little in a "text of becoming" comprised of a field of forces, as opposed to a narrative centered on a protagonist. Marion's scream signals the flight of the body, his and hers. It is the operation by which her entire body escapes through the mouth and the same route by which Norman disintegrates into the field of abjection—the realm beyond which forms no longer remain intact. Interestingly, one particular painting Deleuze points to as a way of illustrating the body in Bacon escaping from itself presents an image that seems straight out of Hitchcock. Deleuze selects the *Figure at a Washbasin* to convey Bacon's "approximation of abjection": "clinging to the oval of the washbasin, its hands clutching the faucets, the body-figure exerts an intense motionless effort upon itself in order to escape down the blackness of the drain"

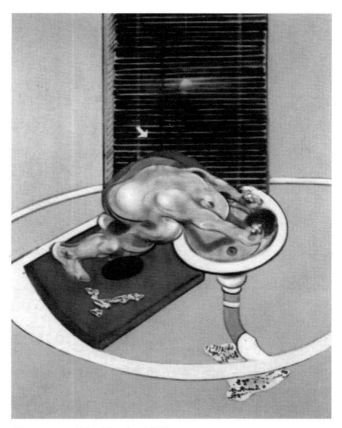

Figure at a Washbasin, 1976

(Deleuze, 2003, 15). Just as Bacon's Figure is sucked down into a black drain hole, Hitchcock's spectator too is pulled into *Psycho*'s myriad drains and black holes, and incited to scream. Audiences, too, "were screaming like never before" (Williams, 1998, 103).

Deleuze stresses the absolute proximity of the field (which functions as a ground) and the Figure, both being on a single plane in painting. We can read Norman Bates similarly as coterminus with the filmic field that surrounds him, as being commensurate with everything else the camera focuses on, no more privileged than any non-diegetic element in the film. Focusing on asignifying traits can begin to undermine the legibility of Norman's story. I am suggesting, in the spirit of Deleuze, that we look at *Psycho* in a way that frees its lines, shapes, shades of color, sounds, and movements from the demands of representation, liberating all the figures from figuration, and attend instead to sensations. Actually, Deleuze defines the Figure itself as "the sensible form related to a sensation; it acts immediately upon the nervous system, which is of the flesh" (Deleuze, 2003, 31).

From the moment of Norman's peeping through the hole in his Bates Motel room's wall, the sort of hole through which the Deleuzean-Baconian body deteriorates and the flesh descends, the Figure/Norman passes through a vanishing point in, and to escape from, Deleuze's "contour." In *Psycho*, I take the contour to be the combination of the Bates Motel and the haunted house on the hill, an enclosed dual space within which the dominant characters tend to circle. From this space, Norman dissipates into the materiality of what is outside the contour, as well as external to all figuration. The contour, then, contains a point of disappearance, through which the Figure becomes a deformed body that escapes from itself, as Norman not only desubjectifies from this point on but disintegrates into an interminable outer space. And just as in Bacon the body waits to escape from itself by means of a scream or a spasm—which act of fleeing is, to Deleuze, Bacon's encoding of abjection—in *Psycho*, the body attempts to escape from itself to rejoin the field or the material structure at two key points (one auditory, the other spastic): midway through, when Marion lets out her blood-curdling scream (as mentioned), and at the end when Norman evaporates, leaving his mother to inhabit his body. That is, in the final shot of "Norman," wrapped (maternally) in a blanket/shawl and sitting on the side of a stark room at the police station, in unmistakable Baconian isolation, Norman's mother is all that remains. She refers condemningly to Norman now as "he," rather than "you," which would have indicated the double personality exhibited earlier. This complete maternal takeover of Norman, a total immersion in abjection, I am suggesting, pushes Norman out, into an outer field, allowing him to flee.

In sum, in this Deleuzean reading of *Psycho*, we are privy to its rhythm—the vibration that flows through the Body without Organs, the Body submerged under the organism, the deformed Body comprised of indiscernible forces, the violent forces of inorganic processes—a rhythm generated by two movements. In the former, the contour isolates the Figure. As I have indicated, I read roughly the first half of *Psycho* as pressing on the Figure of Norman, as the pressures of Marion's visit to the Bates Motel, her warmth and appeal to Norman, Lila and Sam's investigation of the Motel and invasion of the haunted house, and Detective Arbogast's interrogation and intrusion—all zero in on Norman as a kind of target of their attention. Consequently, Norman passes through a hole, inducing a scream. In the latter movement, the Figure gives way to material exteriority. He experiences becoming-animal, or, in the case of *Psycho*, becoming-mother.

In Bacon, the Figure lacks a face; Bacon paints heads, not faces. Deleuze proposes that Bacon dismantles the face, "to rediscover the head." "[T]he Figure, being a body," Deleuze elaborates, is not the face, and does not even have a face. It does have a head, because the head is an integral part of the body. It can even be reduced to the head.... For the face is a structured, spatial organization that conceals the head, whereas the head is dependent on the body, even if it is the point of the body, its culmination.... the head ... is a spirit in bodily form, a corporeal and vital breath, an animal spirit.

(Deleuze, 2003, 19).

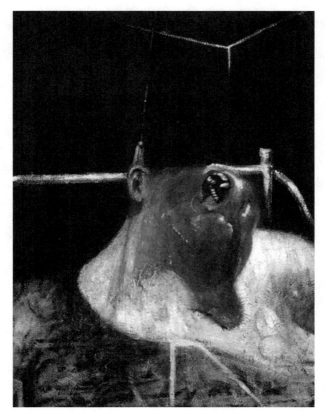

Head, 1948

Likewise, Norman-in-the-guise-of-his-mother lacks a face. When she rushes in to slash away at Marion, we see her wig, her robe, but her face is missing: it becomes another of the film's multiple black holes.

And we eventually encounter her ghastly skeletal, toothy head. The face in *Psycho* transforms into death's head, like the chunks of meat at the top of Bacon's Figures' bodies. The zone of indiscernibility in Bacon is found in meat, where man and beast coalesce. In *Psycho*, man and mother interpenetrate.

From this Deleuzean perspective, *Psycho* can be read as a "film of becoming." In Deleuze's notion of "becoming," the body escapes from itself by undergoing multiple transfigurations. "Becoming-animal" or, as in *Psycho*, "becoming-mother" is one stage in the more profound process of becoming imperceptible, first through the screaming mouth. Beyond the scream—a force that has little to do with the visible spectacle that sets it in motion but, signifying Nothing, emanates from a victim of invisible and insensible forces—is the smile, which (to Deleuze) in Bacon fulfills the function of securing the disappearance of the body. Bacon's smile, we are told, is hysterical, an abjection of a smile. Watching Marion's car, with Marion entombed inside, sink into the muck of the swamp in which Norman buries his victims, Norman gives us a crazed grin, reflecting his awareness, and bliss in the thought, that all things seem now to be moving toward a zero degree. Abjection transports Norman to zero. Here *Psycho* allows us to observe the transformation of the abjected to Nothing. Dissolution challenges the ability of abjection to retain its identity as such. Infinitized, *das Ding* becomes Nothing. The scream and the smile prefigure "the shadow" toward the end, which Deleuze describes as "the body that has escaped from itself" (Deleuze, 2003, 16)—or Norman, who now collapses into the field at large, finally peeled away from himself in the guise of his mother.

At least in Bacon's painting, if not all painting, Deleuze suggests, abjection becomes splendor. The horror of life becomes a pure and intense life. Such a conversion of abjection might seem to be the aim of Hitchcock's film as well. Surpassing figuration, Norman Bates, at the end of *Psycho*, escapes his pain-ridden body/psyche (*Psycho* too would seem to have pity for flesh) by donating it to his mother, so that he can vibrate into the outer field of forces.

Fully becoming-mother is a way of detaching: abjection ironically becomes the mode of leaving stress, pain, anguish—abjection itself—behind. Norman abandons his abject relation to his mother by radiating out into a broader field. Through the embrace, or even pursuit, of abjection, through in a sense its affirmation, *Psycho* (the ideal mother) converts this malady of the soul to splendor, expanding it to infinity. Rather than erecting defenses against the abject, *Psycho* can be read as heading in its direction in an effort to open up presence that acts immediately on the nervous system, to liberate forces that are otherwise invisible, forces that in exerting themselves on the body/psyche of the spectator produce an array of sensations. Most significantly, for my Kristevan emphasis, Deleuze's splendid abjection or abject splendor underscores that it is immersion in the abject that opens up *Psycho* to the *Zeitlos*. Deleuze on Bacon allows us to see, through *Psycho* (which confronts its spectator with the timelessness of melancholia), that *withdrawing* from a melancholic fixation involves *drawing* from the black pool of abjection to reach and sustain desire.

Putting Deleuzean sensation to use

It is noteworthy that Deleuze makes an anti-psychological case for neutral fields of forces and Baconian desubjectification within them yet employs psychoanalytic terminology and concepts especially to comment on the liberation that such a dissolution effects. Is Deleuze's reading of Bacon outside or inside a psychoanalytic framework, after all? I hope to have shown how his reading exposes the Body without Organs in a way that can allow us to observe the spreading of a *jouissance*-propelled *das Ding* across a work of art. Using Deleuze to read *Psycho* enables us to register the pervasiveness of Norman's abject melancholia on the non-diegetic level of the film, where it manifests itself within lektonic traces, which have the sensuous power, in turn, to pull the spectator's own abject melancholia into the film. Our melancholia collides with Norman's. In fact, what Deleuze tends to highlight in examining the semiotics of film—

the nature and dimensions of the framed space, the distribution of moving and fixed objects, the angle of framing, the lens, the chronometric duration of the shot, the light and its degrees, its tonalities, and also figural and affective tonalities (not to mention the colour, the sound, the speech and the music)

(Deleuze, 1986, 44),

factors that vary in relation to particular images—facilitates a more technical description of Kristeva's lektonic traces. Through such *semiotic* traces, we experience Norman's fundamental fantasy of fusion with the mother streaking across the film in the specific forms of Deleuze's *semiotics* of film.

Epitomized by Marion's infamous scream, a certain violence can be located in *Psycho*'s filmic elements of sensation that act directly on the spectator's nervous system (that the film triggers actual screaming in the audience testifies to this level of engagement). The notorious "theme-song" (or screaming violins) is obviously one of the most prominent and piercing of those elements. Accessing *Psycho* through such intense sensation, the spectator is able to undergo a working through of his/her traumatic encryptment. Being within Kristeva's semiotic register, "Deleuzean" sensations are a most appropriate aspect of *Psycho* for us to attend to, given their potent capacity to thaw a melancholic encryptment. Turning to science, Kristeva hypothesizes in *New Maladies of the Soul* that the "imaginary level of semiotic *meaning*...can act as a relay" between "the lower layers of the brain," where drive representatives are housed, and "the cortex that controls linguistic production, thereby constituting supplementary brain circuits able to remedy any psychological deficiencies." Hence the semiotic serves as a "way of gaining access to...archaic affective representations," a "way of accessing the drama that underlies these representations" (Kristeva, 1995, 104). Kristeva's semiotic, which "consists of drive-related and affective *meaning* organized according to primary processes whose sensory aspects are often non-verbal (sound and melody, rhythm, color, odors, and so forth)," is put into play by the very components of art that Deleuze tends to concentrate on, to bring out the way art operates at the level of sensation. Attending to images and sensation(s) in the spirit of Deleuze necessarily engages Kristeva's semiotic modality, in which "psychic representatives are displaced from affects as well as from the drama of desires, fears, and depressive fits" (Kristeva, 1995, 109). So it is no surprise that Kristeva acknowledges Deleuze (along with Merleau-Ponty) for "bringing forth the sensorial fundaments of expression" (Kristeva, 2010, 303).

Deleuze's reading of Francis Bacon, with its stress on sensation(s), to apprehend *Psycho* gets us exactly where we need to be to realize the psychoanalytic function of the film's lektonic traces. In absorbing the spectator's melancholic fundamental fantasy that barricades him/her from desire, they deflate that fantasy by luring the spectator into an encounter (or perhaps even various encounters) with the gaze. But we must note well *to what end* such a deflation takes place. It is by sucking the spectator into the "narcissistic throes of the 'mirror stage' and the paradises, both perfumed and abject, where 'I' [depends] on the mother" and is "more or less indistinct from her," as a way of catapulting the spectator beyond this "stage," that a film can enact "the ultimate seduction" (Kristeva, 2002, 72). Deleuze helps us to apprehend that and how *Psycho* ubiquitously brings the psychosis induced by the mother to its untenable logic and limit—so that the loss of the mother may be experienced, as she is finally left behind in a body that no longer houses Norman, in a film from which Norman seems freely to have vanished into thin air.

A Deleuzean reading of *Psycho*, modeled on his approach to the paintings of Francis Bacon, helps us to apprehend how Hitchcock produces, through an immersion in abjection, an "out-of-field" that extends "on to infinity" (Deleuze, 2003, 18). Having achieved infinite space, through the dissolution of Norman-as-mother, the end of *Psycho* can transport the spectator with a fixation similar to Norman's to a space of radical negativity or Nothingness, with the potential then of releasing the spectator from a controlling, psychically draining fantasy into an infinite condition of desire. A fantasy akin to Norman's certainly cripples the subject's ability to access his/her creative psychic potentialites. Especially through Deleuze, however, we can understand *Psycho* as a film that moves into the realm of abjection as a way of confronting and dissolving the fantasy that solders the psyche to the maternal Thing in order to escape that fixation into infinite potentiality.

By releasing the melancholic spectator from a maternal attachment that impedes desire through an intense experience, at the level of sensation, with Deleuze's Body without Organs that culminates in an infinite outer field, *Psycho* gives the gift of psychic vitality. Kristeva insists that the copresence of Nothingness in Being must be engaged. One form it takes in Western texts, as she points out, is "a familiarity with psychosis." *Psycho* advances "this interrogation into Nothingness and negativity" that Kristeva describes as an "[e]rasure of subject/object borders, [an] assault of the drive," where "language becomes tonality (*Stimmung*), memory of being, music of the body and of matter" (Kristeva, 2002, 9). *Psycho* joins psychoanalysis in reconstructing the "border region of the speaking being that is psychosis" (Kristeva, 2002, 10), where meaning is unveiled at the level of sensations and drives. Through this cinematic journey into psychosis, Hitchcock's film invites the spectator to experience *anamnesis* with the eventual aim of the infinite re-creation that psychic reconfiguration and rebirth can enjoy. The terrors of *Psycho* are thus surpassed as a more imaginative, polyvalent relation to the world (than what Norman's was) can now come into being.

In fact, even in Deleuze, catastrophe is to be passed through rather than perpetuated. Deleuze defines a painting's diagram, "the operative set of traits and color-patches, of lines and zones," as indeed...a violent chaos in relation to the figurative givens, but it is a germ of rhythm in relation to the new order of the painting. As Bacon says, it 'unlocks areas of sensation.' The diagram ends the preparatory work and begins the act of painting.

(Deleuze, 2003, 83)[6]

Deleuze asserts that the diagram's chewing away of the entire painting

must remain limited in space and time. It must remain operative and controlled. The violent methods must not be given free rein, and the necessary catastrophe must not submerge the whole....[T]he Figure, should emerge from the diagram and make the sensation clear and precise. To emerge from the catastrophe....

(Deleuze, 2003, 89)

If the diagram were to spread across the entire painting, that would be, to quote Deleuze quoting Bacon" 'sloppy'":

Being itself a catastrophe, the diagram must not create a catastrophe. Being itself a zone of scrambling, it must not scramble the painting....The essential point about the diagram is that it is made in order for something to *emerge* from it, and if nothing emerges from it, it fails.

(Deleuze, 2003, 128)

Immersed in the *jouissance* of his maternal cathexis, Norman enjoyed a childhood that *exceeded* happiness. He confides to Marion: "This place is my home...this place happens to be my only world. I grew up in that house up there. I had a very happy childhood. My mother and I were *more than happy*" (my emphasis). Insisting that something Deleuzean emerge from this excess, refusing to fail, *Psycho* becomes a film about becoming as Norman is released at the end into Deleuze's "out-of-field" infinite space.

Having captured and represented both Norman's and the spectator's melancholia, having folded the stuff of such encryptment into the time of the film as a way of bringing it to a crisis point, *Psycho* turns into a passageway through the looking-glass of the spectator's fantasy of fusion to fresh possibilities of desiring. The ideal mother, the ultimate seducer, *Psycho* liberates the spectator who has crossed this threshold now to seek his/her own reincarnations of the lost Thing. Read along the lines of Deleuze's engagement with Bacon, melancholic Norman Bates, upon dispersing at the end, would seem to become a part of, and have the force to open up, an unconstrained field of infinite meanings. His vanishing, his encounter with Nothing, invites the spectator's unconscious to join him in entering an infinite space of creativity that can lead to an experience of complex desire, in all its movement and singularity, the infinite re-creation essential to Kristeva's intimate revolt.

Something else, too, much less abstract, emerges (besides Norman as he is shot into space) at the very end of the film: Marion's white car provides the final image. Signaling finally a move from a jubilatory to a fortifying anality, this white car is ponderously pulled out of the swamp from behind. *This* is "The End," the film announces in the last seconds—just *after* showing Norman's face with his mother's corpse's teeth superimposed on it. Caked with mud, this white car half-surfaces from the gaze-like space of the swamp and thus indicates an insertion of non-life into life, the slow, excruciating withdrawal of timelessness from excitation, locating it within conscious temporality—yet without fully abandoning it. *Psycho* in the end is poised, and situates its spectator, at the intersection of timelessness and time. Such a paradoxical positioning "transits through the specular" (Kristeva, 2002, 38), here and now a maternal force, an ideal speculum.

Notes

1 In a provocative essay titled "Discipline and Distraction: *Psycho,* Visual Culture, and Postmodern Cinema," Linda Williams perceives a suspicion of the visual in French theory as well as ironically in film studies. She also refers to a general anxious sense that the visual is fundamentally pornographic in that it effects "rapt, mindless fascination" (this notion springs primarily from Jameson's *Signatures of the Visible*). Such a position is, to Williams, problematic in opposing "sensual pleasures of vision and the abstraction of critical thought, as if thought could never take place in and through a body." Kristeva's theory of the "thought specular" responds directly to this challenge. Williams faults film studies for "demonizing the power of moving images to move the bodies of spectators" (Williams, 1998, 91); Kristeva celebrates such power to transform the psyche of spectators. Even as she takes the dominant psychoanalytic position that opposes fetishism and favors lack/castration, Kristeva is absolutely not antiocular. Visual pleasure plays an indispensable role in the power of the thought specular to absorb the spectator's traumatic material and release the spectator finally into the sensuous world as a desiring subject.

2 For a different sort of, perhaps more queer, reading of anal spaces in Hitchcock, see D. A. Miller's "Anal Rope," published in *Representations*, 32 (Fall, 1990): 114–33. This well-known essay was reprinted in *Out Takes: Essays on Queer Theory and Film*, edited by Ellis Hanson (Duke University Press, 1998), 97–125, as well as in *inside/out: Lesbian Theories, Gay Theories*, ed. Diana Fuss (Routledge, 1991), 118–41.

3   The Lacanian as well as Kristevan psychoanalytic concept of castration is
    hardly a "punishment," as Linda Williams reads it in the psychoanalytic
    criticism of *Psycho* that she critiques in her essay "Discipline and
    Distraction." If the viewer emerges from the film accepting his/her lack or
    as "castrated," rather than punishment he/she has undergone an experience
    of *jouissance* facilitating desire. Likewise, cutting, as we have seen, of
    flesh or film opens a space for desiring subjectivity, rather than shuts
    down pleasure or "fun," as Williams suggests. It is striking, though, that
    Williams attacks Kaja Silverman for seeming to support "punishment" when
    Williams celebrates the Foucauldian "discipline" operating in her view in
    Psycho. Actually, however, using Stephen Heath for support, Silverman, in
    The Subject of Semiotics, mainly explains that "cinematic coherence and
    plenitude emerge through multiple cuts and negations" and points out that
    such "castrating coherence" is put on display in *Psycho*, which "deliberately
    exposes the negations upon which filmic plenitude is predicated" (Silverman,
    1983, 205–6). Although Silverman does assert that Hitchcock's "cinematic
    machine," during the shower sequence, is "lethal" ("it too murders and
    dissects"), her primary theoretical point, concerning cutting, is that it
    inscribes lack, a blessing rather than a penalty. Even more inconsistently
    (beyond her denigration of punishment and praise for discipline), Williams,
    it turns out, celebrates the film's "secret" and its sadomasochistic effects:
    "*Psycho*'s secret that gender is often not what it seems … helped produce
    an ironic sadomasochistic discipline of master and slave with Hitchcock
    playing the sadistic master and audiences playing the submissive victims"
    (Williams, 1998, 106). So it is not, after all, that Williams dislikes punishment
    or reads the film as "fun" rather than punishment but that she applauds
    Psycho for turning punishment into "fun." (Given that sadomasochism
    involves a master and a slave, it is hard to regard it distinctly as "discipline"
    rather than "punishment.")

4   Although a distinction can be made between the melancholic and a person
    suffering from abjection, on the grounds that the latter, termed "the deject"
    in *Powers of Horror*, puts up defenses against the abject, I am joining the
    two pathologies here. Both melancholia and abjection result from something
    having gone awry at the border of subject-object relations. Both involve a
    fraught relation with the maternal object. I have taken the liberty of using these
    maladies of the soul for the most part interchangeably, given their structural
    similarities. Norman Bates's melancholia certainly renders him abject.

5   In "Hitchcock with Deleuze," Sam Ishii-Gonzáles elaborates his sense
    of what Deleuze means by the "mental-image," which Deleuze believes
    predominates in Hitchcock's films. Developing his idea from the work of
    American philosopher-logician Charles Sanders Peirce, Ishii-Gonzáles takes
    the mental image to involve an "interpretant." In Hitchcock, we have a sign,
    signified, and then this third or "interpretant," who is in this film scenario
    (of course) the spectator. It is especially striking to me that Ishii-Gonzáles
    brings in here, through Deleuze's concept of the mental-image, an insistence
    in Hitchcock on the viewer's production of meaning. "For Hitchcock," he
    writes, "the spectator must also be inscribed within the fabric of relations.

Hence, the director's version of suspense which is based on the co-efficient to involve, to implicate" (Ishii-Gonzáles, 2004, 134–5). Deleuze writes in *Cinema I*, "In Hitchcock, actions, affections, perceptions, all is interpretation, from beginning to end" (Deleuze, 1986, 200). This emphasis on Hitchcock's interpretant and his/her interpretation, making it seem as though Hitchcock's films absolutely depend on an engagement with the spectator at the level of "thought," dovetails with Kristeva's notion of the thought specular, helping us to understand why she singles out Hitchcock as one of its primary practitioners. As if to arrange for an experience of intimate revolt through his films, Hitchcock also refused to allow entry to late spectators.

6 Deleuze certainly gives signals that he wishes to distance himself from psychoanalysis—for example, he writes, "There is no painter who has not had this experience of the chaos-germ, where he or she no longer sees anything and risks foundering: the collapse of visual coordinates. This is not a psychological experience, but a properly pictorial experience." Yet this passage proceeds to acknowledge the impact the "experience of the chaos-germ" can have on the painter through words that may as well be Kristeva's: "Painters here confront the greatest of dangers both for their work and for themselves. It is a kind of experience that is constantly renewed by the most diverse painters.... [P]ainters pass through the catastrophe themselves, embrace the chaos, and attempt to emerge from it" (Deleuze, 2003, 83–4).

Works cited

Barr, Charles (1999) *English Hitchcock*. Moffat, Scotland: Cameron and Hollis.

Bellour, Raymond (2000) *The Analysis of Film*. Bloomington: Indiana UP.

Deleuze, Gilles (1986) *Cinema I: The Movement-Image*. Trans. Hugh Tomlinson and Barbara Habberjam. Minneapolis: University of Minnesota Press.

—(2003) *Francis Bacon: The Logic of Sensation*. Trans. Daniel W. Smith. Minneapolis: University of Minnesota Press.

Ishii-Gonzáles, Sam (2004) "Hitchcock with Deleuze." In *Past and Future Hitchcock*. Ed. Richard Allen and Sam Ishii-Gonzáles. London and New York: Routledge.

Kristeva, Julia (1989) *Black Sun: Depression and Melancholia*. Trans. Leon S. Roudiez. New York: Columbia UP.

—(1995) *New Maladies of the Soul*. Trans. Ross Guberman. New York: Columbia UP.

—(2002) *Intimate Revolt: The Power and Limits of Psychoanalysis*. Trans. Jeanine Herman. New York: Columbia UP.

—(2010) *Hatred and Forgiveness*. Trans. Jeanine Herman. New York: Columbia UP.

Lacan, Jacques (1981/1973) *The Four Fundamental Concepts of Psycho-Analysis: Book XI*. Ed. Jacques Alain-Miller. Trans. Alan Sheridan. New York: W.W. Norton & Co.

Mulvey, Laura (2004) "Death Drives." In *Past and Future Hitchcock*. Ed. Richard Allen and Sam Ishii-Gonzáles. London and New York: Routledge.

Silverman, Kaja (1983) *The Subject of Semiotics*. New York: Oxford UP.

Smith, Daniel W. (2003) "Translator's Introduction: Deleuze on Bacon: Three Conceptual Trajectories in *The Logic of Sensation*." In *Francis Bacon: The Logic of Sensation*. Trans. Daniel W. Smith. Minneapolis: University of Minnesota Press.

Williams, Linda (1998) "Discipline and Distraction: *Psycho*, Visual Culture, and Postmodern Cinema." In *"Culture" and the Problem of the Disciplines*. Ed. John Carlos Rowe. New York: Columbia UP.

Žižek, Slavoj (2004) "Is There a Way to Remake a Hitchcock Film?" In *Past and Future Hitchcock*. Ed. Richard Allen and Sam Ishii-Gonzáles. London and New York: Routledge.

Filmography

Psycho (1960) Alfred Hitchcock. Paramount Pictures (1960–8); Universal Pictures (1968–present), U.S.A.

7

Intimate *Volver*

Kristeva's semiotic/Almodóvar's signature

Pedro Almodóvar's *Volver* can seem to embody so many components of
Kristeva's recent work that it may look like the quintessential Kristevan
thought-specular film. It is as though Almodóvar made *Volver* to fulfill her
theoretical dreams, both demonstrating and making legible Kristeva's theory
of intimate revolt. (Almodóvar is known to have likened this film to therapy.)
That is, *Volver* can be experienced as a thought-specular film that gives rise to
the spectator's intimate revolt and at the same time is *about* such a process,
about the benefits of intimate revolt.

Thematically, *Volver* works through a double trauma of sexual abuse
committed by the father and the psychically crippling loss of the mother
that follows—in a way that accords with Kristeva's emphasis on a process
of *anamnesis* that reaches all the way back to an encounter with the
"dead mother." *Volver* clearly shows an "aptitude to return" that pushes up
against the very boundary of what is representable, thinkable, and tenable.
Almodóvar's film pulls time into the timeless and subsequently weaves the
timeless into time, befriending death in myriad ways that are analogous to
the embrace of death on the part of the Spanish women villagers featured at
the beginning of the film, as they clean and polish coffins in a festive Spanish
cemetery in La Mancha. *Volver* champions, by putting into play, Freud's idea
that every human act, utterance, and symptom needs to be opened up at an
unconscious, prepsychical, and somatic level. Chronos is shown to be limited.
In *Volver*, the "work of the *Zeitlos* that scans it...essentially upset[s] time's
flight forward" (Kristeva, 2002, 32). Illustrating Kristeva's theory of intimate
revolt, Almodóvar's film insists on the immanence of "time unbound" within
"bound living time" (Kristeva, 2002, 33)—unbound time being what "presides
over working out and sublimation" (Kristeva, 2002, 32).

Featuring colors, shapes, and music, or in other words being thoroughly semiotic, replete with absorbent lektons, *Volver* has the potential to capture psychic material locked inside the unconscious of the spectator, in turn facilitating the insertion of that non-life into representation. Moreover, *Volver* attacks the society of the spectacle for blocking such a vital movement. That is: clinching its Kristevan perspective, *Volver* even points to the society of the spectacle as what subtracts death from life. Like Kristeva, Almodóvar's film targets the society of the spectacle as the most insidious enemy of the *Zeitlos* and replenishes what the society of the spectacle takes away.

Being much more than a narrative about abuse and alienation, being flagrantly sensuous, *Volver* presents a postmodern explosion of color, patterns, and music. As a thought-specular film, *Volver* operates heavily, if not primarily, on the level of sensation. The film is therefore semiotically well equipped to receive the spectator's unconscious turmoil through its dynamic lektonic traces. Like the white paper towel that slowly absorbs Paco's blood early in the film, *Volver* lektonically draws out and soaks in the spectator's psychic pain. In its opening scenes, *Volver* swoops the spectator into a splendid vision of colorful flowers and incantatory women. Later on, the camera takes time to offer shots of, or we might say to caress, random objects such as a yellow, green, and red, old-fashioned tea set, with six charming cups, sugar and cream bowls, and a tea pot. Agustina's mother's collection of plastic jewelry, to give another example, becomes the apple of the camera's, and in turn our, eye. Especially Raimunda's but Paula's colorful clothing as well arouses our senses, as do the green, white, and red striped curtains hanging in Agustina's home and the glistening blue and white tiles that decorate Aunt Paula's spacious entry hall.

The Almodóvarian color red dominates. Close-ups of hot red, voluptuous tomatoes at a vegetable stand grab our attention, along with the red peppers Raimunda slices cleanly for the film-crew banquet. Raimunda wears an outstanding red and white apron and later (when she sings) a red-checked jacket; Paula sports a red and white striped shirt. The Madrid bus is red and white; the family car is unmistakably all red. Even at Aunt Paula's funeral, red and white tiles on the floor are emphasized via an overhead shot. Colorful, surreal graffiti; a multi-colored dolly used to remove the refrigerator to the restaurant and the deep freeze to the truck; a bright, rainbow-colored, tube-like decoration that Paula nails up at the restaurant; colorful straws carefully placed in the mojitos; a creamy, plump dessert turned over and plopped onto a plate encircled by colorful flowers—all of these decorative, thing-oriented shots seduce the spectator's psyche at a subliminal level.

At the very end of *Volver*, as the final credits roll, shapes and colors alone explode onto the screen, unfolding for several minutes various, mainly floral, configurations. Accompanied by heart-wrenching music, red, white, pink, and black flowers emerge and recede. Squiggly lines appear that grow more flowers. Geometrical shapes of various sorts, including red stripes, are followed by blue and red flowers as well as black, white, and red lines that trace trees. Leaves evolve, and then numerous colorful circles burst forth, filling up the screen, until the film ends with black and white flowers. Just as, to Deleuze, "the broken lines and contrasting black and white structure of *Psycho*" serve as a "signed image" for Hitchcock (Deleuze, 1983, 21) (such primary geometric shapes and colors also appear during the *Psycho* credits), here we have at the finale of *Volver* Almodóvar's signature, which picks up on myriad images (such as flowers from Raimunda's striking black and red skirt) that stood out earlier in the film. Almodóvar signs his film through its lektonic traces, illustrating "Godard's formula, 'it's not blood, it's red,' ... the formula of colourism" (Deleuze, 1983, 118), as *Volver* transforms traumatic blood to semiotic color.[1] And through what I am calling Almodóvar's signature—the semiotic expressibles of *Volver* that galvanize primary processes—the spectator's suffering is planted in the film. These semiotic components of *Volver* render the spectator susceptible, at the level of the unconscious, to Raimunda's story, which then carries him or her to the end of the night. The sensuousness of the thought-specular film lektonically prompts the spectator's (timeless) traumatic memory to come forward, so that, through a subsequent encounter with the gaze, his or her unconscious is further absorbed into the film.

Thought-specular film enables a transformation of flat filmic images into containers of symptoms, putting into play primary processes. Such cinema, Kristeva believes, provides a skeleton and a logic for the spectator's psychic material, through its themes, the rhythm of its images, as well as through laughter. The specular encodes the drive via its "network of lektonic elements: sounds, tone, colors, space, figures" (Kristeva, 2002, 77). Yet, as became unmistakable in our analysis of *Psycho*, what we see is not what fascinates us. The thought specular ultimately offers the spectator an encounter with his or her constitutive lack—as a way of immersing the viewer in that "psychotic" space conducive to psychic regeneration. Cinema seizes us at this place of the gaze: "This is its magic" (Kristeva, 2002, 73).

Volver a sentir: Papa

Faithful to its title ("to return"), *Volver* is a rehearsal—of extremely traumatic material. At the beginning of the film, though, Raimunda (the central, Penelope Cruz character) appears ebullient as she is trapped in a delusion about her past—that her parents were happily married and that they died in each other's arms. "Mom was lucky," she announces gleefully to her sister Sole, "she died in Dad's arms, and she loved him more than anyone." Such a false, sugar-coated sense of her past denies the truth of Raimunda's having been incessantly raped by her father, with the result of a pregnancy that produced her now fourteen-year-old daughter and sister, gorgeous Paula. The opening scenes of *Volver*, in which Raimunda greets her friend Agustina, at the cemetery, with gaiety and, later on, visits her Aunt Paula with big smiles and effervescence, present this traumatized woman as upbeat.

However, upon seeing Raimunda's appalled reaction to a fire burning on Aunt Paula's TV (which reminds Raimunda at some level of the fire in which her parents supposedly were killed and possibly of the true conflagration that fire was caused by—her mother set the fire soon after hearing about the father's abuse of young Raimunda), we realize that there is a buried layer of trouble simmering in Raimunda's psyche. Almodóvar's *Volver* presents a working through of all this catastrophic psychic material as the storyline centered on it is "treated" by the non-diegetic, lektonic components of the film itself. *Volver* progresses from the present in which Raimunda's trauma is repressed (Raimunda has not sung at least since the birth of her daughter; she idealizes her parents when in fact her father was an incestuous rapist) to a new time, outside of time, in which Raimunda's singing takes place as a means of confronting her past.

Raimunda's eventual critical breakthrough into song is enabled by the killing of a father-figure. That is: what catalyzes the film's penetrating engagement with the trauma of incestuous rape, of a daughter by her father, is the killing by another daughter (herself the product of that incestuous rape) of a "father" who attempts to rape her. Paco, Raimunda's daughter's (Paula's) apparent father, ogles her early in the film. We watch him eye her crotch as she lounges at home in a comfortable chair with her legs, wrapped in pink tights, splayed childishly, though for Paco alluringly, before him. (That Raimunda perceives the scene as at least disturbing in itself is revealed when she orders her daughter to sit with her legs closed.) We also observe Paco glance into Paula's bedroom as she is undressing, catching the slightest glimpse of her naked, young breast. Here then we have a crucial repetition. With Paco's compulsion to rape his own "daughter" (he is her non-biological father), *Volver* re-presents, repeats, returns to the original traumatic incestuous act of Raimunda's father's multiple rapes of Raimunda.

This time around, though, the victim (Paula) defends herself, by stabbing her abuser with a knife. The killing is taken seriously. When Paula tells her mother about the incident, the girl's face wrinkles up like a raisin, revealing the excruciating pain and torment she has undergone during the incident and its immediate aftermath. But this fatal violence is also methodically and thoroughly mopped up. We watch Raimunda's mop and paper towels absorb Paco's bright red blood in a way that suggests the film's own absorption of trauma into its sponge-like cinematic elements. This is the essential filmic activity of Kristeva's thought specular: such absorption demonstrates Kristeva's notion that "the imaginary captures fear [and] appeases it," eventually restoring it to the Symbolic Order (Kristeva, 2002, 78–9).[2]

Significantly, at this point, Raimunda in a sense takes credit for the violence: "Remember, I killed him," she insists to Paula. On the one hand, here Raimunda behaves as a protective mother (taking the blame for her child), but on the other she embraces the act psychically, to seize it from her daughter as a way of grappling with her own father's abuse of her. Paco's attempted rape of Paula and its outcome restage Raimunda's trauma and thus enable her to begin the process of extracting that trauma from its encasement in timelessness and the unconscious and trans- planting it in time and consciousness. Paco is the psychoanalytic scapegoat for Raimunda's father's abuse of her. His body is sacrificed, his blood mopped up, and his corpse stuffed in a deep freeze to pay for the sins of the father. (This actual freezer in which Raimunda temporarily stores Paco's body clarifies imagistically that the death of Paco displaces the stuff of Raimunda's encryptment, that it takes the killing of Paco to begin to thaw Raimunda's psychic freezer.) Yet, Paco in his own right, a beer-drinking, TV-sports addict, is nothing more than a pathetic member of the society of the spectacle. Devoid of intimacy, sex for Paco is mere "work": when Raimunda rebuffs his invitation in bed, he volunteers to do "all the work." Then, worse, he fulfills her sense of him as a mere "pest" in flaunting his masturbatory activity as he lies next to her. Killing Paco serves as a means of acknowledging the earlier abuse; it also seems tantamount to stepping on an insect. Paco is presented as an ugly specimen of the mindless society of the spectacle that advocates through images the objectification of, and disrespect for, women and girls.

But, while men need to be killed, women's harmonious relation to death is celebrated. *Volver* inscribes death from its very first scene with singing women cleaning and polishing gray-silver, unburied coffins. It is a gorgeous and, especially because of the potent east wind, animated depiction, with its abundance of flowers and cheerful women. The sensory intimacy of women, constantly giving each other loud, succulent kisses on the cheek, is unmistakable from the onset of *Volver*, along with their closeness to death. Here too Almodóvar overlaps with Kristeva, who also discovers in women a more sensuous, poetic, caring, and supple relation to power and meaning (distinct from mastery or even significance) as well as a rapport with death. And, insofar as this is the case, both thinkers locate in the "universe of women…an alternative to the robotizing and spectacular society that is damaging the culture of revolt" (Kristeva, 2002, 5). "Their women" oppose the society of the spectacle—in which *bios* (political life) has overtaken *zoë* (natural life)—in fact, through their embrace of Kristeva's conception of the sacred, which is located at the crossroads of dichotomies such as body versus soul, life versus death, or bios versus zoë, as well as where "meaning" emerges through the inextricability of these ostensible antitheses. Kristeva regards the body of a woman in particular as "a strange intersection between zōō and bios, physiology and narration," flesh and Word (Kristeva and Clement, 2001, 14).

In the opening scene, Agustina arrives at the cemetery to clean her coffin and to free herself from time: she tells Raimunda, Sole, and Paula that she often visits the cemetery to sit on her own, and "time goes by." In this way she befriends death and enters the *Zeitlos* (both of which eventually return her embrace). Plagued by cancer, especially Agustina injects the fruits of death into *Volver*. Cleaning one's coffin, we are told, is the custom in this quaint Spanish village, although a man dusting off his coffin would seem odd. At Aunt Paula's funeral service, the men appear cordoned off. They look clueless, standing in a drab social space of their own. They wear gray, white, and black, reflecting colorlessness in contrast with the vibrant colors, frame by frame, that for the most part surround the women of the film, in the form of clothing, furniture, interior decor, stray props, etc., the lektonic expressibles of *Volver* that suck us in.

Aunt Paula's death follows immediately on the heels of Paco's demise, which puts death, a funeral, a funeral procession, and mourning at the center of this bittersweet film. On the "sweet" side, in sync with Kristeva's stress on the liberatory function of laughter in thought-specular films, there is a comic quality to every scene in *Volver* connected to batty Aunt Paula's passing, if not to just about every scene in the film. Laughter greets death. The grieving village women dressed in black, sitting in a circle with somber faces, while rapidly fanning themselves, resemble a swarm of agitated bees. When Sole enters the room, and the women rush up to express their condolences, the scene seems ludicrous, perhaps in part because of the clash between Sole's coldness toward her aunt (who regards Sole as a "sourpuss") and the grief-stricken mood of the ritual. Next, a self-conscious, heavily stylized, stiff funeral procession creeps across the screen, led by a limo decked out in rings and bouquets of colorful flowers, with women walking behind in a straight line, the men following—all of which can seem hilarious. Almodóvar's depiction of death in scenes that evoke laughter comports with Kristeva's sense that it was "inevitable…that cinema itself should openly become the privileged place of sadomasochistic fantasy, so that fear and its seduction explode in laughter and distance" (Kristeva, 2002, 80).

I take the funny funeral of Aunt Paula, as it follows the death of Paco, to complete the first phase of *Volver*'s process of working through. Indolent Paco, sports-TV addict, cruel masturbator, child-molester, sunk to the level of a "pest," is killed off to avenge the abuse committed by the real father. As a corpse Paco is, also humorously, dragged from the household refrigerator to a deep freeze in Emilio's restaurant. He is later buried, in that freezer-coffin, in a hole in the ground that two women have the muscle to dig. Through Paco's bad deeds, his demise, and his proper burial, the trauma of the incestuous father is confronted, instead of remaining buried psychically, and brought to closure. Paco's death merges with that of Aunt Paula (Raimunda's surrogate mother), and a general funereal ambience is comically established, making way for a more shattering confrontation.

Volver a sentir: Mama

The second phase of *Volver*'s enactment of working through engages the central mother-daughter relation. Raimunda rejected her mother for being blind to the abuses her father inflicted upon her. After the birth of her daughter, Raimunda moved with Paco out of Alcanfor de las Infantas to Madrid and avoided her mother. Irene, Raimunda's mother, even announces to her granddaughter Paula that Raimunda did not love her. Raimunda put her mother away psychically, incorporating Irene in a melancholic crypt that in turn crushes Raimunda's desire. Raimunda shows no interest whatsoever in men: Paco, needless to say; handsome Emilio (who apparently wanted her as a partner); or the young, attractive film-crew manager (who in one scene, as though mesmerized, stares at Raimunda chopping food). Now her mother returns. As I see it, young Paula's brave act of defending herself against her father-molester/monster vicariously allows Raimunda to face her rejected and reincarnated mother. Acknowledgment of her father's abuse opens the door to recognition of the mother's role in that trauma, as Raimunda's reified psyche continues to undergo a gradual process of excavation. Although in the story the question is whether or not the mother is a ghost, on the psycho-analytic level of *Volver*, the mother's apparitional return indicates a further dilation of Raimunda's psyche that allows her psychic encryptment of her mother to end.

Humor again is key. Irene returns as a phantom of Raimunda's psyche, in a state between incorporation (psychic taking in) and introjection (psychic pushing out), as an externalization of the mother that is often ridiculously presented. When Sole hears her mother's voice calling from the trunk of her car ("Let me out, Sole! Let me out! I'm your mother"), a shocked Sole asserts, with excess deliberateness: "My mother is dead.... You are her ghost or spirit." The ghost replies, "Whatever you say but get me out of here." The next shot of Irene, disheveled, in a fetal position and a bright blue dress, lying wide-eyed and cramped on her side in the trunk, has the charm to amuse every viewer. Other scenes in the film involving Irene mix the senses with humor. Raimunda detects her mother early on by smelling her flatulence. Conjoining humor with sensory intimacy, the mother's propensity to "fart" gives all the prominent women in the film a hearty laugh. And, in a scene that hints at the very point of the introjection of Irene from Raimunda's psyche, humor takes precedence. Raimunda inquires of her mother, "You're not a ghost are you? You're not dead?" Irene responds: "No love, I'm not." And Raimunda comments, "That's such a relief." Psychoanalytically, for Raimunda, it is an enormous relief. The silliness of the exchange, the lightness with which such heavy subject matter is discussed, along with the little burst of laughter it evokes in the spectator—all demonstrate Kristeva's assertion that "evil is only representable insofar as you can laugh at it, with full knowledge of the facts" (Kristeva, 2002, 80). A comedy about incestuous rape and a prolonged, painful alienation of mother and daughter, *Volver* supports Kristeva's notion, intrinsic to intimate revolt, that laughter is the most salubrious means to gain the distance that results from working through.

Volver also demonstrates Kristeva's psychoanalytic concept of forgiveness, placing it at the center of its cinematic working through of the mother-daughter trauma. In *Intimate Revolt*, Kristeva points out that forgiveness has not been a psychoanalytic concept. She attaches it, rather, to a Christian line of thinking about guilt, which "only achieves its full meaning retroactively, in forgiveness" (Kristeva, 2002, 15). But, in contrast to Christian forgiveness, which follows judgment, Kristeva's idea of forgiveness "suspends judgment and time" (Kristeva, 2002, 16). Kristeva's forgiveness is offered by an-other, who must listen in a way that forgoes judgment, in the mode of an analyst rather than a priest in a confessional. "My unconscious," she explains, "is reinscribable beyond the gift that someone else is giving me of not judging my acts" (Kristeva, 2002, 21), in a way that grants meaning to suffering. The inexpressible becomes the expressible as an-other (now the film) offers forgiveness through silence and love by turning the disturbing senselessness to sense. In this way "complex and intraverbal experiences" are "brought to the other"—here the film, which draws forth and receives the specta-tor's psychic turmoil. Psychoanalysis then is obviously an experience of forgiveness. Sublimation likewise serves as a process of forgiveness, given that it brings preverbal material, wounded emotions and bodies, to words or other forms of expression, with the bonus of meaning. And so does *Volver*. Forgiveness in *Volver* entails an alleviation of suffering—suffering due to the lost, yet psychically retained, desire-impeding maternal object—as the real mother emerges into the realm of time.

Over soup after Aunt Paula's funeral, Agustina and Sole sit down together to converse about the return of the dead. Superstition in their Spanish town preserves the possibility of ghosts, a tradition Raimunda's mother takes advantage of, in that she is a murderer (having set fire to the hut in which her husband and Agustina's mother had just made love) on the run and fleeing justice by pretending to be a ghost, and getting away with it. (Being in the Imaginary register, everything up to this point in *Volver* takes place outside the law.) In fact, Irene (Raimunda's mother) appears in the film itself, to the spectator, as an unreal presence, looking asocially haggard, with long, ugly gray locks, dumpy clothes, and seeming a bit (hilariously) crazed. Viewers tend to take a while before they realize she is "real." For a long stretch of time, daughter Sole assumes that her mother is supernatural. This cinematic depiction of Irene as a spirit fits perfectly with a Kristevan reading of the mother in that Kristeva conceptualizes the soul as the psyche. Irene as a ghost or spirit can be read as a psychic phenomenon, an incorporated maternal object that materializes, as Raimunda, after having disavowed Irene for several years, gradually comes to acknowledge her mother's non-ghostly, real presence. Irene-as-ghost serves as Irene-as-incorporated maternal object resurrecting from the dead, from unbound time, to enter into the narrative. By transporting the mother from an unconscious place of disavowal to consciousness (avowal)—at the same time, leaving a trail—*Volver* enacts Kristeva's definition of forgiveness.

It is noteworthy, in this connection, that Raimunda's mother seeks forgiveness explicitly. When Raimunda, upon encountering her mother (as "ghost") for the first time, asks her, "Aren't you dead?" the mother, Irene, replies that she has returned to receive Raimunda's forgiveness—"for being blind." Irene's request, however, is for conventional forgiveness. Even as she raises the topic of forgiveness, Raimunda's mother is not presented as being involved in a process of transforming her unconscious into consciousness or timeless trauma into time (although we must credit Irene with broaching the topic of forgiveness so that it can be recognized as psychoanalytically relevant to *Volver*). But Raimunda is. Forgiveness for Raimunda transpires through the semiotic. The traumatic material embedded in her unconscious awakens in a sense through the lektons that constitute *Volver*. As she becomes disentangled from past traumas that gripped her psyche, Raimunda plunges into the sensuous world of food. As soon as Paco is buried, *Volver* cuts to a vivacious scene of Raimunda carefully slicing red peppers and feeding dozens of people with appetizing food and drinks. To slice the peppers, Raimunda uses a sharp knife that resembles the one that killed Paco, its purpose transformed. (Having stabbed Paco, the knife, too, is now free to chop vegetables.) Such lektons in turn provide pockets of absorption of the viewer's psychic trouble and the opportunity for the spectator's identificatory experience of forgiveness.

Although Raimunda used to sing, Raimunda's daughter, Paula, has never heard her mother's singing voice. Much is made of this fact, since it means that Raimunda stopped singing, at least by the time she gave birth (to her own sister) or after her father's rape produced a child. The deepest "note" of the film is Raimunda's performance at Restaurant Emilio. In the middle of the festive, colorful film-crew banquet, Raimunda has the brainstorm of joining a small band of gypsy musicians assembling to play. (That the group Raimunda feeds and performs for is a film crew italicizes *Volver*'s implication that through film trauma can be thawed out.) Full of anticipation expressed by a wide grin on her beaming face, Paula is eager to make up for her deprivation. Raimunda then lets go, singing soulfully lyrics of a song titled, of course, "Volver," whose meaning itself bears an uncanny relation to Kristeva's theory of intimate revolt.[3] Herein lie the Kristevan heart and lungs of Almodóvar's film.

The resemblance is astonishing. It is as though Almodóvar deliberately selected these lyrics to articulate Kristeva's theory. Raimunda seems to have an inkling that she is on the verge of an intense experience with an earlier segment of her life. Of this she sings:

> I'm afraid of the encounter
> with the past that's coming back,
> to confront my life.
> I'm afraid of the nights
> that, filled with memories,
> enchain my dreams.

Sensing that now she is being summoned by her past, a shaken Raimunda uses her voice to experience a terrifying encounter that has the potential to release unbearable memories that have precluded her dreams from being realized. Raimunda now completes the journey to the dark night of her soul. Unlocking her memories of the sexual abuse by her father has paved the way for a renewal of relations with the mother. Significantly, at this critical point in the film, the mother rolls down the window of the red car (parked outside Emilio's restaurant where Raimunda sings), exposing herself, making her presence known to Raimunda, even, we might say, attempting to burst forth from Raimunda's unconscious into consciousness, to rise from the dead.

Despite her trepidation, Raimunda now feels compelled to bring her flight from her past to an end. To do so, she must first return to it—meet her past face-to-face. Raimunda can "see the twinkling of... lights in the distance" that "mark her return." Those are the prefatory lyrics she sings that seem to well up inside Raimunda before she launches into a full expression of her need to end her disavowal:

> But the fleeing traveler,
> sooner or later,
> must come to a halt.
> And even though oblivion,
> which destroys everything,
> has killed my old illusions,
> I still retain a humble hope
> hidden away.

At this point in the song, the mother, Irene, shows herself framed in the car window, as though the collision of daughter and mother is happening at this very moment, as though Raimunda's flight has now ceased. Having fled from her mother physically and cut her off consciously, Raimunda psychically remained unconsciously glued to her. Her mother persisted in her psyche as the source of deep pain, as an obtuse, negligent, inert figure brutally ignorant of Raimunda's suffering. As she sings of her "humble hope," Raimunda gives the impression of looking beyond the restaurant, as though she senses, if not perceives, the presence of that previously buried mother. This is Raimunda's "moment of grace," a sign of rebirth through a contracting of timelessness and time that inscribes death in "lived actuality" (Kristeva, 2002, 36).

The song "Volver" then proceeds hopefully, as Raimunda's encryptment continues to break up:

> And that is all
> of my heart's fortune.
> Coming back
> with a wrinkled forehead.

Framed in the car window, the mother now begins to look nervous about being observed. Before entering the restaurant, Sole had warned her mother Irene to remain in the car and to avoid letting anyone see her. Irene had replied, "No one can see me in here," insinuating that she occupies a realm of the unseen, that to grasp her presence is to embrace something beyond conventional viewing. Having solicited Raimunda's unconscious, the mother retreats from the window to leave the gaze as the residue of her withdrawal. The next camera shot of the empty car window has the radical effect/affect of a shock, illustrating Kristeva's theory of the thought specular that what we visualize on the screen is not the locus of our most intense fascination. By framing the mother's face and then following that close-up with the empty frame of the car window, *Volver* presents the psychoanalytic idea that the most magnetizing "thing" in the film (both for Raimunda and the spectator) is the Nothing lurking behind, the reminder/remainder of the now lost maternal object—in Lacanian terms, the lack that enables the production of *objet a*, or the cause of desire. And (to offer my own reminder) that this remainder is simultaneously a reminder is essential to Kristeva's way of thinking. Such progression away from the mOther—as it depends on her receding after Raimunda's encounter with her, as we see vividly illustrated here—forges a connection to that object.

In the midst of her song, upon sensing the presence of Irene outside in the car, Raimunda experiences a provisional psychosis of being, the dark night of the soul. At the end of her song, Raimunda's face reflects overwhelming exertion and pain; she completes her singing in tears. Through her encounter with the gaze—the Nothing that remains after separation from the maternal Thing, her constitutive lack—Raimunda carries out the psychoanalytic premise that the subject must "agree to lose" the mother to "imagine" and "name her" (Kristeva, 1989, 41) and that to imagine and name her is to experience the loss of her. Glimpsing Nothingness in the place of the desire-blocking mother, who no longer fills up that space, directly after having at long last apprehended her, enables Raimunda to continue to sing, of hope and time. Her psyche is released to enter time as she sings passionately a song that transports her past suffering into discourse.

Raimunda even sings *about* her effort now to name what she seeks. In addition to setting intimate revolt in motion for the spectator—insofar as Raimunda's experience of the gaze that enables her to commit psychic matricide is offered to the viewer—*Volver* promotes the concept:

> And the snows of time
> Silvering my brow
> Feeling
> That life is an instant,
> That twenty years is nothing,
> That the feverish eyes
> Wandering in the shadows
> seek you and name you.

Raimunda participates in Kristeva's "pardon" by "reuniting with affect through the metaphorical and metonymic rifts of discourse" (Kristeva, 2002, 26). She is able to access her formerly encrypted mother and begin to defrost her psychic trouble ("the snows of time" that made twenty years seem like "an instant"), to separate from her, by translating her into the semiotic poetry of song. Raimunda discovers her mother in language. Raimunda's song enacts, articulates, and celebrates that process of forgiveness and presents it as a paradigm.

Raimunda breaks through a destructive oblivion, to "seek" and "name," so that she can return to a "sweet memory" rather than be plagued by a buried traumatic past that forever sabotages her desire:

> Living,
> With my soul clinging,
> To a sweet memory,
> That I weep for again.

This song "Volver" itself, given that the mother taught it to Raimunda as a child, is even part of that sweet memory. (It is strangely as though Irene at some level had foreknowledge of Raimunda's psychic turmoil, in that she exposed her daughter to this very song about the necessity of intimate revolt.) Irene metamorphoses from being "dead" (a haunting ghost) to being a real presence. And because the mother disappears after her appearance to Raimunda, as twenty years of pain turn to "nothing," giving way to the gaze, she becomes in the end a supportive real absence. Insofar as Irene's subsequent status as a daily presence in Raimunda's life is preceded by Raimunda's intense, shattering encounter with her as a real absence, enabling "the copresence of nothingness in being," Raimunda achieves an intimate revolt.[4]

Curiously, what Giorgio Agamben writes about archaeology in *The Signature of All Things* pertains here. It is not quite a process of bringing into consciousness all the repressed content of the unconscious: "it is a matter of conjuring up its phantasm, through meticulous genealogical inquiry, in order to work on it, deconstruct it, and detail it to the point where it gradually erodes, losing its originary status." Intimate revolt, we might say, still using Agamben's words, returns, not to a specific "content but to the modalities, circumstances, and moments in which the split, by means of repression, constituted it as origin." Intimate revolt wills the past "to let it go, to free itself from it, in order to gain access beyond or on this side of the past to what has never been, to what was never willed" (Agamben, 2009, 102–3). Agamben unwittingly captures the paradox of Kristeva's intimate revolt, where an Imaginary past fusion is experienced through an undergoing of its loss.

Indicting American capitalism

Beyond thematizing and putting into effect Kristeva's concept of intimate revolt at the level of the spectator, *Volver* targets the society of the spectacle as the most formidable threat to intimate revolt. Completely on Kristeva's wavelength, Almodóvar's film presents intimate revolt as an antidote to the Western obsession with facile images and objects of quick consumption. *Volver* takes up the topic of the society of the spectacle overtly. In Sole's illegal beauty salon, her clients analyze and condemn what they call "trash TV." Seeming to agree with Kristeva's view that "the images flooding TV viewers…stop the flow of thought in a sort of hypnosis" (Kristeva, 2010, 281), they note in particular its addictive quality: "Once I start watching it, I can't stop. I feel worse and worse, but I'm hooked. It's like a drug." They comment on its assault on one's sensibility, observing that trash TV keeps you from sleeping and that all the shouting "drives you crazy."

Shortly after Sole's clients' explicit critique, a parodied television talk show, "Wherever You Are," run by Agustina's sister, Brigida, attempts to treat Agustina's relation to her mother, needless to say crudely, by bribing Agustina to speak out with the reward of a trip to a cancer-treatment center in Houston. Agustina is invited, and pressured, to sacrifice her soul to gain her biological life (what would then be a controlled "bare life"). The crass talk-show host throws at Agustina a barrage of rude, invasive questions about her mother: Was she a single parent? Was she mentally imbalanced? And who was the friend that died in the fire on the day Agustina's mother disappeared? "Wherever You Are" concerns itself with what is most intimate in Agustina's life. The show is exposed in *Volver* as cheapening that intimacy by reducing it to entertainment. The host of "Wherever You Are" expects Agustina to tell the story of her mother's connection to Raimunda's mother—to reveal their private family secrets and even, we might say, to enact a superficial "intimate revolt" on TV. Agustina is turned into a freak, an object of fascination for the audience and TV viewers, especially as she grows alienated by the show's rough, if not abusive, handling of her most personal issues.

In this ghastly scene, *Volver* sets up a clash between delicate psychic life and the commodification of that life in the society of the spectacle. In the interest of unveiling a murder mystery for profit, the show and its host batter Agustina with questions, pretending to be her friend. At a point of particular frustration with Agustina's unwillingness to cooperate, the host announces that Agustina is "among friends" and urges the audience to offer "a big hand for Agustina!" The applauding audience is portrayed mechanically, as monstrously fake. The film exhibits an abyss between the artificial applauding audience and a frail, suffering Agustina, a cancer victim tempted pathetically, though understandably, to win a cure. The grotesque applause awakens Agustina to what she is doing—selling her soul/psyche to save her body. With obvious deliberation, she marches off the live show, causing a great deal of commotion. Though in a fragile state, Agustina resists the pull of the bribe, walks humbly and honestly off the show, and in effect chooses literal death over the "death" of her psyche/soul. *Volver* lays bare the horror of the show, its cruel bribe, and the way it mangles and destroys intimate life—chiefly by supporting Agustina's last-minute choice, instead, to die, peacefully and gracefully.

Volver represents the society of the spectacle as a virtual killer, making real, natural death preferable. At supper at Aunt Paula's after the show, Sole states bluntly to Agustina: "You shouldn't have done it." Agustina returns a humiliated "I know that." Raimunda contributes her approval with a nod. We watch in awe over the choice they are making. By concluding with Agustina's acceptance of literal death, the film further injects death into "lived actuality," both on the level of the figures within the film—Raimunda, Sole, Paula, and even Irene—and on the level of the spectator. Toward the end of *Volver*, Agustina becomes more and more ghostly. Her ethereal figure seems to float, in a white nightgown, through the domestic spaces of her home. She greets Irene as though Irene were an emissary from the heavenly realm that Agustina is on the verge of entering. However, Agustina trades places with Irene, who has, at the end, living in Madrid, given up her supernatural status, her phantasmatic self having materialized within the everyday world of her daughters.

Volver is framed by Agustina's rapport with death. Agustina will soon slip into the tomb she had found solace in visiting and cleaning in the opening scene. Enclosing all the material of the film in this way, *Volver* conveys Kristeva's idea that death as "a temporality heterogeneous to linear time (Zeitlos)" must not be "subtracted" from "the logic of the living" (Kristeva, 2002, 32). Leaving temporality behind, Agustina enters the *Zeitlos*, just as Irene emerges from the *Zeitlos* into time, a two-way crossing that itself well illustrates, and activates, Kristeva's favored intersection of life and non-life. Irene, the mother who has emerged from the dead, plans to conduct daily conversations with her daughter, Raimunda. When Raimunda announces to her mother that she has "so much to tell" her, Irene assures Raimunda: "I'll see you every day." Having encountered Irene at the level of the gaze and thus having pulled herself out of her psychic deep freeze, Raimunda now can engage with her on a regular basis—in time.

For all we know, at the end Irene herself may be on the verge of an intimate revolt through film. *Volver*'s final displacement of the society of the spectacle hints at the potential for this process. Near the end of *Volver*, the society of the spectacle seems supplanted as Irene watches Luchino Visconti's *Bellissima* on television. While caring for the dying Agustina, Irene takes in what appears to be a thought-specular film with the capacity to enable Irene to face her past mistakes. For *Bellissima* indirectly reflects on Irene's life. The main character, Maddelena, is abused by her husband, who has a sweet relationship with their young daughter (though it is not even implied that he abuses her). The mother too, like Irene who taught the song "Volver" to Raimunda for a "casting for child singers," teaches her daughter, Maria, a song, in the hope that Maria will be selected for a central acting part in a film.

After a great deal of duress, finally Maria is offered the role, but Maddelena, the mother, having realized the ruthlessness of this cinema world, rejects the contract she so desperately craved at the outset. Maddelena learns that "Dreams of stardom have made many people unhappy," observes corruption (the giving of acting favors for sex and money), and experiences the crude insensitivity of the judges, who remark that her daughter is "a real dwarf." Maria, the little girl, breaks down in a heavy bout of tears during her audition. Disillusion is the only outcome of Maddelena's fierce passion to have her daughter star at Cinecittà. A meta-cinematic film, in the category of *neo-realism rosa* (a sub-genre of comedy), *Bellissima* condemns the society of the spectacle or Hollywood-style cinema. Just as Agustina sacrifices a trip to Houston for cancer treatment, Maddelena sets aside her wish for a better future for her daughter rather than sell out to American capitalist values.

By putting *Bellissima* on TV at the end of his film, Almodóvar substitutes an attack on the society of the spectacle for that spectacle. He completes his already multi-tiered Kristevan message of intimate revolt versus the society of the spectacle. The kinship between Kristeva and Almodóvar is close. Distinguishing between films produced at Cinecittà and films like Visconti's *Bellissima*, Almodóvar goes so far as to honor Kristeva's contrast between the spectacle and the thought-specular—her sense that, while the society of the spectacle generates images that fail to liberate us, that abolish our psyches, the visible is nevertheless the port of registry of the drive. All film is not a mindless bombardment of images that wipe out the psyche. Thought-specular film can, in fact, be effective psychoanalytic resistance to the threat of psychic demise posed by "trash TV" and its cinematic counterparts.

Notes

1 The way *Volver* employs color to *absorb* spectatorial psychic content puts to use Deleuze's "colour-image," in *Cinema I*, which is defined by its "*absorbent* characteristic": "the colour-image does not refer to a particular object, but absorbs all that it can." Deleuze regards "colour" as "the affect itself" that has the capacity to absorb the characters, "situations," and the spectator. In the work of film director Minnelli, "colours" are more than absorbent: "the splendour of colours" here (interestingly) has an "almost carnivorous, devouring, destructive ... function" (Deleuze, 1983, 118–19).

2 Calling attention to the absorption of impurities that takes place as the film engages the spectator's psyche, *Volver* contains several washing scenes: Raimunda washes dishes as well as the knife that kills Paco, both before and after it kills him; as part of her job, she cleans the spacious floor and does laundry at the Madrid airport. Sole washes women's hair and instructs her mother on how to do it properly.

3 "Volver," originally a tango by Carlos Gardel, was transformed into flamenco. It is sung by Estrella Morente; lyrics by Alfredo Le Pera.

4 *Volver* underscores the initial real presence of the mother through a joke on the Eucharist. This Catholic Mystery plays an amusing role in the film through the lektonic trace of the wafers. When Paula, Sole, and Raimunda visit Aunt Paula at the beginning of *Volver*, they are served a plateful of "wafers," baked, unbeknowst to them at the time, by Irene, the "dead" mother. The tasty wafers appear, and are enjoyed periodically, throughout the film, keeping the Real Presence of the mother alive. They are a material trace of her reality, just as her odors allow her daughters to sense her real existence. Sole and Raimunda smell their mother and, in a sense, taste her, as a Catholic takes in the Real Presence of Christ during Communion. "Do this in remembrance of me," the priest utters as he holds up the host for the communicant to consume. Likewise, Raimunda's mother bakes wafers for her daughters to partake in remembrance of her. It is all a joke. Nevertheless,

the taste of the wafers ties the mother to her daughters through sensory intimacy. Serving on behalf of working through, the pun on wafers inserts non-life (the "dead" mother) into life.

Works cited

Agamben, Giorgio (2000) *Means Without End: Notes on Politics*. Trans. Vincenzo Binetti and Cesare Casarino. Minneapolis: University of Minnesota Press.
—(2009) *The Signature of All Things: On Method*. Trans. Luca D'Isanto with Kevin Attell. New York: Zone Books.
Debord, Guy (1995) *The Society of the Spectacle*. Trans. Donald Nicholson-Smith. New York: Zone Books.
Deleuze, Gilles (1983) *Cinema I: The Movement-Image*. Trans. Hugh Tomlinson and Barbara Habberjam. Minneapolis: University of Minnesota Press.
Kristeva, Julia (1982) *Powers of Horror: An Essay on Abjection*. Trans. Leon S. Roudiez. New York: Columbia UP.
—(1989) *Black Sun: Depression and Melancholia*. Trans. Leon S. Roudiez. New York: Columbia UP.
—and Catherine Clément. (2001) *The Feminine and the Sacred*. Trans. Jane Marie Todd. New York: Columbia UP.
—(2002) *Intimate Revolt: The Powers and the Limits of Psychoanalysis*. Trans. Jeanine Herman. New York: Columbia UP.
—(2010) *Hatred and Forgiveness*. Trans. Jeanine Herman. New York: Columbia UP.

Filmography

Bellissima (1951) Luchino Visconti. Film Bellisima. Italy.
Volver (2006) Pedro Almodóvar. Sony Pictures Classics. U.S.A.

8

The virtue of blushing: turning anxiety into shame in Haneke's *Caché*

Das Ding is totally indefinable and is as blurry as it is tantalizing, terrifying, and like a stalker. It is for this reason that in phenomenology, anxiety is presented without a defined object. The subject says he or she is anxious without knowing from what, or who, or why he or she is suffering.

ROBERTO HARARI, *LACAN'S SEMINAR ON "ANXIETY"*

Anxiety is no doubt the most puzzling (as well as the most promising) affect in Lacanian theory. Is it triggered by fear of loss or by a loss of loss? In her book *On Anxiety*, Renata Salecl asserts that "Lacan agreed with Freud that anxiety is the subject's response to the threat of castration" (Salecl, 2004, 30). In Chapter 4 of *On Anxiety*, titled "Love Anxieties," she invokes a commonplace notion of anxiety in reminding us that "when we have found a partner and established a love relationship, we are then often anxious that we may lose their love" (Salecl, 2004, 72). Yet Salecl also claims that "anxiety is not incited by the lack of the object but rather by the lack of the lack" (Salecl, 2004, 51). In other words, anxiety has been taken to be a response to loss as well as to, what would appear to be its opposite, the lack of loss or lack of lack.

In his *Anxiety* seminar, *Seminar X*, Lacan clarifies that "anxiety is not the signal of a lack but of something that you must manage to conceive of...as being the absence of this support of the lack" (Lacan, 1962–3, 5 Dec. 1962). It is not, in other words, the anticipation of a loss (or the loss itself) of an object that is anxiety-producing (as at least a simple understanding of castration anxiety in Freud might suggest) but a lack of lack or lack of desire. Likewise, it is not the absence of the mother that induces anxiety in the child but her suffocating presence. Extending this explanation, by putting it in terms of representation, Charles Shepherdson writes (in his introduction to Harari's book) that it is precisely the "failure to register...lack—its 'foreclosure' or nonemergence—that gives rise to the experience of anxiety." Anxiety surfaces when "the order of symbolization (substitution and displacement) is at risk of disappearing" (Shepherdson, 2001, xxxii).

Although from a (rudimentary) Freudian viewpoint fear of castration causes anxiety, so that what might be lost is unambiguous, in Lacanian theory whether or not anxiety even has an object of loss is a tricky issue. In *Being and Time* (to shift to philosophy momentarily), Heidegger states, "[t]hat in the face of which one has anxiety is not an entity within-the-world" (Heidegger, 1927/1962, 231); in harmony with Heidegger's position that anxiety has no visible cause, *although his view may initially seem antithetical*, Lacan phrases the idea very deliberately this way: anxiety is "not without an object." He elaborates in *The Other Side of Psycho-Analysis: Book XVII*:

> What I insist upon when I address the affects is the affect that is different from all the others, that of anxiety, in that it's said to have no object. Look at everything that has ever been written about anxiety, it's always this that is insisted upon—fear has a reference to an object, whereas anxiety is said to have no object. I say on the contrary that anxiety is not without an object.
>
> (Lacan, 2006/1968, 147)

Then, in a subsequent critical move, clearly agreeing with Heidegger, after all, *on the point that anxiety is not triggered by an entity within-the-world*, Lacan fills in the blank of his litotes with "surplus *jouissance*"—which is "not nameable, even if it's approximately nameable, translatable" (Lacan, 2006/1968, 147). That is, Lacan's "object" of anxiety turns out to be an "object" without a name, an overwhelming excess, a surplus—of *jouissance*, consonant with *das Ding*.[1] Keeping the focus on surplus *jouissance*, as a way of explicating the concept of anxiety as lack of lack, Harari points out that, with anxiety, "Something that should not have been exposed, as something meant to remain hidden, becomes present" (Harari, 2001, 56). Lacan conceives of anxiety as the result of a "lack of lack" rather than simply as no lack—as though "lack of lack" possesses its own ontology. In other words, a lack of lack produces the presence of the hidden: where Nothing should reign, the subject encounters something overwhelming.

Undergirding the idea of anxiety as lack of nothing but lack itself, Joan Copjec's formulation gives the non-object of anxiety a status *higher* than that of objecthood in claiming that "anxiety is precipitated by an encounter with an object of a level of certainty superior to that of any object of fact, to any actual object." Copjec refers to "the moment of extimacy" as when "we discover an 'overpopulated' privacy, where some alien excess adheres to us" (Copjec, 2006, 99). We may assume, then, that the "object" of anxiety is something hidden that rises to the surface as an "alien excess." Anxiety occurs when the subject, or perhaps even society, runs up against what is usually missing or set behind the scenes—*jouissance*—as he/she senses the presence of a stalker, *das Ding*.

The so-called object of anxiety is therefore not a real, or actual, object but an "object" in the Real. Because of its location in the Real, Lacan characterizes it as "what does not deceive" (Lacan, 1962–3, Dec. 19, 1962). In fact, Harari takes the extreme view that anxiety "has a crushing degree of certainty since it is the 'only connection' to the Real, and, as such, constitutes the 'only ultimate grasp . . . as such of any and all reality" (Harari, 2001, 264). One consequently has a great deal to gain from an eruption of anxiety. Obviously this indescribable affect can be debilitating, as the promiscuous use of anxiety pills these days testifies. But what might such an attack open up?

According to Heidegger and Lacan, such a seizure has the power to pry open what is most vital. In *Being and Time,* Heidegger proposes that "[a]nxiety throws Dasein back upon that which it is anxious about—its authentic potentiality-for-Being-in-the-world": "anxiety discloses Dasein as *Being*-possible" (Heidegger, 1927/1962, 232). Resulting from the disappearance of Being, Heideggerian anxiety thus ironically indicates Being. From a Lacanian perspective, of course "[w]ithout lack, the subject can never come into being, and the whole efflorescence of the dialectic of desire is squashed" (Fink, 1995, 103); yet anxiety appears "at a very primitive level in the constitution of the subject, in a primordial relation to desire." And so, it makes sense (as Shepherdson explains) that Lacan situates anxiety "as the threshold that the subject must cross on the way toward desire and symbolic mediation" (Shepherdson, 2001, xxxiii, xxxii). It is for this reason that in *The Seminar of Jacques Lacan: Book I* Lacan characterizes anxiety as "the fertile moment" (Lacan, 1991/1975, 188). Although for Heidegger it is running up against the Nothing that causes anxiety—"that in the face of which and for which we were anxious was 'properly'—nothing. Indeed: the nothing itself— as such—was there" (Heidegger, 1929/1977, 101)—and for Lacan it is the condition of lack of lack, for both, anxiety can be revelatory and productive.

In Copjec's estimation, the experience of anxiety is set in motion by a surplus (= lack of lack) that

> provides the subject with an opportunity to break from the grip of the Other, from the intersubjective relations the Other defines and in which it catches us up. And yet, in so far as this surplus evades assimilation by us, it binds us in turn in an even stronger, more terrifying grip.
>
> (Copjec, 2006, 104)

Confronting and assimilating one's anxiety rather than fleeing from it, even simply by trying to keep it at bay, has the potential (in Lacanian theory) to escort one to a lacking/desiring subjectivity, to a state of vitality *predicated on* (rather than immersed in or overwhelmed by) the Real. Such an experience is apt to disturb a false state of self-sufficiency, unbarred subjectivity, that precludes desire and in turn *a relation to jouissance*.

Anxiety—a lack of lack that has reached a boiling point—therefore has the potential to carve out a lack and establish a relation (rather than a fusion) with the Real not only in the personal but also in the political arena. In *The Other Side of Psycho-Analysis: Book XVII*, Lacan

> claims that anxiety is the 'central affect' around which every social arrangement is organized; every social link is approachable as a response to or transformation of anxiety, the affect which … functions as a counter-weight to existing social relations.
>
> (Copjec, 2006, 106)

Likewise coupling social relations with anxiety, Yannis Stavrakakis sounds an alarm over the drive within politics to crush loss, which again is apt to produce anxiety (lack of lack). (No transformation here.) His book *Lacan & the Political* is centered on the notion that "all ideological formations, all construc- tions of political reality, although not in the same degree or in the same way, aspire to eliminate … loss, to defeat dislocation, in order to achieve fullness" (Stavrakakis, 1999, 82). Stavrakakis points out that especially the hegemony of nationalism is predicated on such an anxiety-producing exclusion, as is (I would add) that of the society of the spectacle, which fetishistically upholds a fantasy of plenitude. As Kelly Oliver puts it, in her book *Women as Weapons of War:*

The media has fueled the fetishism that confuses reality and fantasy and disavows loss and separation, including the separation or distance necessary to sublimate loss into meaningful forms of signification.... When visual media presents itself as reality immediately accessible and in need of no interpretation, it encourages spectators to fetishize aggressive, violent, and sexual impulses rather than interpret them. And by turning reality into a fetish object[,] we thereby disavow loss and separation.

(Oliver, 2007, 93)

But anxiety erupts as soon as an ideological formation is faced historically (again to quote Stavrakakis) "with a situation totally alien to [its] experience of normality, ... with unfamiliar hazards [such as plagues, famines, the Crusades]"—and I would add September 11th as well as suicide bombers— "dislocating [its] constructions of reality," when it, in other words, feels the emergence of the Real (Stavrakakis, 1999, 103). Radical democracy is then a possibility. Stavrakakis's ideal democratic society, where the whole is missing, since it is crossed or barred "by the impossible real," is ultimately an anxiety-free Lacanian social structure (Stavrakakis, 1999, 138), as it is *based on* lack rather than constituted by a lack of lack. In contrast, shutting out loss rather than being traversed by it, our society of the spectacle is certainly not anxiety-free in this ideal sense. The question may be whether it is even anxiety-ridden in a potentially useful or ideal sense.

"Shame is dead"

[M]odern man forgets his subjectivity, forgets his existence and his death. Lacan did not get to the point of saying, 'he watches television,' but he mentions crime novels and other diversions.

JACQUES-ALAIN MILLER, "ON SHAME"

We can study the insidious nature of anxiety in Michael Haneke's 2005 film *Caché*. Diegetically as well as non-diegetically, *Caché* exposes a lack of lack (lack of desire), on both personal and socio-political levels. Desire is in fact so crippled in this film that—through the catalyst of an enigmatic, anxiety-producing videotape, itself a symptom of the society of the spectacle—*Caché* reaches a point of extremity where redemption from that condition can be glimpsed.

The acrimonious, continuously bickering main married couple of the film is numb. Georges Laurent withholds his hunches about their video crisis from his wife, Anne, telling her that "It's not her concern." She complains that they fail to have a "sound relationship" since there is "no trust" between them. Inadvertently spreading the word of Guy Debord, who defines the spectacle as "the opposite of dialogue" (Debord, 1995, 17), diagnoses Western culture as suffering from a "generalized autism" (Debord, 1995, 153), and announces that self-emancipation will remain impossible "until dialogue has taken up arms to impose its own conditions upon the world" (Debord, 1995, 154), Anne inquires rhetorically of a friend, "People talk to each other, don't they?" Conversation between affectionless husband and wife has crumbled. Desire is dead.

Caché exhibits a microcosm devoid of "living desire" within the broader context of the (in this case French, racist) society of the spectacle, in which the main couple survives and which they support. Absence of "living desire" is an emphasis of Debord, who in *The Society of the Spectacle* attributes such a deprivation to the unending artificiality set in motion by rampant commodification. In the film a comatose Georges drives a BMW and moderates a TV talk show (which has to be clipped upon becoming "too theoretical") whose surrounding shelves are filled with fake books. After his tragic visit to Majid's apartment (the home of an Algerian man who was once George's adoptive brother), Georges has the audacity to emerge from a movie theater. Georges's mother has befriended her remote control, and his son's room is plastered with a typical teenager's society-of-the-spectacle rubbish. The chic family living room contains a large, centrally located television (in the place of any windows), on which violent news items, about, for example, the Israeli-Palestinian conflict and the (ongoing) American war with Iraq, run as *background* noise. Georges seems as insensitive to Arab-Western relations now as he was as a six-year-old boy. The tomb-like spaces the Laurents inhabit reinforce Debord's point that the society of the spectacle fosters a "false consciousness of time"—history and international relations, actually all relations, are out the window.

One of Lacan's most striking points in his *Anxiety* seminar is that "anxiety is framed," which idea he metaphorizes as a "painting [rather than a TV that] is placed in a window frame." The point is not to perceive more vividly what is in the painting (that would be an "absurd technique") but, "whatever may be the charm of what is painted on the canvas, not to envision what can be seen through the window" (Lacan, 1962–3, Dec. 19, 1962). Keeping this window closed, so to speak, and thereby producing an eruption of anxiety, the video camera in *Caché* is devoid of "tracking shots, close ups, pans, or cuts," as Kalpana Seshadri has written about its technique. Seshadri observes further that, in fact, this "camera does not even focus on any particular object. Objects pass in and out of the camera eye, and the pure contingency of what is filmed suggests the camera eye here is not exactly staring...but is a dead eye. And this certainly adds to the overall sense of the videos as harbouring a vague menace" (Seshadri, 2007, 36). From start to finish, from the opening frozen shots of the Laurent neighborhood to the last prolonged shot of Pierrot's school, *Caché* self-consciously foregrounds its frames, creating a visual sense of haunting claustrophobia. The film's lack of music, too, enhances its eerie, timeless, traumatic, very chilly feel.

But why even consider interpreting a film so apparently resistant to interiority, so insistent upon surfaces, psychoanalytically? Most glaringly, its title, *Caché*, presents the initial invitation, luring us to discover what lies "hidden" beneath its thin veneer. The title (like anxiety) teases us with the prospect that something sequestered is about to become present. The main character, Georges, undergoes two unignorable nightmares: one devastating, of young Majid approaching young Georges with an axe; the other from which we never see him awake. Georges's unconscious reels with tempestuous activity, unmistakably catalyzed by the videotaping. It might even be assumed, insofar as the tapes and related drawings appear to be a function of Georges's unconscious, that Georges is the videotaper. From what other figure in the film might have originated the two childish drawings that recur throughout the film—one of a round face from whose mouth blood pours forth and the other of a bloody chicken? These are images that spring from young Georges's lies about young Majid, as they seem to surface fully realized in Georges's adult flashbacks and nightmares. Who else might be aware of young Georges's lie to his parents about young Majid's tuberculosis and his lie told to and acted on by little Majid that Georges's father wished for him to chop off the rooster's head?—fibs that return to haunt Georges through the drawings attached to the tapes. It can seem that only Georges's unconscious could be privy to such disturbing detail.

If we look hard, in other words, the psychoanalytic dimension of the film is impossible to miss. There is also a curious and complicated disjuncture between Georges's childhood—which is presented mainly in terms of a classic Imaginary rivalry with Majid for the attention of the mother—and the political effects his childhood misdeeds produce. Here we have a split, worth analyzing, between a psychoanalytic episode and the political content of the film that it generates. Rather than the political eclipsing the psychoanalytic, psychoanalysis and politics in *Caché* are intertwined. In addition, the words "Nothing" and "Nobody" are repeated to the point that negativity/lack becomes a background motif, pressuring the hermetically sealed film to allow it some breathing room. The first words of the film are "Well?" (spoken by Georges) and then "Nothing" (Anne's response). The anxiety-producing, mysterious videotaping that gives *Caché* its cachet remains hidden. As James

Penney observes, in a smart essay titled "'You never look at me from where I see you': Postcolonial guilt in *Caché*," the missing camera "incites our desire as viewers to solve the perplexing enigma of its 'impossible' hidden camera" (Penney, 2011, 79). But, while *Caché* tempts the viewer to regard it as a moral tale—as a didactic allegory that reveals French guilt over its colonization of Algeria, and in particular over the 1961 FLN massacre and all its horrific effects, especially the orphans of the roughly 200 corpses that floated down the Seine—the film finally does *not* reward such an obvious reading. (This assertion, however, is absolutely *not* to insinuate that these political atrocities are peripheral.) Psychoanalytically, *Caché* has something, concerning them, much more disturbing, opaque, and inarticulable in mind.

Haneke's film is a post-9/11 tour de force in which the main male, French figure, Georges, believes he is being terrorized by Algerian Arabs videotaping his private life. No doubt most spectators take a moral perspective on *Caché,* interpreting it as a condemnation of chiefly Georges's but also French society's unwillingness to accept responsibility for its brutal racist mistreatment of Algerians. In this reading, the videotaping lays bare French insensitivity, aloofness, and culpability—to stamp the French as *guilty*. This perspective might even embrace the false hint, given at the end of the film when the two sons chat affably together on the steps of the school, that Majid's son and Pierrot shot the videos as a way of redeeming the sins of the fathers.

Such an interpretation would have the ostensible advantage of transforming something bizarre (another term that gets reiterated, in significant tones, in the film) into a (false) sense of what is knowable—or, anxiety into guilt. In an essay titled "May '68: The Emotional Month," Joan Copjec points out that "The guilt-laden, anxiety-relieved subject still experiences *jouissance*"; however, "this *jouissance* is characterized by Lacan in *Book XVII* as a 'sham', as 'counterfeit'" (Copjec, 2006, 109). Copjec stresses that Lacan wants us to relinquish "our satisfaction with a sham *jouissance* in favour of the real thing," which can never be "dutified" or "controlled, regimented: rather, it catches us by surprise, like a sudden, uncontrollable blush on the cheek" (Copjec, 2006, 110).

Copjec's reference here to a blush is, I am guessing, an allusion to the "flush" of the boy from Bologna whom Giorgio Agamben writes about in *Remnants of Auschwitz*. This is my speculation especially since soon after referring to "a sudden, uncontrollable blush on the cheek," Copjec invokes the topic of shame, which Agamben exemplifies through Robert Antelme's Italian boy who blushes upon realizing that the SS are on the verge of shooting him—upon registering, in other words, his own desubjectification. To Agamben, Antelme confirms that shame is distinct from guilt, having "a different, darker and more difficult cause" than a bad feeling over surviving in someone else's place. Antelme recounts that when World War II was on the brink of ending, as prisoners were being transferred from Buchenwald to Dachau, with the Allies resolutely on their way, the SS extinguished anyone impeding their progress as well as anyone they randomly felt like eliminating. When the SS soldier summons the boy from Bologna, he flushes pink. The boy "is not ashamed for having survived"; his rosy color is the consequence of his certain realization that he is about to die. Agamben writes that "it is as if he were ashamed for having to die, for having been haphazardly chosen— he and no one else—to be killed" (Agamben, 2002, 104), exemplifying Agamben's ontological (counterintuitive) conception of shame.

Likewise, Joan Copjec privileges shame over guilt since shame, which entails the interplay between subjectification and desubjectification (in Agamben), to her holds open a gap, whereas guilt stifles enigma with firm knowledge. Copjec reminds us that the superego, to Lacan, dissolves or blocks "the disturbing enigma, the enigma of being, which *jouissance* poses" (Copjec, 2006, 109). While anxiety overwhelms one with surplus *jouissance*, guilt stamps real *jouissance* out. Also ranking shame as superior to guilt, James Penney reads *Caché* as exploring "through the character of Georges how intuitions of guilt work as a defense against the uncomfortable visibility that lies at the root of the affect of shame"; "Georges finds it easier to wallow in guilt and the denial of guilt, the one being inseparable from the other....What renders the encounter that Georges orchestrates with Majid so traumatic is therefore Majid's refusal to accuse, his insistence that it is not from his perspective...that Georges appears guilty. Equally important, of course, is Majid's refusal to exonerate Georges" (Penney, 2011, 89, 90).

Caché tempts the spectator to consider it in terms of French guilt; but that would reductively transform the riddle of anxiety into a transparent, controllable object of knowledge. The much less stifling way to read the film is in terms of shame, which assimilates the anxiety that suffuses the film—in bearing witness to the trauma of Algerians, in a way that has the further huge benefit of challenging the society of the spectacle, as it resists being punctured. *Caché* opens up Copjec's gap, maintains the bizarre, and revives the "enigma of being"—all for broad ethical and political (anti-racist) reasons. It is necessary, as Agamben argues, to expand the ethical field to life beyond the limit of dignity. Agamben champions "a new ethics, an ethics of a form of life that begins where dignity ends." *Remnants of Auschwitz* insists on this point—and *Caché* italicizes it, especially in its gentle presentation of Majid's depression, the hole into which he sinks—that "it is possible to lose dignity and decency beyond imagination," but "there is still life in the most extreme degradation" (Agamben, 2002, 69). *Caché* demands that we look down there, into the abyss that prompts the boy from Bologna to "flush" and Majid to commit suicide.

Lacan himself regarded shame as an antidote to our image-driven, image-mediated society, diagnosing it in pronouncing, "There is no longer any shame." "[S]hame is dead" (Miller, 2006, 15). As Miller, ventriloquizing Lacan, writes in his essay "On Shame," "the disappearance of shame alters the meaning of life…because it changes the meaning of death" (Miller, 2006, 18). To Lacan, when shame vanishes, "the ethics of psychoanalysis is called into question" (Miller, 2006, 19): the ethical possibility of the second death— the point at which "the false metaphors of being (*l'étant*) can be distinguished from the position of Being (*l'être*) itself" (Lacan, 1992/1986, 248)—drops out.[2] Instead, one merely "kicks the bucket." According to Miller, Lacan's "fundamental debate" was not with ego psychology or his colleagues but (as is evident in *The Other Side of Psycho-Analysis: Book XVII*) "has always been…with civilization insofar as it abolishes shame, with the globalization that is in process, with Americanization or with utilitarianism" (Miller, 2006, 26). In accord, then, with both Agamben's philosophy and Lacan's psychoanalytic theory, *Caché* deploys anxiety (lack of lack) to restore shame. *Caché* blushes, and in doing so hopes to prompt the spectator to do the same.

Agamben as well, in *Means without End*, promotes blushing as a strategic gesture that resists the society of the spectacle. Blurring "the shame of the camps, the shame of the fact that what should not have happened did happen" with the shame we experience today, Agamben regards shame as a politically effective way of responding when we are

> faced by too great a vulgarity of thought, when watching certain TV shows, when confronted with the faces of their hosts and with the self-assured smiles of those 'experts' who jovially lend their qualifications to the political game of the media.
>
> (Agamben, 2000, 132)

He celebrates "such a shame" as constituting "the beginning of a revolution and of an exodus of which it is barely [possible] to discern the end" (Agamben, 2000, 132). Flattening the subject, to the cool dimensions of a contemporary TV screen, robotizing him/her, the society of the spectacle keeps us from taking in suffering. This is Kristeva's central point as well: that "the modern world besotted with pleasure-performance-excellence" leads us to forget vulnerability (Kristeva, 2010, 174). Hence she adds, in *Hatred and Forgiveness*, a fourth term—vulnerability—to "the humanism inherited from the Enlightenment (liberty, equality, and fraternity)," pointing out that "analytic listening inflects these three toward a concern for sharing, in which, and thanks to which, desire and its twin, suffering, make their way toward a constant renewal of the self, the other, and connection" (Kristeva, 2010, 42).

Inducing shame

My reading is paradoxical, reflecting the duplicitous nature of the affect it discerns (anxiety)—a lack of lack with the potential to generate lack. In *Caché*, what is caused by anxiety or lack of lack (the video, an alien excess that looms large as a strange symptom of the society of the spectacle) as well as, in turn, causes anxiety (again, the video, which becomes, like *das Ding*, a stalker) can be said ultimately to generate shame. Anxiety, in *Caché*, brought to the limit of its lack of lack produces a symptom, the taping, which serves as a witness at the intersection of destruction and survival—a site of chaos that it helps to bring about.[3] Various scenes shot by the video—which at times, and eventually, becomes indistinguishable from the film itself[4]—emblematize and stage the incomprehensible or in other words bear witness to "a new ethical material" being "touched upon in the living being" (Agamben, 2002, 104). Might we not look at the uncanny authorless videotaping as situated finally in the place of shame—or Agamben's remnant—which does not take on the knowability and responsibility of guilt but sustains the inarticulable and speaks back to the seamless and flat society of the spectacle, insofar as shame carves out a lack, acknowledges desubjectification, death?

Shame, it must be clarified, as Agamben and also Lacan conceive of it, is unrelated to wrongdoing. Agamben regards it as an experience of intimacy. Referring to the boy from Bologna, Agamben contends that "certainly the intimacy that one experiences before one's own unknown murderer is the most extreme intimacy, an intimacy that can as such provoke shame." The Italian boy experiences shame as he confronts death's threshold that he is about to cross. Agamben stresses that in shame the subject "has no other content than its own desubjectification; it becomes witness to its own disorder, its own oblivion as a subject." The Bologna boy's "flush" is for Agamben "the remainder that, in every subjectification, betrays a desubjectification and that, in every desubjectification, bears witness to a subject" (Agamben, 2002, 112). Agamben's key idea here is that "in shame we are consigned to something from which we cannot in any way distance ourselves" (Agamben, 2002, 105). The boy from Bologna is forced to face what he is not—to which he is nevertheless consigned. Shame, according to this strictly ontological definition, entails "being consigned to a passivity that cannot be assumed" (Agamben, 2002, 110); in *Idea of Prose*, Agamben characterizes it as "the index of an unheard of, frightening [shuddering] proximity of man with himself" (Agamben, 1995, 84).

Interestingly, Lacan suggests, in *Book XVII*, that the analyst's task is to induce shame. To translate this into Agambenian terminology: the analyst strives to put the analysand into relation with what cannot be assumed. To his seminar members who question such a use of shame, thinking, "[i]f that is what the other side of psychoanalysis is, we don't want any," Lacan replies,

'You've got enough to open a shop.' If you are not yet aware of this, then do a bit of analysis, as they say. You will see this vapid air of yours run up against an outlandish shame of living.

(Lacan, 2006/1968, 184)

Shame—"not a comfortable thing to put forward.... not one of the easiest things to speak about"—is to Lacan "the hole from which the master signifier arises." Consequently, shame is not "useless" for subverting, or even just rotating, the master's discourse (Lacan, 2006/1968, 189). In fact, Lacan has been attempting to produce this very affect in his seminar interlocutors: he concludes *Book XVII* with the bold assertion that he has tried to make his seminar members "ashamed, not too much, but just enough" (Lacan, 2006/1968, 193)! The videotaping in *Caché* and in turn the film itself are focused on this same site, on the place of the analyst or *objet a*, that is, the gaze in the register of the visible, the Real, and are therefore able to effect a fundamental shift, through an inducement of shame.

Caché deploys this menacing invisible eye to uncover incomprehensible destruction—hardship, forms of desubjectification, suicide, death, all unacknowledged by our fetishistic society of the spectacle—again, to witness "new ethical material" blanketed by contemporary society. As Debord points out, the society of the spectacle puts commodities and images in the place of the lack that constitutes living desire. It fetishistically plugs that gap. The carving out of such a gap is tantamount to the film's transformation of anxiety into shame. That aim backfires for Georges, who becomes only more callous, but it can operate at the level of the spectator.

While Georges resists his unconscious memories, just as the society of the spectacle attempts to shrink psychic life to zero, *Caché* clears a space for the psyche also by revealing the terror of the demise of psychic life. What is most terrifying in the world of *Caché* is certainly not the gentle Algerians—the only figures in the film with integrity, as well as a polite and compassionate wish to connect, which contrasts with the rampant lying that seems customary among the French (Georges lies to Anne repeatedly throughout the film, as he also lies to his mother; it is intimated that Anne in turn betrays him with Pierre, and lies about that betrayal to her son Pierrot, who senses it). Georges is outrageously off-track in referring to Majid's "campaign of terror" and accusing Majid's noble son of "terrorizing" the Laurent family with his "stupid tapes." (The tapes, moreover, are hardly stupid.) "You terrorize my family," Georges obtusely reiterates to Majid's well-raised son, using post-9/11 diction robotically. What *is* terrorizing, instead, is the sheer exteriority, the complete lack of intimacy in the vapid and cold, secularized, imperialistic, capitalist world of *Caché*. *This* is the terror that *Caché* points to as the cause of distrust and loss of "living desire" between Georges and Anne. Insufficient intimacy is the terror that leads as well to the rough extraction of Majid from the French family that once adopted him. The film herein makes Kristeva's point that listening to vulnerability, or the primary activity of psychoanalysis, has political meaning. She ties the vulnerability of people like Majid to "our dreams, our anxieties, our romantic and existential crises," to the "*lack of being* that invades us when our resistances crumble and our 'interior castle' cracks" and believes that only upon recognizing and exploring that psychic territory will we be able "to construct a common life project" (Kristeva, 2010, 44).

That the political turmoil of the film, as it relates to the Laurent family, stems from an Imaginary rivalry between two six-year-olds vying for the attention of the mother is perhaps our first major hint that *Caché* points to a cause deeper than what we normally think of as politics to explain its inhuman relations. Such an origin, in other words, grounds the film's political content in a psychoanalytic register. Majid complains to Georges that he talks as though they are "strangers," testifying to Debord's notion that the society of the spectacle is the very "expression of estrangement, of alienation between man and man" (Debord, 1995, 151). To mollify that estrangement, Majid quite deliberately invites Georges to witness his suicide, an "authentic act,"[5] pronouncing to him, as Georges enters the flat, "I wanted you to be present," just prior to slitting his throat with a knife and spraying blood all over the wall. Georges regards his disastrous childhood experience with Majid as a mere "interlude," refuses to take "responsibility" for it or to compensate Majid for it, and, what is far worse (I am suggesting), resists being "present"—or I should say "absent"—at the event of Majid's death. Georges declines a vital encounter with the desubjectification that witnessing Majid's suicide shamefully would have offered him. He turns away from the gaze that Majid's demise could have opened for him, the site of his constitutive lack that, had he engaged it, would have enabled a transformation. Like an analyst at the end of analysis, Majid vanishes, but Georges fails to experience this loss. He remains impervious to the death that had the potential to move him to a state of desire predicated on Nothing. Georges fails to take advantage of the awesome opportunity Majid offers to rid himself of his spectacular racist, robotic selfhood, constituted merely by images and objects and founded on the repudiation/fetishization of the Arab Other.

Instead, Georges proceeds to take sleeping pills and to climb into bed, where he is haunted by his second nightmare—of young Majid being violently wrestled away from his adoptive home. (Georges goes naked to bed but manages not to feel exposed, not to recognize his nakedness as something he cannot flee, defying Levinas's sense that nakedness brings shame since we are unable to cloak what we wish to remove from the visual field.) Unlike the boy from Bologna who exhibits a shameful flush, Georges refuses to budge in relation to chaos, to this suicidal scene of utter turmoil and despair, Majid's literal desubjectification. Totally defensive, Georges maintains an absolute denial, refusing even one moment of reflection. Georges boasts to Majid's son: "You'll never give me a bad conscience." He asserts fatuously: "I am not to blame." He asks Anne to turn off the lights in their bedroom, and like the screeching bats that fly over their Paris domicile, he remains blind. Georges will have no part in Majid's death, far less claim it as his own. Although he is seized with anxiety, Georges rejects the shame through which he could have put his anxiety (rather than himself) to bed—by engaging *das Ding*, rather than running from it, in a way that would have called up genuine *jouissance* (the kind without which psychic life cannot thrive, rather than the sham *jouissance* generated by anxiety) and thereby forged a relation with the Real and, in turn, with raw and struggling life beyond the limits of the ethics of dignity as well as beyond the stupidity of the spectacle.

But Haneke's attentive film zooms right in on Majid's suicidal act, as do we, to acknowledge this heightened moment of potential shame in which pure intimacy takes place (like that between the boy from Bologna and his murderer). At this point *Caché* sets up *our* (the spectator's) stark encounter with Majid's shattered subjectivity: Georges is moved off screen for a short time, leaving us alone to face Majid's ruin. Earlier, when Georges demands of Majid, "Tell me what you want," Majid replies, "Nothing, nothing." Now Majid achieves that Nothing and gives it in turn as a gift (a Derridean gift of death) to Georges (and to us) wanting him (and us) to be present at this absence, allowing a move into the space of lack so as to transfigure anxiety through the shame of an encounter with death.

Instead, George recoils, illustrating the "false consciousness" and "breakdown in the faculty of encounter" that Debord perceives the society of the spectacle imposing "at every moment on an everyday life in thrall to the spectacle" (Debord, 1995, 152). Georges is Debord's Homo Spectator:

the consciousness of the spectator can have no sense of an individual life moving toward self-realization, or toward death. Someone who has given up the idea of living life will surely never be able to embrace death....The social absence of death is one with the social absence of life.

(Debord, 1995, 115)

Georges's refusal of Majid's invitation to experience his death ruins Georges's chance to detach from the images and consumer objects fetishized in the society of the spectacle and to open up a psychic space of lack/desire. Witnessing Majid's suicide, moreover, had the potential to remove Majid as the founding Other on whom Georges bases his superiority. *Caché* suggests that the raced Other is woven into Georges's collapsed psyche in a way that enables Georges to establish his (false) sense of rotten self-sufficiency. Had Georges permitted himself to visit the shameful space on which his subjectivity rests, and is filled, through the subjugation of Majid, then no doubt the coordinates of his racist, unbarred subjectivity—subjectivity devoid of lack and so plagued by anxiety—could have been reconfigured.

However, by filming the Laurent family, the video in *Caché*, and undeniably *Caché* itself, both produce for the audience the potential for a missing "privacy, an interiority unbreachable even by ourselves" through shame, which is "*a flight into being*" and so "does not sacrifice *jouissance*'s opacity, which is finally what 'keeps it real'" (Copjec, 2006, 111). Located both inside and outside the society of the spectacle, the video in *Caché* has the power to provoke extreme anxiety and is thereby able to instill in the specular register a lost dimension by opening up various spaces wherein subjectification can encounter desubjectification and desubjectification can contact subjectification, thus generating shame. For shame is "what is produced in the absolute concomitance of subjectification and desubjectification, self-loss and self-possession, servitude and sovereignty" (Agamben, 2002, 107).[6]

Caché's enigmatic videotaping—vehicle of the stalker *das Ding*, the excess that fills in the lack, only to explode it—serves as the index of the film's shuddering proximity to itself, thereby opening up a strip. It keeps us from forgetting that we are consigned to various things we cannot assume. *Caché* gives birth to the video as a way of bringing the lack of lack of the society of the spectacle to a crisis point of anxiety, which affect is assimilated in the film, as the video and in turn the film itself (as it becomes identified with the enigmatic video it contains) feature material threatening to the hermetically sealed spectacular society. Of course I have in mind here primarily the ghastly scene of Majid's suicide that rips open the society of the spectacle. But we can add Majid's weeping (which the video camera tapes for more than two hours after Georges departs from Majid's apartment); Georges's nightmares and weeping; the haunting, dark, unmoored snippets of little Majid coughing up blood; the creepy postcards as well as the videos marked by images of blood; and the bitterness between husband and wife as well as between parents and child. All of this unignorable turmoil in *Caché* chisels cracks in the monolithic society of the spectacle that release the raced Other from the space of the subject's lack, the site of the subject's "not-I."

After staging intersections between numb bourgeois life and the inner disruptions that "life" generates but then immediately disavows, *Caché* is in a position to witness disorder and distress. Acknowledging "new ethical material" being "touched upon in the living being," it thereby turns into the remnant that works against robotization and its accompanying racism, on behalf of what is becoming more and more terrifyingly fragile and rare—subjectivity and the psychic life on which it depends. *Caché* conveys that only upon reclaiming our desiring subjectivity—subjectivity predicated on Nothing as well as on its founding experience of the loss of the Imaginary mOther, that is, only upon reseizing our sense of ourselves as unknown to ourselves—will we be able to bear witness to, and enjoy intimacy with, the pain of others and hence no longer capture and subordinate anyone in the dehumanizing role of the Other. And only then will we be able to celebrate the wedding of the freedom of desire (for "objects, knowledge, and production") and the freedom of "intimacy and mystical participation."

Notes

1 Actually, it is Freud (and here I quote from *Beyond the Pleasure Principle*) who assumes that fear "requires a definite object of which to be afraid," whereas anxiety might be due to the expectation of or preparation for an unknown danger (Freud, 1961, 6). So, although Freud's concept of castration anxiety indicates an object to be lost, it turns out that later Freud associates anxiety with an indefinite, unknown object; and Lacan's view likewise shifts from the assumption of an object of anxiety to that "object" being the amorphous *das Ding*. Freud's conception of anxiety is a complicated topic, obviously, beyond the scope of this chapter.

2 Lacan takes up the concept of the "second death" in *The Ethics of Psychoanalysis (Seminar VII)*.

3 Agamben defines "the remnants of Auschwitz—the witnesses" as "neither the dead nor the survivors, neither the drowned nor the saved. They are what remains between them" (Agamben, 2002, 164). The flush of the boy from Bologna likewise is a remnant of Auschwitz that acts as "a mute apostrophe flying through time to reach us, to bear witness to him" (Agamben, 2002, 104).

4 Seshadri offers this succinct explanation: "There are several moments in the film . . . where we simply do not know what we are looking at (whether it is the video, a dream, a memory) if only because the shots lack a point of view

or purpose" (Seshadri, 2007, 34). The reader should also consult the essays in *Screen* dedicated to *Caché* since they tend to touch in similar ways on the technique of the film, underscoring its depthlessness. I found especially noteworthy the distinction Martine Beugnet makes in her piece "Blind spot" between the dream sequences and the film otherwise: "It is images from a different visual regime that suggest that the events are having a deeper effect on Georges: the dream sequences, the only moments where the past—memory or fantasized reminiscence—resurfaces, are conveyed with the depth of field and visual lyricism that is denied to the rest of the film" (Beugnet, 2007, 227).

5 In *Welcome to the Desert of the Real*, Slavoj Žižek defines the "authentic act" as a gesture that draws the line, that indicates a refusal to participate. He proceeds to explain, drawing from St. Paul and Plato, that "this 'No!' designates the miraculous moment in which eternal Justice momentarily appears in the temporary sphere of empirical reality" (Žižek, 2002, 116). An "act" can aid one in breaking out of a vicious cycle insofar as it touches the Real and thereby has the potential to alter "the very co-ordinates of the conflict" (Žižek, 2002, 128). It always "involves a radical risk, what Derrida, following Kierkegaard, called the *madness of a decision*: it is a step into the open, with no guarantee about the final outcome – why? Because an Act retroactively changes the very co-ordinates into which it intervenes" (Žižek, 2002, 152).

6 While I use both Agamben's and Lacan's conceptions of shame, I do not consider them to be identical. Facing one's constitutive lack, the gaze, produces shame in Lacan, whereas in Agamben the interplay between subjectification and desubjectification is key, implying a perpetual motion rather than any sort of foundational gap. I am appropriating from Agamben's notion of shame his emphasis on desubjectification to make my own case regarding the gaze.

Works cited

Agamben, Giorgio (1995) *Idea of Prose.* Trans. Michael Sullivan and Sam Whitsitt. Albany: SUNY Press.

—(2000) *Means without End: Notes on Politics.* Trans. Vincenzo Binetti and Cesare Casarino. Minneapolis and London: University of Minnesota Press.

—(2002) *Remnants of Auschwitz: The Witness and the Archive.* Trans. Daniel Heller-Roazen. New York: Zone Books.

Beugnet, Marine (2007) "Blind spot," *Screen*, 48 (2): 227–31.

Copjec, Joan (2006) "May '68, the Emotional Month." In *Lacan: The Silent Partners.* Ed. Slavoj Žižek. London and New York: Verso.

Debord, Guy (1995) *The Society of the Spectacle.* Trans. Donald Nicholson-Smith. New York: Zone Books.

Fink, Bruce (1995) *The Lacanian Subject: Between Language and Jouissance.* Princeton: Princeton UP.

Freud, Sigmund (1961) *Beyond the Pleasure Principle*. Trans. James Strachey. New York: W. W. Norton & Company.

Harari, Roberto (2001) *Lacan's Seminar on "Anxiety": An Introduction*. Trans. Jane C. Lamb-Ruiz. New York: Other Press.

Heidegger, Martin (1927/1962) *Being and Time*. Trans. John Macquarrie and Edward Robinson. New York: Harper & Row.

—(1929/1977) "What is Metaphysics?" In *Martin Heidegger: Basic Writings*. Trans. David Farrell Krell. New York: HarperCollins Publishers.

Kristeva, Julia (2002) *Intimate Revolt: The Power and Limits of Psychoanalysis*. Trans. Jeanine Herman. New York: Columbia UP.

—(2010) *Hatred and Forgiveness*. Trans. Jeanine Herman. New York: Columbia UP.

Lacan, Jacques (1962–3) *The Seminar of Jacques Lacan: Book X: Anxiety*. Trans. Cormac Gallagher from unedited French typescripts.

—(1991/1975) *The Seminar of Jacques Lacan: Book I: Freud's Papers on Technique: 1953–1954*. Ed. Jacques Alain Miller. Trans. John Forrester. New York: W. W. Norton & Co.

—(1992/1986) *The Ethics of Psychoanalysis 1959–1960: Book VII*. Ed. Jacques-Alain Miller. Trans. Dennis Porter. New York: W. W. Norton & Co.

—(2006/1968) *The Other Side of Psycho-Analysis: Book XVII*. Ed. Russell Grigg and Justin Clemens. Trans. Russell Grigg. New York: W. W. Norton & Co.

Miller, Jacques-Alain (2006) "On Shame." In *Sic 6 — Jacques Lacan and the Other Side of Psychoanalysis: Reflections on Seminar XVII*. Ed. Justin Clemens and Russell Grigg. Durham, NC and London: Duke UP.

Oliver, Kelly (2007) *Women as Weapons of War: Iraq, Sex, and the Media*. New York: Columbia UP.

Penney, James (2011) "'You never look at me from where I see you': Postcolonial guilt in *Caché*," *New Formations*, 70 (Winter): 77–93.

Salecl, Renata (2004) *On Anxiety*. London: Routledge.

Seshadri, Kalpana Rahita (2007) "Spectacle of the Hidden: Michael Haneke's *Caché*," *Nottingham French Studies*, 46 (3): 32–48.

Shepherdson, Charles (2001) "Foreword." In Roberto Harari, *Lacan's Seminar on "Anxiety": An Introduction*. Trans. Jane C. Lamb-Ruiz. New York: Other Press.

Stavrakakis, Yannis (1999) *Lacan & the Political*. London: Routledge.

Žižek, Slavoj (2002) *Welcome to the Desert of the Real*. New York: Verso.

Filmography

Caché (*Hidden*) (2005) Michael Haneke (writer and director). Les Films du Losange. Germany, Italy, France, Austria.

Bibliography

Adams, Parveen (2003) "Art as Prosthesis: Cronenberg's *Crash.*" In *Art: Sublimation or Symptom.* New York: Other Press.

Agamben, Giorgio (1995) *Idea of Prose.* Trans. Michael Sullivan and Sam Whitsitt. Albany: SUNY Press.

—(2000) *Means without End: Notes on Politics.* Trans. Vincenzo Binetti and Cesare Casarino. Minneapolis: University of Minnesota Press.

—(2002) *Remnants of Auschwitz: The Witness and the Archive.* Trans. Daniel Heller-Roazen. New York: Zone Books.

—(2009) *The Signature of All Things: On Method.* Trans. Luca D'Isanto with Kevin Attell. New York: Zone Books.

André, Serge (1999) *What Does A Woman Want?* Ed. Judith Feher Gurewich. Trans. Susan Fairfield. New York: Other Press.

Barr, Charles (1999) *English Hitchcock.* Moffat, Scotland: Cameron and Hollis.

Bellour, Raymond (2000) *The Analysis of Film.* Bloomington: Indiana UP.

Beugnet, Marine (2007) "Blind spot," *Screen,* 48 (2): 227–31.

Bhabha, Homi K (1994) *The Location of Culture.* New York: Routledge.

Butler, Judith with Ernesto Laclau and Slavoj Žižek (2000) *Contingency, Hegemony, Universality: Contemporary Dialogues on the Left.* New York: Verso.

Caruth, Cathy (1996) *Unclaimed Experience: Trauma, Narrative, and History.* Baltimore: The Johns Hopkins UP.

Coming to Power: Writings and Graphics on Lesbian S/M (1987) Ed. members of Samois. Boston: Alyson Publications, Inc.

Copjec, Joan (2006) "May '68, the Emotional Month." In *Lacan: The Silent Partners.* Ed. Slavoj Žižek. London and New York: Verso.

Debord, Guy (1995) *The Society of the Spectacle.* Trans. Donald Nicholson-Smith. New York: Zone Books.

De Lauretis, Teresa (1994) *The Practice of Love: Lesbian Sexuality and Perverse Desire.* Bloomington: Indiana UP.

Deleuze, Gilles (1971) *Masochism: An Interpretation of Coldness and Cruelty.* Trans. Jean McNeil. New York: George Brazillier.

—(1983) *Cinema I: The Movement-Image.* Trans. Hugh Tomlinson and Barbara Habberjam. Minneapolis: University of Minnesota Press.

—(2003) *Francis Bacon: The Logic of Sensation.* Trans. Daniel W. Smith. Minneapolis: University of Minnesota Press.

Doane, Mary Ann (1999) "Film and the Masquerade: Theorising the Female Spectator." In *Feminist Film Theory: A Reader.* Ed. Sue Thornham. Washington Square, New York: New York UP.

Fink, Bruce (1995) *The Lacanian Subject: Between Language and Jouissance.* Princeton, NJ: Princeton UP.

—(1997) *A Clinical Introduction to Lacanian Psychoanalysis: Theory and Technique.* Cambridge, MA: Harvard UP.

Foucault, Michel (1994/1997) *Ethics: Subjectivity and Truth.* Trans. Robert Hurley and others. New York: The New Press.

—(2003) *Society Must Be Defended: Lectures at the College de France, 1975–1976.* Trans. David Macey. New York: Picador.

Freud, Sigmund (1927) "Fetishism." *Standard Edition of the Complete Psychological Works of Sigmund Freud.* Oxford: The Hogarth Press, Vol. I, 295–343.

—(1961) *Beyond the Pleasure Principle.* Trans. James Strachey. New York: W. W. Norton & Company.

Goodnow, Katherine (2010) *Kristeva in Focus: From Theory to Film Analysis.* New York: Berghahn Books.

Grosz, Elizabeth (1995) *Space, Time, and Perversion: Essays on the Politics of Bodies.* New York & London: Routledge.

Harari, Roberto (2001) *Lacan's Seminar on "Anxiety": An Introduction.* Trans. Jane C. Lamb-Ruiz. New York: Other Press.

Heath, Stephen (1998) "God, Faith and Film: *Breaking the Waves.*" *Literature & Theology*, 12 (1): 93–107.

Heidegger, Martin (1927/1962) *Being and Time.* Trans. John Macquarrie and Edward Robinson. New York: Harper & Row.

—(1929/1977) "What is Metaphysics?" In *Martin Heidegger: Basic Writings.* Trans. David Farrell Krell. New York: HarperCollins Publishers.

Ishii-Gonzáles, Sam (2004) "Hitchcock with Deleuze." In *Past and Future Hitchcock.* Ed. Richard Allen and Sam Ishii-Gonzáles. London and New York: Routledge.

Jelinek, Elfriede (1983/1989) *The Piano Teacher.* Trans. Joachim Neugroschel. London: Serpent's Tail.

Kaplan, Louise (1991) *Female Perversions: The Temptations of Madame Bovary.* New York: Doubleday.

Kristeva, Julia (1982) *Powers of Horror: An Essay on Abjection.* Trans. Leon S. Roudiez. New York: Columbia UP.

—(1989) *Black Sun: Depression and Melancholia.* Trans. Leon S. Roudiez. New York: Columbia UP.

—(1991) *Strangers to Ourselves.* Trans. Leon S. Roudiez. New York: Columba UP.

—(1995) *New Maladies of the Soul.* Ed. Laurence D. Kritzman. Trans. Ross Guberman. New York: Columbia UP.

—(1996) *Julia Kristeva: Interviews.* Ed. Ross Mitchell Guberman. New York: Columbia UP.

—(2000) *Crisis of the Euro/pean Subject.* Trans. Susan Fairfield. New York: Other Press.

—(2002) *Intimate Revolt: The Power and Limits of Psychoanalysis.* Trans. Jeanine Herman. New York: Columbia UP.

—(2006) *Murder in Byzantium.* Trans. C. Jon Delogu. New York: Columbia UP.

—(2010) *Hatred and Forgiveness.* Trans. Jeanine Herman. New York: Columbia UP.

Kristeva, Julia and Catherine Clément (2001) *The Feminine and the Sacred*. Trans. Jane Marie Todd. New York: Columbia UP.

Lacan, Jacques (1962–3) *The Seminar of Jacques Lacan: Book X: Anxiety*. Trans. Cormac Gallagher from unedited French typescripts.

—(1981/1973) *The Four Fundamental Concepts of Psycho-Analysis: Book XI*. Ed. Jacques-Alain Miller. Trans. Alan Sheridan. New York: W. W. Norton & Co.

—(1990/1974) *Television: A Challenge to the Psychoanalytic Establishment*. Ed. Joan Copjec. Trans. Jeffrey Mehlman. New York: W. W. Norton & Co.

—(1991/1975) *The Seminar of Jacques Lacan: Book I: Freud's Papers on Technique: 1953–1954*. Ed. Jacques Alain Miller. Trans. John Forrester. New York: W. W. Norton & Co.

—(1992/1986) *The Ethics of Psychoanalysis 1959–1960: Book VII*. Ed. Jacques-Alain Miller. Trans. Dennis Porter. New York: W. W. Norton & Co.

—(1998/1975) *Encore 1972–1973: On Feminine Sexuality/The Limits of Love and Knowledge: Book XX*. Ed. Jacques-Alain Miller. Trans. Bruce Fink. New York: W. W. Norton & Co.

—(2006/1968) *The Other Side of Psycho-Analysis: Book XVII*. Ed. Russell Grigg and Justin Clemens. Trans. Russell Grigg. New York: W. W. Norton & Co.

MacCannell, Juliet Flower (2000) *The Hysteric's Guide to the Future Female Subject*. Minneapolis: University of Minnesota Press.

McGowan, Todd (2004) *Lacan and Contemporary Film*. Ed. Todd McGowan and Sheila Kunkle. New York: Other Press.

—(2004) "Lost on Mulholland Drive: Navigating David Lynch's Panegyric to Hollywood." *Cinema Journal*. 43 (2): 67–89.

Marx, Karl (1887/1967) *Capital: A Critique of Political Economy. Volume I: The Process of Capitalist Production*. Trans. Samuel Moore. New York: International Publishers.

Metz, Christian (1982) *The Imaginary Signifier: Psychoanalysis and the Cinema*. Trans. Celia Britton, Annwyl Williams, Ben Brewster, and Alfred Guzzetti. Bloomington: Indiana UP.

Miller, Jacques-Alain (1996) "On Perversion." In *Reading Seminars I and II: Lacan's Return to Freud*. Ed. Richard Feldstein, Bruce Fink, and Maire Jaanus. Albany: SUNY Press.

—(2006) "On Shame." In *Sic 6—Jacques Lacan and the Other Side of Psychoanalysis: Reflections on Seminar XVII*. Ed. Justin Clemens and Russell Grigg. Durham, NC and London: Duke UP.

Mulvey, Laura (1996) *Fetishism and Curiosity*. Bloomington: Indiana UP and the British Film Institute.

—(2004) "Death Drives." In *Past and Future Hitchcock*. Ed. Richard Allen and Sam Ishii-Gonzáles. London and New York: Routledge.

Nasio, Juan-David (1998) *Hysteria from Freud to Lacan: The Splendid Child of Psychoanalysis*. Ed. Judith Feher Gurewich. Trans. Susan Fairfield. New York: Other Press.

Oliver, Kelly (2007) *Women as Weapons of War: Iraq, Sex, and the Media*. New York: Columbia UP.

Penney, James (2011) "'You never look at me from where I see you': Postcolonial guilt in *Caché*," *New Formations*, 70 (Winter): 77–93.

Reik, Theodor (1941) *Masochism in Modern Man*. Trans. Margaret H. Eigel and Gertrud M. Kruth. New York: Farrar, Straus.

Riviere, Joan (1929) "Womanliness as a Masquerade." *International Journal of Psychoanalysis*, 10: 303–13.

Salecl, Renata (2004) *On Anxiety*. London: Routledge.

Seshadri, Kalpana Rahita (2007) "Spectacle of the Hidden: Michael Haneke's *Caché*," *Nottingham French Studies*, 46 (3): 32–48.

Shepherdson, Charles (2001) "Foreword." In Roberto Harari, *Lacan's Seminar on "Anxiety": An Introduction*. Trans. Jane C. Lamb-Ruiz. New York: Other Press.

Silverman, Kaja (1983) *The Subject of Semiotics*. New York: Oxford UP.

—(1988) "Masochism and Male Subjectivity." *Camera Obscura*, 17: 31–67.

—(1988) *The Acoustic Mirror: The Female Voice in Psychoanalysis and Cinema*. Bloomington: Indiana UP.

Smith, Daniel W. (2003) "Translator's Introduction: Deleuze on Bacon: Three Conceptual Trajectories in *The Logic of Sensation*." In *Francis Bacon: The Logic of Sensation* Trans. Daniel W. Smith. Minneapolis: University of Minnesota Press.

Soler, Colette (2006) *What Lacan Said about Women*. New York: Other Press.

Stavrakakis, Yannis (1999) *Lacan & the Political*. London: Routledge.

Stok, Danusia, Ed. (1993) *Kieslowski on Kieslowski*. London: Faber and Faber.

Walton, Jean (1999) "(White) Female Perversions." Paper at "Women Filmmakers: Refocussing" Conference, Vancouver, British Columbia.

Williams, Linda (1998) "Discipline and Distraction: *Psycho*, Visual Culture, and Postmodern Cinema." In *"Culture" and the Problem of the Disciplines*. Ed. John Carlos Rowe. New York: Columbia UP.

Wyatt, Jean (2006) "Jouissance and Desire in Michael Haneke's *The Piano Teacher*." *American Imago*, 62: 453–82.

Ziarek, Ewa Pronowska (2001) *An Ethics of Dissensus: Postmodernity, Feminism, and the Politics of Radical Democracy*. Palo Alto, CA: Stanford UP.

Žižek, Slavoj (1989) *The Sublime Object of Ideology*. New York: Verso.

—(2000) *The Fragile Absolute: Or, Why is the Christian Legacy Worth Fighting For?* London. Verso.

—(2001) *Enjoy Your Symptom! Jacques Lacan in Hollywood and Out*. New York: Routledge.

—(2001) *The Fright of Real Tears: Krzysztof Kieslowski between Theory and Post-theory*. London: British Film Institute.

—(2002) *Welcome to the Desert of the Real*. New York: Verso.

—(2004) "Is there a way to remake a Hitchcock film?" In *Past and Future Hitchcock*. Ed. Richard Allen and Sam Ishii-Gonzáles. London and New York: Routledge.

Žižek, Slavoj with Ernesto Laclau and Judith Butler (2000) *Contingency, Hegemony, Universality: Contemporary Dialogues on the Left*. New York: Verso.

Index